The Life &
Poetry of
Ted Kooser

MARY K. STILLWELL

University of Nebraska Press
Lincoln and London

Acknowledgments for the use of copyrighted
material appear on page 229, which constitutes
an extension of the copyright page.

Photographs are used with the permission of
Ted Kooser, except no. 24 by Megan Bean/
Mississippi State University; no. 25 by Eileen
Barroso/Columbia University; no. 26, courtesy of
Lincoln Public Schools; no. 27 by Matt Valentine;
no. 28 by Don Unser; and no. 29 by Jon D.
Humiston/University of Nebraska–Lincoln.

Publication of this volume was assisted by a
grant from the Friends of the University of
Nebraska Press.

Library of Congress
Cataloging-in-Publication Data
Stillwell, Mary K.
The life and poetry of Ted Kooser /
Mary K. Stillwell.
pages cm
Includes bibliographical references and index.
ISBN 978-0-8032-4386-6 (cloth: alk. paper)
1. Kooser, Ted. 2. Kooser, Ted—Criticism
and interpretation. 3. Poets, American—20th
century—Biography. 4. Poets, American—
Nebraska—Biography. 5. Poets laureate—United
States—Biography. I. Title.
PS3561.O6Z86 2013
811'.54—dc23   [B]   2013011893

Set in Lyon by Laura Wellington.
Designed by Nathan Putens.

Frontispiece: Ted Kooser in his art studio in
Dwight, Nebraska. Photo by Matt Valentine.

For Frank,

for Wil and Anna,

and in memory

of Susan J. Rosowski

Contents

List of Illustrations

Acknowledgments

As an epigraph for his 2004 collection, *Delights & Shadows*, Ted Kooser chose a line from Emily Dickinson's letter to Thomas Wentworth Higginson: "The Sailor cannot see the North—but knows the Needle can." Dickinson was looking for literary guidance from her friend and mentor; Kooser was reminding his readers of how knowledge of death informs our lives. Dickinson's words also suggest the kind of support and guidance, seen and unseen, that I have received as I turned my interest in Kooser's poetry into the book that is before you.

Like that sailor setting forth, I have many to thank for pointing me in the right direction both before and after the announcement of Kooser's laureateship. The late Susan J. Rosowski, scholar and editor of Willa Cather's scholarly edition, a careful listener, provided insight, feedback, and an opportunity for financial support by nominating me for a UNL Presidential Fellowship to complete my doctoral study of Nebraska poetry. Although she was too ill to attend graduation, her friendship continued, and I have felt her presence long after her death several months following Kooser's appointment.

Early in my college career I had the good fortune to study with Sr. Ernestine and Mike Novak at (then) St. Mary College, who praised my early attempts at writing even when my test scores indicated a future in the sciences. Later William Packard, poet, teacher, and editor of the *New York Quarterly*, encouraged me to give poetry writing a try in his master class at New York University. He introduced me to the work of Nebraska poet Weldon Kees and those who came after him, including Ted Kooser. Two decades after that first class Packard wrote my recommendation for graduate school. I also owe thanks to Michael Benedikt, who, when he served as poetry editor of the *Paris Review*, published my early poetry and in this way encouraged my writing.

Happily many of those who nurtured me and influenced my work are alive and well. Writing any long work is at times a lonely task, and yet it cannot be accomplished without support and assistance every step of the way. Thanks to the other members of my doctoral committee: in English, Paul Olson, who suggested that I write a book on Kooser's work, and Plains scholar Frances W. Kaye, as well as Nelson Potter, in philosophy, who steered and listened, prompted and were silent in just the right doses. Special thanks go to Susan Naramore Maher, advisor, teacher, and former chair of the English department at the University of Nebraska at Omaha, for her encouragement, mentoring, and for including *Weather Central* on her Plains literature syllabus many years ago.

Librarians compose a special tribe, always helpful and always quick; special thanks to the librarians at Love Library, especially to Amy Heberling, UNL Interlibrary Loan; Denise Matulka, *Lincoln Journal Star*; and various staff members at the Ames Public Library, Guttenberg Public Library, Cedar Rapids Public Library, Des Moines Public Library, Marshalltown Public Library, and the Valentine Public Library. I also wish to thank Alan Spohnheimer, Ames Historical Society, and Kathy Svec, Iowa State University, along with Kim Stafford and Paul Merchant, director, William Stafford archives, and Stephen Meats, editor of the *Midwest Quarterly*. Norton and Edward Mezvinsky, Susan Allen Toth, and Larry H. Christie were helpful in providing a sense of the Ames of Kooser's childhood. Iowa State faculty, including Richard Herrnstadt, provided recollections of their colleague Will Jumper, Kooser's first mentor.

Various poets and scholars have also provided information or pointed me in its direction; among them are Gregory Fraser, Glenna Luschei, Robert Phillips, Detrich Oostedt, Henry Taylor, Steve Cox, Norbert Krapf, and the late Don Jones, and, closer to home, Greg Kosmicki, publisher of Backwaters Press, Hilda Raz, Bill Kloefkorn, Todd Robbinson, Roy Scheele, Greg Kuzma, Don Welch, Mark Sanders, Lee Lemon, and Mordicai Marcus, along with *ausländer* Steve Hahn. A special thanks goes to Danielle Glazner, my plains literature seminar partner, when I was just launching this leg of my journey at the University of Nebraska at Omaha. I would also like to extend my gratitude to the Nebraska Foundation for a fellowship that allowed me to reduce my teaching load for a year, particularly important to a lecturer, and to Joy Ritchie and Deborah Minter, then chair and vice chair of the English department, for lending their support. Thanks, too, to my students who read and shared their insights about Kooser's poetry with me over the years.

Fortunate for me, Andrews Hall reverberates with poetry past and present. Not long after I began this book, Ted Kooser dropped by my office on the first floor of Andrews. "You know," he began, "this was Karl Shapiro's office in the 50s, only it was much larger, a suite of offices. *Prairie Schooner* was located here too." He went on to say that my old upholstered chair in the corner, where students sat when they came to visit, was probably his too, the place where "Karl sat to read his mail, . . . where he sat to read *Howl* when it came in the mail, and where he announced to Glenna Luchsi, his grad assistant, 'This will change everything.'" Being able to work in this environment enriched the text and texture of this project.

Kooser's friends have been generous with their time, filling in blanks and providing helpful insights into his life. Among them are Patty Lombardi, Burke Casari, and Mij Laging. Diana Tressler, Kooser's first wife, has become a friend as well as a well-spring of information and encouragement. In addition to providing insights into their lives via interviews and e-mails, she generously passed along Kooser's early letters that tell the story of their courtship and dreams, and that document her former husband's desire for a life of poetry. Kooser's sister, Judith Langmack, has also been helpful in affording a look into the house on West Ninth Street where she and her brother grew up.

Since my first query of Ted Kooser in 1997 when I was a master's degree student, he has generously given time and attention, answering questions by e-mail, phone, and in person, first for a seminar paper, later for my dissertation, and then for this work. I am extremely fortunate to have had an opportunity to be among Kooser's first poetry tutorial students at the University of Nebraska–Lincoln. I appreciate in particular his personal tour of Guttenberg, Iowa, that included his grandparents' home and the Mississippi River Lookout to which he returned in his imagination when he was being treated for throat cancer. I am also grateful for his assistance in making sure the manuscript was accurate, for filling in the gaps that Ancestry.com could not. He has also graciously allowed me to include his poetry, letters, and photographs in this work. Kathleen Rutledge, Kooser's wife and wordsmith in her own right, has been generous with her time and attention. She has also been helpful in my gaining an understanding of the daily life of the poet and provided insight into their lives together.

Personal thanks go to Kathy O'Connor, who urged me to undertake graduate work and then cheered me on through thick and thin. I appreciate the friendship and continuing support of the Dish Diners, Kathy Rutledge, Lynn Wake, and Anne Whitney, who have helped keep me grounded through the many years of research and writing.

Very special thanks go to my husband, Frank Edler, with whom I set sail, literally and figuratively, on the two-masted *Ventura* in Manhattan Bay many years ago. He has, since our first meeting, offered me new ways to think about new things. His own scholarly work has informed mine in ways that go beyond the conscious acumen of this sailor but are surely present.

My deep thanks also go to my children, Wil and Anna, who have provided their own inspiration along with a good deal of fun. They have accompanied me to more readings and discussions of poetry than any child need ever attend and have entered into the spirit of

this project as great listeners and companion travelers, whether to
Ted Kooser's office in Dwight to climb his maple, to have lunch at
Cy's, to tour the grottos behind the Catholic church, or to Garland
to investigate the ionic columns of the Germantown bank.

I thank all of you, named and unnamed, who have accompanied
me on this journey. With that said, neither Ted Kooser nor anyone
mentioned above should be held accountable for any mistakes or
red herrings that may have crept or swum into the final product.

Chronology

Full-length collections and prose works indicated by bold.

APRIL 25, 1939 Theodore John Kooser born in Ames, Iowa

1962 Earns a BS in English education from Iowa State University

1962–1963 Teaches high school in Madrid, Iowa

NOVEMBER 17, 1962 Marries Diana Tressler in a church ceremony

1963 Moves to Lincoln, Nebraska, to pursue full-time graduate study in English with Karl Shapiro at the University of Nebraska

1964 Joins Bankers Life Nebraska

JULY 17, 1967 Son, Jeffrey Charles Kooser, born

1967–PRESENT Founds and operates Windflower Press

1967–1975 Edits and publishes *Salt Creek Reader*

1968 Receives MA from University of Nebraska

NOVEMBER 1969 Ted and Diana Kooser separate

1969 ***Official Entry Blank***

1970 Becomes part-time instructor in creative writing, University of Nebraska

1971 *Grass County*

1973 *Twenty Poems*

1974 ***A Local Habitation & a Name***

1975 *Shooting a Farmhouse/So This Is Nebraska*

1976 *Voyages to the Island Sea*, with Harley Elliott

1976 ***Not Coming to Be Barked at***

1976 National Endowment for the Arts Fellowship

SEPTEMBER 24, 1977 Marries Kathleen Rutledge

1978 *Old Marriage and New*
1978 **Hatcher**
1979 *Cottonwood County*, with William Kloefkorn
1980 Edits *The Windflower Home Almanac of Poetry*
1980 **Sure Signs: New and Selected Poems**
1980-1981 Edits and publishes *Blue Hotel* magazine
1981 Publishes *The Blue Hotel*, volumes 2 and 3: *Seventeen Danish Poets: A Bilingual Anthology of Contemporary Danish Poetry*
1984 National Endowment for the Arts Fellowship
1985 **One World at a Time**
1986 **The Blizzard Voices**
1994 **Weather Central**
1998 *Journey to a Place of Work*
JUNE 1, 1998 Diagnosed with tongue cancer
FALL 1998 "Lights on a Ground of Darkness: An Evocation of a Place and Time"
1999 *Riding with Colonel Carter*
1999 Retires from Lincoln Benefit Life

2000 **Winter Morning Walks: One Hundred Postcards to Jim Harrison**
2002 **Local Wonders: Seasons in the Bohemian Alps**
2003 **Braided Creek: A Conversation in Poetry with Jim Harrison**
2004 **Delights & Shadows**
2004 August 2004 Named U.S. poet laureate consultant in poetry
2005 **The Poetry Home Repair Manual**
APRIL 2005 Pulitzer Prize for *Delights & Shadows*
2005 **Flying at Night: Selected Poems**
2005 **Writing Brave and Free** with Steve Cox
2005 **Lights on a Ground of Darkness**
2005-2006 Second term as poet laureate
2008 **Valentines**
2009 **The Poets Guide to the Birds,** edited with Judith Kitchen
2010 **Bag in the Wind** (children's book)
2012 **House Held Up by Trees** (children's book)

THE LIFE AND POETRY OF TED KOOSER

One

Growing Up in Iowa,
1939–1963

CHAPTER ONE

Official Entry

The peonies are up, the red sprouts
burning in circles like birthday candles,
for this is the month of my birth . . .
everything ready to burst with living.

—From "Mother"

Vera Deloras Moser Kooser and Theodore Briggs Kooser welcomed
their first child into the world at Mary Greeley Hospital in Ames,
Iowa, on Tuesday, April 25, 1939. All across town peonies were
sending up bright red sprouts along fences and sidewalks, and the
tall, well-established elms that would soon provide shelter from
the Midwest summer sun were coming into leaf. A few days later
the couple paid their hospital bill of $47.38 and carried Theodore
John, named for his father and maternal grandfather, a few blocks
south to their upstairs apartment across from Bandshell Park on
Carroll Avenue.

Not long after the young family moved to the modest white frame
house at 109 West Ninth Street where Teddy, or Little Ted, as he
was called, grew up. The neighborhood, now part of the Historic
Old Town, was already well known to Ted Sr. He had been born in
the house to the immediate west, currently occupied by the Mallo

family; the Mezvinskys lived to the east of the honeysuckle hedge. The area was comfortably middle class, its residents hardworking and optimistic despite the temporary setbacks that life and weather might bring their way. By 1939 the United States was emerging from the Great Depression, and the residents of West Ninth, like their counterparts across the nation, felt the stirrings of prosperity. Ted Sr. was drapery manager of the Tilden Department Store, located at 203 Main Street, where he had met his future wife when she came to work there as a clerk. Vera became a full-time homemaker when they married.

Members of the Kooser family were among the early white settlers of Story County, Iowa. Originally from Württenberg, Germany, Hans Michael Kosser (1717–1774) and Anna Maria Sybilla (1720–?) married in 1748 and a year later packed up their possessions, and set out to the New World on the *Dragon*, sailing from Rotterdam and arriving in Philadelphia October 17. The Kossers (spelled variously as Koser, Kuzer, Koozer, and Kooser) settled in Reading, Pennsylvania.

During the 1840s and 1850s more than 632,000 settlers from the east, primarily from Indiana, New York, and Pennsylvania, poured into Iowa, which was first named a territory and then became the twenty-ninth state of the union in December 1846. These new-comers saw themselves, at least by some accounts, as "children of destiny, called to fulfill the promise of a chosen nation" and there-fore "fortified by an irrepressible optimism." Among the new arrivals were Hans and Anna's great-great-grandson George W. Kooser (1834–1896) and his wife, Margaret Elizabeth Boucher (1836–1919), listed with their nine children on the 1860 US Census Story County (Iowa) rolls.

Commerce in the area thrived, and by December 1864, the town of Ames was founded as a railroad stop on the south branch of the Skunk River and its tributary Squaw Creek in the midst of the county's rich farmland. By 1905 the poet's grandparents, Charles F. Kooser (1873–1942) and Grace E. Lang (1876–1948), whose family had moved to Iowa from Illinois, married and lived in Ames at 1023 Clark Street with their two young sons: Herold Lang (b. 1900) and

Theodore Briggs (b. 1902). A third son, Derral Charles, was born in 1909.

Early on, the Koosers' middle son, named for Theodore Roosevelt, whose campaign train stopped in Ames during his mother's pregnancy, and for his paternal grandfather, discovered an interest in shopkeeping and exhibited a creative flare. The ingenious young boy set up a millinery shop in his grandmother's barn and began collecting old, unwanted hats that he would transform with new ribbons, feathers, and flowers and resell to many of the same customers.

Business in Ames prospered as Theodore grew to adulthood. Montgomery Ward and J. C. Penney opened stores on Main Street providing Ames' residents a wider selection of goods and Tilden's with competition for the shopper's dollar. With the end of World War I came the end of farm subsidies, and land prices, along with production costs, soared. Over half of the state's farmers were forced to mortgage their land and, as a result, lost it during the Great Depression.

Nearly two hundred miles to the east, the large Moser clan, Vera Kooser's family, worked hard throughout the Depression to hang on to their land and scrape a livelihood from the hills and meadows along the Mississippi River in Clayton County, Iowa. Her parents, like their forebears, were thrifty people. The youngest of five children born to John R. Moser (1874–1972) and Elizabeth D. Morarend (1879–1962), Vera (b. 1908) struck out on her own after graduating from Guttenberg High School, joining her sister Mabel (1902–1990) in Iowa City, where she attended the University of Iowa. Two years later Vera moved to Ames, where her older sister, Florence (1899–1966), and her first husband, Calvin Lake, had relocated. Her brother, Alva (1905–1980), known as Elvy, remained at home. The fifth child, Millard Laurel (1904), died in infancy.

Once settled in Ames, Vera enrolled at Iowa State College of Agriculture and Mechanic Arts (now Iowa State University), where she studied French for two years. She also attended classes at the Templeton Business College before taking a job at Tilden's. There the shy young woman from Clayton County met the gregarious shopkeeper, Theodore Briggs Kooser. They married October 17, 1937, in Clinton, Iowa, not far from Guttenberg, in the home of her sister and brother-in-law, Mabel and Carl Allen.

Ames celebrated its diamond jubilee the year of Teddy's birth. About one-fifth of the size it is today, the town boasted a population of nearly 13,500—not counting 6,500 college students. The three-day celebration consisted of a maze of concessions and rides at the city park, concerts, old settler get-togethers, a citizenship induction ceremony, a jubilee dance, plus a round of artillery fire, as though to ward off news of Germany's invasion of Poland.

Despite the impact of World War II, Vera and Ted Sr. were able to provide Teddy and his sister, Judith, born in 1942, with a secure home environment. The war did touch their lives, however. Derral C. Kooser, the children's uncle Charlie, was inducted into the army at Camp Dodge (Johnston, Iowa) in 1942. During part of 1944 and 1945, Vera's sister Mabel, with her daughter, Janice, moved into the Kooser home while her husband served in the navy. A total of 882,542 young Iowa men were drafted, and, for the first time, women saw active duty during war. Ted Sr.'s cousin Margaret became a member of the Army Nurse Corps and served in the Pacific. Herold, known to the family as Uncle Tubby, was forty-two at the time of the attack on Pearl Harbor and served at home as a civil air patrol observer. Ted Sr., forty, with a wife and a child, was not called up.

"It would eventually be proven that our fifteen thousand citizens had always been safe from Axis Powers," Kooser writes in *Local Wonders*. However, he continues, "we weren't to relax until peace was declared." Despite Iowa's location in the center of North America, many citizens feared attack by the Japanese or at the very least by the subversive work of spies living undercover among them. Capitalism and patriotism mingled, producing "Spotter Cards" sold by the U.S. Playing Card Company, enabling citizens to memorize the silhouettes of enemy and friendly aircraft while playing pitch. Kooser adds, "Though we were never to hear the searing whistles of V-2 rockets or feel the ground-shuddering thumps of falling blockbusters or smell any smoke other than that of our own leaf fires on peaceful October evenings, we had been warned that there was always the possibility we might be attacked from the air by long-range German bombers, and we watched the skies, ready to huddle under the basement stairs when we heard the roar of the Luftwaffe and the blitz came hurling down."

His parents and their neighbors, he writes, because they were descended from immigrants, had "learned from their forebears to prepare for the worst. A Nazi air attack was just one of the many horrible things that might happen to a family along the long, hard, Calvinistic trail to life's end." During blackouts, the Kooser family listened for their neighbor, Mr. Posey, like Uncle Tubby, a local civil defense observer, to make his rounds, checking to make sure no light showed below the drawn blinds. They followed the progress of the war in the newspapers and on the radio as the poet recalls in the poem, "Zenith," from *Delights & Shadows*. woi and who radio brought *The Jack Benny Show*, *One Man's Family*, *The Romance of Helen Trent*, along with big band music led by Glenn Miller, Duke Ellington, Tommy Dorsey, and Benny Goodman, into their homes.

CHAPTER TWO

An Emerging Imagination

So, you never can tell what will happen
when you learn to play the harmonica.

—Robert McCloskey, *Lentil*

Even with the threat of attack "by the Germans from one direction or the Japanese from the other," Teddy and his sister grew up feeling safe. They looked forward to coming home from school to the scent of molasses cookies baking in the oven. If their parents argued, it was away from the children. They were, Kooser writes, "very formal; there wasn't a whole lot of physical affection in our house. Everybody understood we all loved each other but there was not a lot of hugging."

Vera Kooser was a supportive mother. "I could do no wrong. . . . She was always on my side," her son says. Judith describes their mother as more formal than her father. Teddy and their mother were "soul-mates," she says, as she and her father were. Homemaking, informed by the Depression and then by rationing during the war, was for Vera Kooser both a skill and an art. "Mother's the type of woman," Kooser wrote many years later in a tribute, "who patched torn clothes and darned socks and *made do* . . . Like many Midwestern women of her generation she thrived on doing without."

She cooked and canned, made jellies and jams, and made nearly all of her own clothes and those of her children. He has written about her careful management of family resources, recording "every cent they spent from 1936 till the day she died."

Teddy "adored" his father and as a young boy loved to watch him get ready for work each morning, his hands fluttering like birds before the mirror, as the adult son will describe in the poem "The Necktie." As evening fell, Teddy waited at the living room window for him to return, bringing stories of the day at Tilden's. One long afternoon when he was four or five, the boy set out to visit his father at work. "Those four blocks were a very long way for a little boy to travel," Kooser writes, "and I underwent many fearful trials before I got there.... A woman found me crying as I stumbled along Main Street, not knowing quite where Tilden's was."

Ted Sr., his daughter reflects, "worked hard to become very successful in his retail career." She adds, "His profession was People! ... He talked to everyone." His son adds, "He was extremely good at describing people," so good that a friend told his son, that she'd rather hear his father describe someone than see the person for herself.

Ted Sr., who was promoted to general manager of Tilden's, was from all reports well liked throughout the community. In 1942, after over twenty years at Tilden's, he was named manager of the Younker Brothers store, also on Main Street.

V-E Day took place two weeks before Teddy Kooser's sixth birthday. Japan's surrender, following the U.S. bombing of Hiroshima and Nagasaki, brought the war to a close in August but not until over 8,300 Iowa men and women lost their lives. The Cold War followed. Teddy and Judy, along with other American school children across the nation, prepared for surprise atomic strike. "Whatever you do, don't lose your head," advised *Survival under Atomic Attack*, a booklet widely circulated to local teachers and students by Iowa Power and Light.

Despite occasional dire warnings, life was interesting and often fun. Ames was, by many accounts, a wonderful, even idyllic, small midwestern town in which to grow up during the 1930s and 1940s. Girls and boys spent long summer evenings running across wide green lawns catching lightning bugs in Mason jars and searching the hedges for crickets. In winter, stuffed into snowsuits, the same children threw themselves down onto the snow to fan angel wings or fashion large balls of snow that they stacked into men and women with coal smiles and carrot noses. Year round children felt free to bicycle all over town.

Saturday afternoons, for a quarter, Disney movies and cowboy pictures—inspiration for young Ted's cowboy shirt that his mother for made him when he was fourteen—were shown at the Collegian Theater. The Koosers belonged to a play-reading group, called the Playmakers, who met in the houses of members. Listening to the reading was, Kooser recalls, "my first experience of literature as fun." The household had a small library of about twenty books, including Balzac, Ibsen, and the popular fiction of John Fox Jr. (1862–1919), whose *Trail of the Lonesome Pine* is best known. Kooser read them all.

The Koosers, married under the auspices of the First Methodist Episcopal church in Clinton, Iowa, attended church infrequently. The basement of the First Methodist Church was, however, where Teddy took ballroom dancing lessons; just outside, he writes, is the site of the "snow-bank punch and maraschino cherry up-chuck that followed." Kooser has remarked that he believes in "a universal order," although he was not influenced by "by anything in any way churchly."

In many ways Teddy was a typical young boy of the times. During the school term the children attended Beardshear Elementary at 920 Carroll Avenue, a block north of their grandmother's home. In the evenings Teddy watched from Judy's upstairs window as a neighbor boy, Gary Mallo, enacted puppet dramas of stabbings and hangings for the Kooser children's delight. A favorite game was "Miniature Animals," in which Teddy and his friends "dreamed up fantastic adventures" starring small "glass creatures . . . from the five-and-dime."

Herold, Teddy's uncle Tubby, a warm and continuing presence in his nephew's life, inspired the game with his collection of elephants; he owned hundreds of them, "big and small, glass and porcelain and carved from stone and ivory and wood." He gave Teddy his first elephant, a small china pachyderm, Pinky.

Teddy's uncle was a life-long bachelor. After receiving his degree in mechanical engineering from Iowa State University in 1923, he went to work for his alma mater; in 1925 he was named director of Visual Instruction Service, where he built a valuable collection of industrial documentary films. Kooser remembers his uncle hosted a weekly classical music program broadcast on WOI, located in the same building as Visual Instruction Service.

In addition to educational documentaries, Uncle Tubby purchased prints of early animated cartoons, including Steamboat Willie that Iowa State would later sell back to Disney Studios. Before television was common and even cartoons were relatively rare, Uncle Tubby set up his projector at his niece's and nephew's birthday parties, delighting the children with animated figures displayed on the side of his mother's garage.

Kooser describes his uncle as "a kind of elephant himself, ponderous and solitary, so clumsy at his weight that one winter, when he'd dropped his car keys into a snowdrift, he snapped a twig from a nearby tree" to mark the place until the next thaw. Herold shared a house a few blocks away from his brother with his mother; Kooser's grandfather had died in May 1942. Mrs. Kooser hadn't wanted any of her three sons to marry, but the two younger sons, Theodore and Derral, had "broken free."

Judy and Teddy spent many a Saturday afternoons with their grandmother, a "large woman," Kooser writes, who liked to gossip on the telephone. Sometimes, when the children grew restless, they explored their grandmother's house, including the kitchen where Fiji, her black-and-white bull terrier, growled if they dared to come too close. Some Saturday nights Uncle Tubby would whisk Teddy, Judy, and his mother downtown in his 1937 Ford to park on Main Street and watch shoppers. Stores stayed open late on Saturday night during the 1940s and 1950s; farm and town families mingled, shopping, strolling, and exchanging the news. Older folks, like Grandma Kooser, sat in their cars waving their handkerchiefs to passersby.

Grace Kooser had not approved of her son Theodore's marriage and had not attended his wedding in Clinton. However, she was moved into the Koosers' home for care after she fell and broke her shoulder. Complications set in, and she died at Mary Greeley hospital on August 17, 1948, of a coronary occlusion. When Teddy, who was nine, woke the next morning, he wandered into the living room to find it filled with "silent, dark-suited old men of her generation. They carried the faint odor of mothballs. This was a kind of solemnity of which I had never before been part." Services were held at the First Methodist Church, with interment at the Ames Municipal Cemetery.

Uncle Tubby auctioned off his mother's furniture at 804 Carroll and moved into Cranford Apartments, nearer his office at Iowa State. Although this took him farther from his brother's home, he remained close to the family, joining them for Sunday dinners and for the holidays for the next twenty years. "He had," his nephew recalls, "the loveliest whistle of anyone I've ever known. He could twitter and warble and flutter, the notes rising and falling, and then he would break off into beautiful, clear, sustained notes that pierced the air."

About this time family friends gave Teddy *Lentil*, a children's book written and illustrated by Robert McCloskey, which was to have profound influence on his life and his writing. The narrative, advanced both by text and black-and-white drawings, presents a dilemma familiar to many young readers and offers an optimistic story of good triumphing over evil. The story's hero, a boy about Teddy's age, by hard work and persistence, finds his place in the community.

It is hard to imagine a better gift for a boy who already loved to draw and write. Lentil's home town, Alto, was based on the streets and sites from McCloskey's own midwestern hometown of Hamilton, Ohio, and is strikingly similar—with steepled churches and storefronts that line streets radiating up from the Great Miami River—to the Ames of Teddy's youth. What resonated most with the fourth grader was Lentil's predicament: neither boy felt he fit in. Kooser, years later, elaborated, pointing out that he was small of build, not an athlete, the standard of male acceptance in those days. "I tried hard," he writes; "I strapped on the football helmet my parents had lovingly bought me and got run right over as if I'd been a sandbag somebody had left on the playground. . . . I knew I'd never fit in."

McCloskey's drawings of Lentil, with his suspenders, rolled pants legs, and bare feet recall Huckleberry Finn and offer the reader a picture of quintessential Midwest innocence. Lentil's story, however, is an appealing one for nearly all readers wherever they live; the town, good versus evil, the old man, the trickster, and Lentil himself are archetypes that children and adults everywhere recognize. Like every child, Lentil wants to be special. Not only can he not sing, "when he opened his mouth . . . only strange sounds came out." Undaunted, Lentil saves his pennies to buy a harmonica and sets out to "become an expert." *Lentil*, like life and all good stories, includes complications, including "Old Sneep," a cantankerous old-timer who "didn't like much of anything or anybody."

It is Sneep who opposes plans for the welcome home party for the town's benefactor, Colonel Carter, but Lentil saves the day by pulling out his harmonica and playing "Comin 'round the Mountain When She Comes." "So," McCloskey concludes, "you never can tell what will happen when you learn to play the harmonica."

Lentil, with its gentle humor and well-intended hero, was a story in which young Kooser found hope. He bought himself a harmonica and began practicing. Though he mastered "Red River Valley," he knew his musical talents were a distant second to Lentil's. Eventually, Teddy would discover his own music; the ideas of becoming accomplished through a dedication to an art and art as a public service that we find in McCloskey's *Lentil* stayed with the poet and influenced his approach to poetry, which, to be of value to the community, requires diligence and a good deal of hard work.

The archetypal quality of *Lentil* will become a consistent hallmark of the poet's own work. Like McCloskey's stories and illustrations that reflect his youth in Ohio, Kooser's poetry and prose are inseparable from Iowa where he grew up and Nebraska where he now makes his home. Many of his poems address the reader directly or draw the reader into the poem just as McCloskey does with Lentil.

"This book belongs to Teddy Kooser," the boy wrote with his newly acquired cursive on *Lentil*'s title page, and he added it to his library, which would, over time, grow to include thousands of volumes of children's books, poetry, fiction, and nonfiction, which, the poet estimates, comprises the largest private library in Seward County, Nebraska.

CHAPTER THREE

Summers in Paradise

That hill's hard core of yellow stone held steady at 43 degrees
all year round, just warm enough in winter to work in shirtsleeves
stacking the milky slabs of ice sawed from the lid of the river
and sledged uphill with horses, then blanketed with sawdust
to hold the cold, to keep the past from trickling into the present.

—From "Ice Cave"

As soon as the last bell of the school year rang, Ted Sr. drove Vera and their children across the state to visit their maternal grandparents, John and Elizabeth Moser. Located about 180 miles east of Ames, Guttenberg, Iowa, rests in the heart of the verdant upper Mississippi River valley. In striking contrast to the flat, rich farmland the Koosers had just crossed by car, the Paleozoic Plateau of Clayton County contains little of the silt, clay, sand, gravel, and rocks left behind by retreating glaciers during the Wisconsin glaciation. Unlike the deep loess material that provides much of the state with a rich and stable farmland, the Driftless Area is known for its outcrops of bedrock that form the limestone cliffs and, in summer, its lush canopy of trees. Springs, sinkholes, and caves are common. River valleys in this area are deep and steep, and the view of the

Mississippi as the Great River Road, U.S. Highway 52, winds down into Guttenberg is breathtaking.

Kooser returns to the area in his poetry and prose, describing it with great affection. When faced with cancer in 1998, the valley was a source of comfort and healing. In his essay "Lights on a Ground of Darkness," Kooser distills his childhood visits, preserving his memories and providing a window into his cultural inheritance, the origins of his art, and the pastoral quality found throughout his work. Originally published in 1998 in the *Great River Review*, the narrative is set in 1949 when Teddy was about the same age as Lentil. Kooser braids geography, history, and family stories in an attempt to bring to life the essence and importance of these early visits.

The valley's beauty did not escaped Jacques Marquette and Louis Joliet in 1673. Although these explorers continued their travels north, following the Illinois, Des Plaines, and Chicago Rivers to Lake Michigan, traders and trappers following the same route set up a small outpost where they traded with the Sauk and Mesquakie, who had seasonal camps in the area.

Five years after Iowa became a state (1846), not quite a century before Teddy Kooser's birth, Prairie La Porte, "the door to the prairie," as the town was originally called, was incorporated by its mostly German-speaking residents as "Gutenberg," to honor Johannes Gutenberg, the inventor of moveable type. A printer's error on the first plat of the site filed in county records accounts for the change in spelling of the name and eventually in the pronunciation.

Sometimes referred to as the Switzerland of Iowa, the region's valleys and meadows must have looked very much like home to the German and Swiss immigrants who had settled there. Inexpensive farmland brought the first Germans, the largest immigrant group in Iowa, many aided by the Western Settlement Society of Cincinnati, which had purchased land in Clayton County for newcomers.

Kooser's maternal grandfather's father, Nicholas Moser (1825–1904), was born in Brunnenthal, a small Swiss village outside Berne. In 1851 he boarded the *Westphalia* in Bremen, Germany, and arrived in the port of New York November 16. He settled in

New Philadelphia, Ohio, where he worked as a stone mason. Traveling with him from the old country were Christian and Anna Maria Gisiger, whose daughter, Dorathea Magdalina, became his first wife.

Three years later, Nicholas and Magdalina moved west, heading down the Ohio River, then up the Mississippi. The Mosers came ashore, surveyed the area, and eventually purchased farm land south and a bit west of Guttenberg, near Osterdock, along the Turkey River, a quick-running stream that joins the Mississippi River a few miles downstream. Moser developed the tract in Mallory township, into "one of the valuable farms of the county." As early as 1835, Kooser writes, the Turkey River valley was described as having exceptional soil and woodland. When the Mosers came ashore, Kooser imagines, they took the "soil up into their hands and sniffed at it and crumbled it and planted it with corn and oats and wheat and garden vegetables."

While the Turkey River valley seemed in many ways a virtual Arcadia to the young poet, Teddy heard stories and bore witness to the challenges of the landscape, a counterforce contained within the pastoral tradition that can be traced all the way back to Virgil. Nick Moser's first wife died within a few years of their arrival, leaving him with two young daughters. In 1860 he married Anna Marie Mulett (1830-1903), also from Brunnenthal, a fellow passenger on the *Westphalia*. Anna, widow of his first wife's brother, brought five daughters of her own from Dubuque to the Turkey River farm. John Moser, born in 1874, was the youngest of their fifteen children.

On his visits to Guttenberg, Teddy studied the portraits of Nick and Anna Moser, seated on the porch of their farmhouse, and in his essay he notes his great-grandmother's smile as well as his great-grandfather's angry squint as he looked at the photographer. They died within a month of each other in 1904.

The Morarends, Elizabeth Moser's parents, John Dietrich (1832–1917) and Dorothea Schroeder (1840-1925), hailed from Hanover and Mecklenburg, respectively, in northeastern Germany, where many lives were uprooted as the old feudal system gave way in the 1800s. They married in 1858 in Guttenberg.

After John Moser purchased his parents' home place of just over 180 acres, and he and Elizabeth (1879–1962) married in Guttenberg on December 28, 1898. The Mosers raised their four children on the homestead. In the mid-1930s the brick chimney of the farmhouse caught fire, a moment the future poet will describe through his grandfather's eyes decades later in the poem "Grandfather." In their sixties, the couple had long anticipated leaving the family farm; due to cerebral palsy their son, Elvy, they knew, would not be able to undertake the physical labor necessary to keep the farm running.

The Mosers sold the land to a relative and moved into Guttenberg, where they built a Standard Oil service station and small house on U.S. Highway 52 on the edge of town. By this time the Moser children, save Elvy, had moved away, although they came home frequently to visit. While at the university in Iowa City, about a hundred miles from Guttenberg, Vera met another Clayton County girl, Ruth Stickfort (later Kregel), also a member of the Chi Omega sorority. They became life-long friends, and she became the Kooser children's "Aunt Sticky," whose blue flow china will become the subject of a Kooser poem.

The Mosers' white bungalow, with a screened porch and in the shade of an old catalpa, would be home for nearly thirty years. Next to the front stoop, there was a patch of blue, pink salmon, and yellow irises that, Kooser writes, grew "from roots that have been moved from house to house down the years" and now grow along the side of his own home in Nebraska.

The small sleepy town of Guttenberg that the Mosers' grandson visited in the 1940s and 1950s, Kooser writes,

> is taking a midday nap under the trees on the bank of the river. Its wide streets are quiet, its window shades drawn down against the heat. Old elms sprinkle the deserted sidewalks with lacy, drifting patterns. There's a light breeze off the water, carrying the smell of fish and the soft, regular sound of waves lapping the sides of tied-up boats. . . .

The buildings that face the river all date from the mid-1800s. Nearly all of them are two stories in height, built of cut limestone or of brick, with elaborate stone cornices. The original storefronts with their high windows and recessed entryways have been "modernized," but the original facades still peer over the tops of the glaring spreads of glass and the slick cummerbunds of new signs.

Because Guttenberg was largely composed of German descendants and lay at least partially protected in the river valley, anti-German hysteria during the world wars did not significantly change the town as it did others across the Midwest, where sauerkraut was renamed liberty cabbage and German-American place-names were altered in an attempt to escape prejudice. In Kossuth County, for example, the town of Germania was renamed Lakota. In Guttenberg, however, when the town council voted to change the town's name back to Prairie-la-Porte, citizens balked. Residents continued to call their town Guttenberg, and street signs continued to honor German writers and musicians. Despite the state's various language laws, Kooser remembers attending German-language services at St. Paul's Lutheran Church well into the 1950s.

Teddy relished these boyhood summers in Guttenberg, where he dug worms with Elvy and played with his sister under the watchful eye of his grandmother's "little flock of white leghorn hens, bunched together at our side of their pen," as they invented Swinging Off the Table, a game of "great daring and much squealing and laughing."

The town and the surrounding hills seemed filled with all sorts of stories, serving as an inspiration for Kooser's later writing. The Standard Station, its "pop cooler in which the bottles of soda—Nehi Grape, OhSo Orange, strawberry, cream soda—are submerged to their caps in water cooled by a block of ice," was a gathering place for other retired farmers, "men who have nothing better to do than sit in the shade and swap stories." Teddy listened: "I want desperately to be a part of their company, to tell my own good stories, but it is impossible for a little boy to get a word in edgewise. . . . Though I don't know it yet, I will one day be a writer, and my poems and stories will in many ways be my way of applying for acceptance into this same circle of old men, though they will all be ghosts by the time I am ready to tell them a story."

The Moser clan was known for enjoying life, and when they "sang together after dinner, their voices filled the valley." Teddy's grandfather, even as an old man, remembered the words to "After the Ball Is Over" and many other old-time songs. As a young man, John Moser pitched for the Turkey River Gobblers, and although serious about pinochle, he loved to have a good time and could be called upon to yodel or dance a jig in, Kooser writes, "his shiny black Standard Oil Shoes." According to his wife, despite his bald head as an adult, he had had dark curls when he courted her, "parking his buggy on the road below her farm and stealing up through the woods to meet her in the shadows beside the house."

Summer visits included listening to family stories as the boy traveled along Jolly Ridge Road visiting among the Moser and Morarend relatives who still lived on farms in the Clayton County hills where storytelling was a way of life. Parthenia, his grandfather's niece and mother's childhood friend, with her husband, Clarence Meyer, opened their home, "a huge box of light and laughter and music," to Teddy and his family. Clarence's polka band, the Jolly Ridge Hillbillies, was known up and down Turkey River valley.

Visits to the Noacks, his grandmother's sister Laura and her husband Pete, introduced the boy to other ways of life and another kind of music. Pete, who once worked as the county assessor, and his wife lived without electricity and running water on their farm "elbowed into the edge of the timber along the high ridge that divides the good flat farmland of eastern Iowa from the tumbling, rocky woodland of the Mississippi valley." They raised fruits and vegetables and earned a little bit of money from selling produce.

The Noacks were musicians. In a photograph Teddy discovered at his grandparents' home, his great-uncle Pete is posed with his harp and his sons, Harold and Harvey, with violin and flute, respectively, in hand. By the time the boy met his mother's first cousin Harvey, he had returned with his wife, Helen, to the farm following a career as a classical flutist. His story was to make a big impression on Teddy. At the end of World War I Harvey Noack headed to Cedar Rapids, where he played in theater orchestras that accompanied silent films. By the early 1920s he had moved to Chicago and then on to Paris, where he lived for several years studying with European flutists. According to the obituary in the Guttenberg Press, Noack returned to the States and played concert tours with Florence MacBeth, well-known soprano soloist, and became a member of the Minneapolis and Chicago Symphony Orchestras. He was a member of the Chicago Symphony for twenty-five years, serving as principle flutist from 1944 to 1946. As Noack neared middle age, he was affected by a crippling disease and returned with his wife Helen to Clayton County, where they lived with his parents on the farm.

The Moser home itself was a treasure trove of stories, where most evenings the family sat on the screened porch talking. In "Lights on a Ground of Darkness," Kooser describes the violet shadows that climb the Wisconsin bluffs in the distance as he and his sister wait for the next story to be told. "We are learning," Kooser notes, "the way in which stories end, how they drift into near silence, yet leave an after-ringing, like a bell," a bell that the gravediggers "hear" in "Another Story," and Bashō's flowers continue to sound after the temple bell falls silent.

Other nights other relatives with other stories came by to play pinochle. Soon after they arrived, the boy, safe to listen and to dream, curled up on the porch swing. Like the field mouse who with the young boy's touch jumped awake in the tulip vines, Teddy awakened to family, music, stories, and the sounds and smells of nature even as he fell asleep on the porch swing listening to the snap of the cards, the crickets, and the frogs calling from the backwater across the road and smelling the distant river and the fragrant iris just outside the front door.

CHAPTER FOUR

Looking the Part

You may have seen me. . . .
bleached-out Levis, boots with chains,
a leather jacket, and duck's-ass hair.

—From "Home Town"

When the Guttenberg visits were over, the Koosers returned to Ames, where backyard gardens were at their height and night began to nibble at the edges of summer. The leaves of the great elms began to turn, and the school bell called the town's children back to classrooms. At Beardshear School Teddy loved to draw and paint; his teachers recognized and encouraged his artistic talent. In fourth grade Miss Kirby introduced him to poetry. From the beginning, the young poet wrote about the world at hand: "'I love my dog, his padded paws. / At Christmas he's my Santa Claus. / At Easter he's my Easter bunny,'" Kooser recites, recalling an early poem, "And then I suppose the next line ends with 'funny.'"

Teddy was drawn to dramatic narratives, including "The Listeners" by British writer Walter De La Mare. A stirring account of a lone traveler's ride through the dark night, the poem was one from which, Kooser writes, he "never quite recovered."

"Is there anybody there?" "The Listeners" begins, as the traveler knocks "on the moonlit door, / And his horse in the silence champed the grasses / Of the forest's ferny floor." Although no one answers, the rider senses ghostly listeners who had once lived there, not so unlike the imaginings of Kooser's readers of his early poem "Abandoned Farmhouse." Mystery, rhythm, the solitary journey, and a keen awareness of the reader—key elements of "The Listeners"—continue to sound in his work. As Kooser writes, "In at least a dozen of my poems written over the past forty years you can find me beating on doors and hollering out to the ghosts within. I am in many ways still the Lone Traveler."

As Teddy grew up, he began working for his father at Younkers at Christmas time. On Saturdays and weekday afternoons after school, Teddy made bows for gift packages in the store's basement. His first job beyond Younkers at twelve was making posters for the glass cases in the old entrance of the Ames Carnegie Library. Given his early interest in books and libraries, it should be no surprise that Kooser has become a bibliophile. "A library is like an airport," he writes in *Local Wonders*; "if you wait long enough, everybody in the world will walk past." Kooser chose a small-town library as the setting for an early (unpublished) novel.

Also important to the young boy were the examples of local artists. On one of his walks around town with his father, Ted Sr. pointed out painter Velma Wallace Rayness's house near the Iowa State University campus at 3022 Oakland Street. Although Kooser admits he never met or even saw Rayness, who was a portrait painter and educator, her life, as he imagined it, became a source of inspiration. Though serious about his drawing and painting even as a boy, Teddy did not think to ask for art lessons, yet her importance as an example of a local working artist was profound. "I've spent my life," he writes in *Local Wonders*, "trying to move myself into a house just like the one where Velma Rayness lived."

Teddy grew up in Iowa, a state with a long and varied literary tradition. Authors from the Midwest and the Plains provided important literary role models and later informed the direction his own work would take. His boyhood imagination was captured by the autobiography of the Sauk leader Black Hawk, whose last battle was, according to Kooser, just north of Guttenberg, on the Wisconsin side of the Mississippi. "Pursuing Blackhawk," a long narrative poem, is one of his continuing writing projects, Kooser writes.

Something of a Midwest literary movement had gained national prominence beginning in 1910 and continuing well into the 1930s. Hannibal Hamlin Garland (1860–1940) was, and still is, the best-known Iowa fiction writer of the pioneering days of the state. Four of Garland's early novels take place in Winneshiek and Mitchell Counties in northeast Iowa, not far from Guttenberg's Clayton County. Willa Cather's major works, including *O Pioneers!*, *The Song of the Lark*, *My Ántonia*, *One of Ours,* and *A Lost Lady*, were generally popular as Teddy grew up, as was Sinclair Lewis's *Main Street* and *Babbitt*. Iowa novelist Ruth Suckow, like Kooser's maternal grandmother's family, hailed from Mecklenburg, Germany. Kooser will reflect many of the views Suckow held, including the notion that tragedy is given a particular flavor in the Middle West, where it is "given a local habitation and a name." Frederick Manfred, writing under the name of Feike Feikema until 1951, was another prolific novelist of the Midwest landscape. Kooser, a long-time admirer of Manfred's work, met the novelist in the early 1970s, and they were friends until the novelist's death.

Harriet Monroe, who founded *Poetry* magazine in Chicago in 1912, with the assistance of Ezra Pound, who served as her "foreign correspondent," introduced the nation's readers to the work of Modernist poets. "The Love Song of J. Alfred Prufrock," by T. S. Eliot, an expatriate from St. Louis, Missouri, living in London, appeared in *Poetry* in 1915. Midwestern populist poets, whose works also appeared in *Poetry*, found nationwide audiences. Illinois poet Carl Sandburg published *Chicago Poems* (1916) and *Cornhuskers* (1918). His multivolume biography of Abraham Lincoln appeared between 1929 and 1939. Edger Lee Masters's *Spoon River Anthology* was published in 1915 and remains a classic today. Vachel Lindsey's *Collected Poems* appeared in 1923.

Through his parents' theater group, Kooser was likely to have heard of playwright and novelist Susan Glaspell (1882–1948). Glaspell, born in Davenport, Iowa, is best known for her one-act play "Trifles" (1916), based on a murder case she had covered when she was a reporter for the *Des Moines Daily News*. Ted Sr. was, according to his son, an acquaintance of Meredith Willson, who wrote the score and libretto for the hit Broadway musical *The Music Man*. Willson, a native of Mason City, stopped in to visit when he was in town.

As a freshman at Ames High, however, Kooser's attention was diverted to cars, and, he admits, he was rebellious: "I had a hot rod and walked around with the collar of my jacket turned up and my hair swept back. I wasn't too much into impressing teachers. I had a real serious girlfriend from the time I was a sophomore in high school until I was a junior in college and that sort of went against the grain, too, with the family. They didn't like that, which was fine with me, because I wanted to do things they didn't like."

Ames High brought together students from Downtown and Campus Town. Kooser was well liked, known for his artwork, his love of cars, and his relationship with Nancy Thornton, described by a classmate, memoirist Susan Toth, as a "pretty and popular dark-haired cheerleader."

Kooser and Jack Winkler, a high school and college friend, now an Ames businessman, were charter members of the hot-rodding group the Nightcrawlers Car Club. When Kooser, who served as the group's secretary in 1956, put "a big Chevy engine on a little roadster," it became, according to Winkler, "a major neighborhood attraction." Winkler continues, "Kooser's first drive in the dragster ended with a spin over a neighbor's landscaping." Kooser recalls his first car was a 1949 Ford coupe; "I lowered the front end, put in an Oldsmobile grill, and pinstriped it. I did a lot of pinstriping for hotrodders when I was a teenager." In the 1980s, driving along I-80, Kooser says he came upon a Ford coupe with his own familiar pinstriping. ANTIQUE, the license plate read.

The Kooser family had moved to 1321 Marston Avenue in 1953, when their son, still known as Teddy at home, was a sophomore. By then both Winkler and Kooser were writers as well as hot-rodders. Kooser was guided toward writing by his teachers, and he acknowledges the importance of one high school teacher, the late Mary McNally, who encouraged his writing, including lyrical essays much like those that will appear in his memoir.

Writing, including poetry, was very much alive at every level of Iowa schools. Poet Paul Engle continued as director of the prestigious Writers' Workshop at the University of Iowa, a post he held until 1965. James Hearst, who taught at the University of Northern Iowa for many years, was known as a poet as well as an educator. Mona Van Duyn, born in 1921 in Waterloo, studied with Hearst, went on to teach at the University of Iowa, won the Pulitzer Prize for Poetry in 1991, and, two years later, became the first woman appointed U.S. poet laureate.

Karl Shapiro, who would become the young writer's mentor, was teaching part-time at the Iowa Writers' Workshop, driving over from Chicago, where he was editor of *Poetry*. William Stafford, a doctoral student at the workshop during the early 1950s, lists a host of well-known writers who taught at Iowa as regular faculty or as visiting poets: John Crowe Ransom, Reed Whittemore, Robert Penn Warren, and Randall Jarrell. D. W. Snodgrass and Donald Justice were among his fellow students. None of these poets were, however, as exotic, as ground-breaking, or as flamboyant to the young hot-rodders as the Beats.

"The beatnik [Beat] poets were a big attraction," Winkler says; "They were hot and that's where we wanted to be." In a 1979 interview Kooser identifies Jack Kerouac's *On the Road* and writing by the Beats as the first works he says he took seriously. "I really wanted to be an intellectual," he says, and bought Adolph Harnack's *History of Dogma*, which he calls "impenetrable," to carry around to make a good impression.

Poetry and drawing offered the teenager, as did the harmonica for Lentil, a way to creatively express who he was. Kooser says, "I was always interested in the arts as a way of differentiating myself from other people." He elaborates in the *Nebraska Humanist*:

At some lonely hour when I was a teenager, it struck me like a bolt of lightning that I should set out to become a famous poet, and I fell upon this idea with typical adolescent single-mindedness. There were, it seemed to me, many benefits accruing to such a career. First, but not necessarily foremost . . . there was glory: that moment when the city librarian would weep with joy as you deigned to pass the time of day with her. Second, there was immortality: the lichen-encrusted bust standing throughout all time in a swirl of golden autumn leaves. Third, there was the delicious responsibility of the bohemian life: no more rooms to pick up, no more dishes to do.

It was some time before Kooser realized that in order to be a famous poet, he "should have published at least one famous poem. To me, the writing of poetry didn't have all that much to do with being a poet. Being a poet was mainly looking the part. I took to walking around in rubber shower sandals and white beachcomber pants tied with a rope. I let my hair grow a little and tried to grow a beard."

And there were girls: "I got the idea that being a famous poet made one sexually attractive by reading *Life* magazine. In those days, they occasionally profiled some rumpled, unshaven, drunken and melancholy poet (never a woman, as far as I can remember), and I got the idea from the accompanying text that these fellows were woman-killers (as we used to say). It had to be the poetry that made the difference, because were it not for that, these poets would not have been allowed in the house, let alone be permitted to hold the cool, dry hand of a beautiful girl."

He began writing a ballad each day during study hall for his high school sweetheart. When he and Thornton broke up, she burned the poems, which was, according to the poet, "in many ways a blessing."

During high school, Kooser served as scenic designer for the drama club's *Laura* and acted in several plays, including the Pulitzer Prize–winning comedy *You Can't Take It with You* by George S. Kaufman and Moss Hart, in the role of Donald, Rheba the cook's black boyfriend. In *The Silver Whistle*, a farce by Robert E. McEnroe, he was cast in the role of Emmett. The dancing lessons in the Methodist Church basement when he was a child paid off during the summer of 1959; he and his partner, Pat Bloomfield, were one of three couples who won the rock-and-roll jitterbug contest sponsored by the Ames Gold & Country Club.

Of the 175 students in his graduating class, two—Kooser and Susan Toth—would go on to be well-known writers. The Campus Town Ames about which Toth writes in her 1984 memoir, *Blooming*, is not one the poet says he recognizes. "Susan and I were acquaintances in high school," Kooser remembers, "but our social lives were completely different. She was what we used to call one of the Neat Kids, and I hung out with the car nuts and troublemakers."

Kooser's interest in drawing continued to flourish in formal high school art classes. In the summer of his sophomore year, he began his apprenticeship with J. Laverne Mullica, a local sign painter, from whom, he says, he learned more about painting than in classes. He worked for Mullica, evoked in his poem "Gold Leaf," off and on though out college.

According to Kooser's sister, there was no question that she and her brother would go to college; "The only question was where it was to be." Kooser enrolled in Iowa State University of Agriculture and Mechanical Arts (now known as Iowa State University), matriculating in the architecture program. Located in Ames, ISU—alma mater of both of his father's brothers—was convenient and familiar. As a boy he swung on the branches of the campus trees and visited his uncle Tubby's office. Study at ISU would also allow him to live at home. With its engineering and technical orientation, ISU did not stress the design component of architecture that drew him to the field, however.

Kooser took basic drawing as well as Lawton Patton's watercolor class. Although Patton's class was designed to assist student architects in rendering their models, Kooser says it provided him with the basic painting skills he would build on throughout his life. At the Iowa State Library, he also discovered the nine-mural design (funded by the Works Progress Administration) by Iowa artist Grant

Wood. As did Kooser with his poetry, Wood advised painters to paint things around them, rather than to rely on European themes and subjects.

With Nancy Thornton away studying at Iowa Wesleyan College in Mount Pleasant, Kooser was on his own freshman year. He spent his free time with Jack Winkler and another friend, Jim Stevens, "drinking beer and writing poems." Following "a drunken tobogganing party," Kooser was hospitalized with pneumonia. High fever brought hallucinations: the walls of his hospital room swayed, invented visitors came to see him, fur began to grow on the door to his room, and he began to read an imaginary book that would change his life.

CHAPTER FIVE

King, A Dog of the North

Take what is given, and make it over your way.

—Robert Frost, *Vogue*

King, A Dog of the North, a "richly detailed and absorbing story" about a German shepherd, Kooser recalls, perfectly suited the twenty-year-old patient who had, because of his illness, regressed to half his age. He recounts his fevered reading, following King's adventures as he "made his way through snowdrifts, up and down the sheer faces of mountains, through flooded, ice-choked streams." The young college student was so absorbed in the story that when his girlfriend of four years returned to Ames to break up with him, he didn't argue.

When his fever broke and he was feeling better, Kooser searched his hospital room for the book that had so captured his imagination. He described its cover in detail to his parents, who not only had no recollection of seeing it but also told him that he had been far too ill to read anything. In his delirium, he finally saw, he had written, printed, bound, and published *King* in order "to snatch himself from the jaws of pneumonia." If *Lentil* gave Teddy a way to feel special by serving the community through his music, *King* pointed the young man he had become toward storytelling. "I have been a writer ever since," he says.

Health restored, Kooser returned to school, fell in love with a sorority girl who did not return his affection, and wrote some very melancholy poems. His literary horizons, however, were about to broaden. One afternoon Kooser came across the New Directions paperback edition of William Carlos Williams's *Selected Poems* and discovered, he says, a new way to think about poetry and to write it. As he notes years later, "Most of a poet's education is self education, and most of what you'll learn you'll teach yourself through reading and writing poems." Soon he discovered Edwin Arlington Robinson, Robert Frost, e. e. cummings, May Swenson, Randall Jarrell, and John Crowe Ransom. "I'd read May Swenson to death; I'd read all the books I could get a hold of in Ames," he says. "We had a newsstand there, an odd newsstand [Walt's News Stand] that had books of poetry . . . the Scribner's series, blue and white . . . I was reading what I could get my hands on."

"But the craft of careful writing and meticulous revision *can* be taught," Kooser believes. For him this was very true; Will C. Jumper, with whom the young poet took his first college creative writing course, was committed to both craft and revision. "The first assignment we had was to write thirty lines of natural description in rhyming heroic couplets," the poet recalls. Send it to *Poetry*, Jumper advised when he read "Cold Pastoral," the poem that resulted. Kooser took his professor's advice. John Frederick Nims, then on *Poetry* magazine's editorial staff, wrote the young poet a supportive two-page response, on blue tissue airmail stationary, and although the poem was not accepted for publication, the encouragement served the fledgling poet well. "Cold Pastoral," as revised over the years, is included in his first collection, *Official Entry Blank*, and prefigures much of the poet's work.

Kooser did publish short nonfiction pieces, which the poet describes as "a little sugary," in the Iowa State student literary magazine, *Sketch: Magazine of Student Creative Writing*. "The Chariot

Cometh," which appeared in the Spring 1960 issue, for example, foreshadows in tone and content the short sections in *Local Wonders*, written decades later. He continued to work with Jumper, a serious writer and scholar as well as a devoted teacher, throughout his college career and dedicated his first collection of poems to his mentor. He later commented on Jumper's emphasis on form:

> He [Jumper] believed in a very strict. . . . We began with exercises in which we were to write thirty lines of closed heroic couplets of natural description. Then we wrote ballads and rondels and villanelles and all those things and achieved a lot of technical mastery of all those forms. . . . And because of that I had so much iambic motion drilled into me during that time that it was very hard for me to escape from iambic verse and a lot of my earlier poems are pretty strongly iambic and unvaried—varied only within the frame of the traditional variance.

Even in the early 1970s, when Kooser experimented with meter and developed a more idiomatic voice, he still felt the need for form, a product of his early training.

Jumper, who put a premium on student contact, was the advisor for the Iowa State Writers' Round Table, which consisted of sixteen students. Membership in the group was by invitation and based on work submitted for consideration. Kooser credits the group with helping him hone his craft while providing him with a sense of community with other writers. "That was probably the best learning experience I've had," he has said. "Most of the people were about my age and we would really attack each other. It was very good. The first couple of experiences, we just walked away in tears. . . . There was no false praise going on." Other members of the group during Kooser's time included Senator Tom Harkin (D, Iowa) and Jack Winkler. A rallying point near campus for students and faculty alike was the Sportsman Bar, where Kooser would meet with his college classmates and childhood friends who were also attending ISU, Larry Christie, Billy Stoever, and Joe (Max) Molleston among them.

In 1959, in the Iowa State Campus Union, Kooser first encountered Diana Tressler, who would, in 1962, become his first wife. According to Tressler, Kooser had already taken on the "trappings" of a poet and artist; he wore a beret and, she says, looked like a combination of a French poet and Woody Allen. Their first official date did not take place until March 26, 1960. By April 3 they were "pinned." Tressler, a secondary education major two years younger than Kooser, hailed from Marshalltown, about twenty-five miles east of Ames on old Highway 30. Kooser says that his family accepted her immediately, in part because she was a member of Chi Omega, his mother's sorority.

A cache of Kooser's letters to Tressler, written almost daily during the summers and other separations of the couple prior to their wedding in Marshalltown, provides insight into the poet's world, his poetry, and his painting, as well as their relationship. On the second-month anniversary of pinning (June 3, 1960) he was working as a sign painter for J. Laverne Mullica, and amid protestations of love, he describes a "Big Circus Mural," eight feet long and four tall, he began on his off hours. He is also reading the *Selected Poems of Ezra Pound*. By the ninth of June he reports his continuing work on the mural and, in one of the few times in the correspondence between the two, waxes poetic.

What is remarkable is that Kooser's approach and images are ones that will become familiar to his later readers. "It may rain in Ames (in the heart of the Bible belt)," he begins. "Clouds are forming and rubbing their bottoms on our humble home—Porch swings creak all over America and an old man dies among ash cans—Pigeons shuffle dirty feet and fumble under wings for their pocket watches, and settling there among the neon, to be in night's dark town."

Kooser, in this early correspondence, is also apprising Tressler of his feeling of being alone in the world, often an undercurrent of his work. "I want you to understand that *I am very deeply in love with you*," he wrote June 15, "but that if I seem to be alone within myself that it is not you that cause this but rather that I am forever alone and will so remain. . . . My loneliness is not the usual type (and I despise 'type' as a word) but something ingrown which I must endure—my loneliness which I am without you is of a different scale. It is beautiful in its melancholy—."

Four days later, Sunday evening, June 19, Kooser reports to Tressler that he has completed his circus painting and has started a companion piece, the portrait of a clown. He notes his Romantic inclination in his painting and his move toward surrealism, foreshadowing the shift he will make later in his poetry. "I have reached a barrier in my work which I cannot surpass," he writes. "As I have mentioned innumerable times before," he continues,

> I cannot achieve beyond my clown—Romanticism is, of course, my niche so to speak and *Clown* exemplifies the utmost of my Romantic creativity—This last painting . . . is an attempt to break Romanticism into another facet, Romantic or semi-Romantic surrealism at a point which surrealism loses vivid romanticism for fantasy . . . such as in the late works of Tenguy and certain of Dali's in which the reality of the fable is expressed "photographically," the Romantic is lost—I do not mean to imply that Romanticism is the similarity to the Romantics but the philosophical feeling of Kant, Hegel and Schopenhauer—what my painting is then, is a Romantically oriented still life with the distortion of size and object enclosed in surrealism—

That same month Kooser writes of Baudelaire's *Fleur de Mal*: "I have never read finer poetry—one image is absolutely beautiful—He pictures Hope as a huge bat who is fluttering about a darkened room hitting his head and bruising his 'timid' wings—*magnificent*." On June 22 1960, he notes that his "poetic sublimation is nil—I am afraid to face Jumper . . . (I presume, by now," he continues, "that you've rediscovered my 'standard' definition of poetry ["the spontaneous overflow of powerful feelings"] in Wordsworth's *Preface to Lyrical Ballads*.)"

The roots of Romanticism, a reaction to rationalism of the nineteenth century, were solidly planted in the pastoral tradition that

Kooser will contemporize. Intensity, imagination, and an organic view of nature that includes human beings, hallmarks of Romanticism, will remain hallmarks of Kooser's best work throughout his career, along with his interest in the process of creativity. Relationship within and through time, as it was for the Romantics, is central to his work as is his continuing interest in landscape.

By the end of July the two young college students were looking forward to seeing each other when college resumed. Longing and poetry are intermingled throughout the letters. Friday evening, July 22, Kooser writes that he'd bought a pack of cigarettes and a quart of beer and took a walk that led him to the public library, where he checked out a few books. "*Am I lonely—*," he continues. "I walked down the railroad tracks and sat by a red signal light and read William Butler Yeats—Eccentricity is wonderful, and *so* natural—It seems so trite," he goes on without paragraph break, "but—*wish you were here.*" Finally school started, and Tressler and Kooser were reunited.

Until his junior year (1960–1961), Kooser struggled under the yoke of engineering, mathematics, and physics. Finally he liberated himself from "Theoretical and Applied Mathematics," tossed his $12 slide rule into the campus lake, and moved from the study of architecture to that of another form.

"I switched then to a curriculum called 'Distributed Studies,'" a liberal arts program available at ISU, Kooser explains. After meeting classroom requirements for a degree in secondary education with an emphasis in English, he still needed to complete a semester of student teaching. As he writes in *Local Wonders*, "I was certain that I wanted to be a writer, but I ached all over with the melancholy prospect of facing countless years of acting like a grown up. Writing poems and stories was exhilarating, and I could not foresee any such fun under the ghastly burden of steady employment. Teaching English was the only solution that had thus far presented itself, offering as it did the promise of days spent talking about books and writing."

Letters to Tressler from the summer of 1961 continue the themes of longing and poetry, along with family news and good humor. June 28, writing from Waterloo due to his work with the Iowa highway commission, Kooser writes that he is "doing my best to 'hatch' poems,"

> but with very little luck—I am in a frenzy because I cannot find myself—I think I will have to drop back to basic themes to clear my head—I seem to be mentally withered right now & am extensively worried about *only* two (and very bad) poems since school was out—which brings out another worry—I don't seem to be able to write without available criticism—ah! *Cest la vie*—

> I think I shall excuse myself now—having suddenly remembered Clark Kent Superman's suicide and its ironic occurrence—and *it scans*! "and Superman committed suicide" BRAVO!! [iambic scansion indicated]

Kooser meets a possible pregnancy with equanimity. "Neither good nor bad news," he reassures his "Dearest Diana" from the Sunset Motel in Iowa City on July 17, "will change our future happiness." By August 9, from Carroll, Iowa, he apologizes for his "sorry-for-myself" letters. His depression, "like an eyelid," descended "within the last 3 days—first a flutter, then a raucous wink, then bleak darkness—." Even so, Kooser is hopeful. "I have," he writes, "discovered a volume of Keats in the hotel library . . . [and] I am hoping that I'll stumble across my muse somewhere as my canted invocations by the roadside have done no good."

When Iowa State opened its doors for the fall term, Tressler returned to Ames. Shortly after, however, Kooser moved to Marshalltown, where he had been accepted for student teaching. The couple was formally engaged, and he took up residence with his fiancée's parents, Maurice and Mary Tressler, who ran the Smith Herzog Sewing Service. Kooser recalls that time fondly. Tressler's mother was "a splendid cook, and her father a good storyteller, and we sometimes sat in their living room and drank beer and talked until late in the evening."

While Kooser was in Marshalltown, his parents moved from Ames when Ted Sr. was transferred to the Younker's Lindale Plaza branch in Cedar Rapids. Returning to his hometown, he roomed with Margaret Livingston, widow of his father's friend Arnold, wrote his poetry, and counted the days until graduation.

CHAPTER SIX

Moving Gibraltar

Once you were young along a river, tree to tree,
with sleek black wings and red shoulders.

—From "A Poetry Reading"

The year 1962 was one of important decisions and inevitable change. In love and impatient, Kooser and Tressler eloped the second week of January. Aided and abetted by friends Jack Winkler and Inge Mai Knutson, who serve as witnesses, they drove from Ames to Dixon, Illinois, about 150 miles west of Cedar Rapids, to be married by a justice of the peace on January 12. The marriage was a "prophylactic measure," Kooser says, insurance against the repercussions of a possible pregnancy. Neither the bride's nor groom's parents were ever to learn about the Dixon nuptials.

Meanwhile, what seemed to be the constant, mysterious, and musical world of Guttenberg was beginning to crumble. Kooser's grand-aunt, Laura Morarend Noack, had been laid to rest the previous March; his grandmother, Elizabeth Moser, died after a long illness on January 17, less than a week after her grandson's marriage. Kooser returned with his family to Guttenberg for her funeral; freezing gusts blew in from the river, and the temperature dipped to 22 below.

This was the last time he was to see his mother's first cousin Harvey Noack, the classical flutist. "He was by then so badly stooped," Kooser writes, "that as he sat in a folding chair in the church basement during the after-service luncheon, I had to sit on the floor at his feet to visit with him. Still he was the quiet and friendly, uncomplaining, a farm boy from Clayton County who'd traveled all over Europe."

After returning to Ames, Kooser graduated with his BS in English education in February 1962 and then moved to Cedar Rapids to live with his parents at 2721 Franklin Avenue, N.E. Family obligations frequently interrupted his writing and painting and sometimes interfered with plans to be with Tressler. He impatiently looked forward to spending time with his new bride. "I kept telling myself," he wrote in a letter postmarked Cedar Rapids on February 26, "that I will & must adjust to not being with you but secretly know I cannot—I have just finished a letter to Jimmy [Stevens] telling him about our secret; it was great fun to be able to imagine him reading it—." In the same letter to his wife the former architecture student reports that he had been mentally sketching "a design for a summer house for us someday. I will draw the plan and send or bring it to you for your opinion." In a typed letter mailed the next day he announces that he and his parents split the costs of a typewriter, "an Olivetti just like Aunt Margaret's . . . reduced from $157 to $98. . . OK?" The newly, if secretly, married Kooser reports he was also shopping for a wedding ring. "Please forgive me for your little wait. *I love you very much and want to please you so badly.*"

In a letter postmarked March 1, Kooser announces that his teacher's certificate came in the mail and that he was thinking about looking for a teaching job in the Guttenberg area. He also notes that he filed his income tax, "lying about guess what?"—presumably filing as a single person. "We may be jailed for perjury," he adds wryly. Despite concern about the draft and the dearth of job prospects, he continued to paint "a huge 'cubist' still life for our house someday," write, and read, noting he had picked up a book of old English ballads at the Salvation Army for a nickel.

During the spring Kooser traveled to Iowa City to visit the Writers' Workshop at the University of Iowa, where Paul Engle, the long-time program director, had accepted him for fall. In a letter postmarked March 6, 1962, Cedar Rapids, to Tressler, who was in Ames, he describes his job hunting and sitting in on a class taught by Donald Justice, "where people dressed like Che Guevara and wrote like Donald Justice." The letter, signed "HUSBAND," provides insight into both his view of poetry and his determination to support his wife when the time came. "The Poetry Workshop," he printed in a style he still uses today, "is not and must not be what the poetry of the culture is based on in the future—I need no more academic training to be happy & no more creative ideas than I can find in books & in myself. Mr. Justice is," he goes on, "indeed a finer poet than I will ever be & I am sending his book to you, which I hope you will send on to Will Jumper for me after reading it."

Following an unsuccessful interview with a large commercial sign company, Kooser activated his file at ISU's Teacher Placement Office and requested his credentials be sent to Madrid (pronounced Mad-rid, accent on the first syllable), Iowa, where there was a high school job opening. "This will sound strange to you," he wrote to Tressler, "but I think it best to try to teach (until you graduate at least) so that I can build a little security. Although I have voiced many times my dread of teaching, I am willing to confess that I did so partly out of fear, partly out of an unrealistic attitude, and partly out of rebellion—please accept this for what it is—. . . I think it is important that we have some security—Pray that the draft doesn't catch me before I get a job."

A March 18, 1962, letter announced that he had just signed his teaching contract at Madrid. Pay was to be $370 per month for twelve months, beginning August 29. The bad news was he would have to live in Madrid rather than Ames, where his new wife would be completing her senior year. His letters to Tressler, written nearly every day, record his work for the highway commission, his steady concern with poetry, drafts and fragments of poems, records of submission of a variety of publications, including *Harper's* and the

Hudson Review, his growing collection of rejection slips, his art projects, and his love for his new wife. He reports March 23 that in addition to searching for work, he is writing a poem on musical themes (which he will come back to as a mature poet), writing in syllabics, which, he says, "allows me to use more of my own language than strict meter." On April 21, 1962, the couple became officially engaged.

In an undated letter, "Tuesday Morn," Kooser chafes under the weight of household duties and touches on what will become a guiding aesthetic principle:

> it all comes back. . . . that sense of the overpowering unity of all things physical which is the source and lot of art. But the greatest thing of mystery about it all and again the most wonderful thing is that when some individual attempts to isolate it, explain it, it flattens and becomes mute. I will always hold that hope that someday I will have some small recognition, be it so insignificant as a smile from a small boy when he discovers those poems in an old box instead of a bear he is hunting there.

Financial worries and news of job interviews and car repairs frequently make their way into the correspondence, but poetry is never far from mind. Kooser asks his new wife to "watch the bookstore's poetry shelves for anything by H.D. or Amy Lowell." Two weeks later, he writes that he has returned to an earlier conversational tone in his work . . . "getting rid of a lot of preciousness that I picked up from Will Jumper." Kooser was working for the Iowa Highway Commission; the job would last only into July, but because of the twelve- to fourteen-hour work day, at $1.67 an hour, he looked forward to banking his earnings. In April his work took him along Highway 52 where he was "on a center line painting crew as flagman." He recalls that one day he found himself "flagging right in front of Grandpa's station." His grandfather came out "and stood on the center line with me and when someone would pull up in their car that he knew, he'd say to them, 'This is my only grandson.'"

Kooser has a change of heart about graduate school. On June

9 he writes to Tressler, who was vacationing with her parents at the Shady Lane Resort in Osage Beach, Missouri, "I will answer a question of yours by saying that I would like to go to graduate school when we can afford it but I don't think we could make a try of it next summer—."

As their summer of separation came to a close, Kooser's letters are optimistic, focusing on plans for their formal wedding and on furnishing their new apartment at 204½ South State Street, located above a real estate office in Madrid. "My letter," he writes on August 7, "looking back, seems like a list of great problems, but it's all fun, isn't it. With your help we could move Gibraltar, I am sure."

When the school term began, Tressler returned to Ames for her senior year and Kooser moved into the State Street apartment in Madrid, then a town of about two thousand, twenty miles southwest of Ames.

His first, and as it turned out his last, high school teaching position was "a nightmare.... It was," he says, "a tough school," with "kids fighting teachers, teachers fighting kids." Kooser was extremely shy and had never felt comfortable speaking in front of groups: "Most of the time my intestines were tied in such tight knots that my voice trembled and squeaked."

The high point of the autumn was Kooser's and Tressler's church wedding, a two-ring ceremony in Marshalltown the evening of November 17, at the First Methodist Church. Reverend James K. Delahooke officiated amid, according to the newspaper report, "cymbodium ferns and candelabra decorated with gold wheat and yuletide roses." Tressler's dress was "a floor length gown of ivory opera satin with re-embroidered lace motifs and the skirt ended in a chapel train. Her fingertip veil was held by a single lace rose and she carried a bouquet of red yule-tide roses with accents of gold wheat and ivory satin leaves."

At last the couple could be together. The bride commuted from Madrid to Ames to finish her degree, sharing rides with a veterinary student who lived next door, while her new husband car-pooled with the student's wife, a music teacher at Madrid High. The academic year passed slowly. By the time it was over, "I didn't know what I was going to do with my life. I didn't want to continue in high school teaching," he continues, but "I had no other skills other than that I could paint signs."

Kooser returned to sign painting in June following his high school teaching debut, driving his Jeep pick-up into small Iowa towns that reminded him of Lentil's town of Alto, Ohio. He set to work, painting out of the back of his truck, lettering "the glass windows of storefronts on Main Street. Old men would come out of the taverns and coffee shops, carrying folding chairs, and would sit behind me and watch me work. I was that exotic creature, an itinerant artist, and their attention and admiration warmed my back with a kind of bone-deep sunshine."

As he painted, Kooser mulled over the graduate readership that he had been offered at the University of Nebraska. The move west would take him and his new bride away from their families. On the other hand, it would allow him to study with Karl Shapiro, who was, Kooser has written, "among the two or three most important poets of his generation." Gradually, his choice became clear: "I wanted to throw myself at his feet."

1. Maternal grandparents: John R. Moser and Elizabeth D. Morarend married in Guttenberg, Iowa, December 28, 1898.

2. Vera Deloras Moser, University of Iowa Rush portrait, 1927.

3. Paternal grandfather: Charles F. Kooser.

4. Paternal grandmother: Grace E. (Lang) Kooser.

5. Father: Theodore Briggs Kooser as a young man at Tilden's Department Store.

6. Theodore John Kooser, known as "Teddy" as a boy, in his first official portrait.

7. The Kooser family in Ames, 1944: "Big Ted," as he was known at home, is holding Judith. Teddy is standing in front of his mother.

8. Teddy, like his hero Lentil, wanted to make music. His first "instrument" was a banjo that he made from two pieces of wood with strings drawn on. With it he entertained the family with his "hillbilly act," as his mother described it on the back of the photograph.

9. Teddy at six years of age going fishing in Guttenberg.

10. Teddy's formal grade school portrait.

11. Teddy and the boys in his class, 1948, Beardshear Elementary School. Teddy is wearing his favorite cowboy shirt.

12. Ted, secretary of the high school Nightcrawlers Car Club, pin-striped his hot rod, "Henrietta."

13. Fraternity photograph, Iowa State University, 1958.

14. Portrait of the young artist, 1960.

15. Marshalltown wedding, November 17, 1962: Maurice and Mary Tressler, their daughter, Diana, Ted and his parents, Vera and Theodore Kooser. Courtesy of Diana Tressler.

Two

Nebraska Apprenticeship, 1963–1969

CHAPTER SEVEN
———————

The Move to Nebraska

This is the life I have chosen.

—*Local Wonders*

Ted and Diana Kooser packed up their "wedding gifts and courage" and, in August 1963, "lumbered westward on balding tires" toward Lincoln, Nebraska, three hours southwest of Ames. Situated on rolling hills along the eastern edge of the North American Plains, the state's capital city proved to be a congenial home to the new residents.

Kooser remembers Lincoln as "very much a small town in those days before liquor-by-the-drink and the official blighting of blocks for grandiose development. Grass grew through the runways at the recently abandoned air base. Gateway Shopping Center was at the far east edge of town, overlooking the fields. In a barn to the west, as in some medieval hamlet, there were cockfights on Saturday nights. There was so little violent crime that people talked about the Starkweather killings as if they had happened only the week before."

The couple's new hometown was a major trucking and railroad hub, and the insurance industry, which within the year would become important to Kooser, was booming. "One of those American alphabetical towns," as Karl Shapiro came to describe Lincoln, was home to the University of Nebraska and two private church-affiliated colleges, Union and Nebraska Wesleyan. The Koosers quickly settled into an apartment at 1955 A Street, a short drive from campus. Diana applied for a high school teaching job in Malcolm, a nearby town, and the young poet enrolled in two classes with Shapiro and set up his writing desk in an old refrigerator box in the corner of their bedroom.

The university, where enrollment had reached 11,466, was undergoing substantial change at the time of Kooser's arrival. Clifford Hardin, chancellor since 1954, was determined that the land grant institution would become a first-class research university. He raised salaries in order to keep and to recruit faculty as well as began an ambitious development campaign to refurbish the university's physical plant and to build additional facilities. The Sheldon Memorial Art Gallery, designed as a streamlined, contemporary temple of the arts by architect Philip Johnson, had been dedicated the spring prior Kooser's arrival. An early leader in educational radio, the university had also begun to explore television as an educational tool. The introduction of quality paperbacks under the imprint of Bison Books furthered the reputation of the University Press as well as increasing its sales.

Karl Shapiro, one of the highly visible new faculty members, had served as U.S. consultant in poetry. At twenty-two, he had privately published his first collection, *Poems*. Drafted into the army in 1941 a few weeks shy of graduation from Enoch Pratt Library School, he was stationed in Australia. His second privately printed collection, *Place of Love*, was published in 1942. *Person, Place and Thing*, written while the poet served as a medical corps clerk in the South Pacific, soon followed. *V-Letter and Other Poems*, midwived by literary agent Evalyn Katz, Shapiro's fiancée, established his reputation when it was awarded the Pulitzer Prize in 1945.

Shapiro arrived in Lincoln in 1956 to teach creative writing and to become the second editor of the university's literary magazine, *Prairie Schooner*. A contemporary of Will Jumper's, Shapiro brought both solid editorial and teaching experience to the university. Prior to a year of teaching at the University of California–Davis, he served as editor of the prestigious *Poetry* magazine (1950–1955) in Chicago and taught as a visiting poet at the Iowa Writers' Workshop.

His presence alone brought the *Prairie Schooner* a wider public and literary visibility. Although initially created for writers living in the region—"the finest writing of the prairie country" had been its original motto—founding editor Lowry Charles Wimberly soon renounced the journal's geographic exclusivity. Kenneth Patchen, Eudora Welty, Tennessee Williams, Jessamyn West, Truman Capote, and many other writers from "afar" had already found welcome in its pages. Shapiro's own preference for the subjective style and personal idiom is reflected in his selections for the journal; poets he published included Josephine Miles, Isabella Gardner, Richard Eberhart, and William Carlos Williams. Many would not have come to the *Prairie Schooner* had Shapiro not been editor.

Shapiro seemed to enjoy the slower pace of Lincoln, as well as the sudden storms of the Midwest, where, he reported, he could shovel snow in his bare feet, chop his own firewood, paint, and learn welding. His years in Nebraska proved to be productive, both in terms of his poetry and prose. By the time Kooser arrived eight years after Shapiro's appointment, the older poet had published *Poems of a Jew* (1958), another book of criticism, *In Defense of Ignorance* (1960), in collaboration with Ernst Lert, a libretto, *The Tenor: Opera in One Act* (1957), in collaboration with department chair James E. Miller Jr. and Cather scholar Bernice Slote, *Start with the Sun: Studies in Cosmic Poetry* (1960), and *Prose Keys to Modern Poetry* (1962).

Nebraska was not Shapiro's nirvana, as he makes clear in his autobiographical novel, *Edsel*, based in large part on his life in Lincoln. By the time Kooser was his student, Shapiro had resigned his post at the *Prairie Schooner*. University administrators, in a move the Shapiro described as a "provincial atrocity," blocked publication of a short story they found "obscene and in poor taste." The editor, bristling under this kind of censorship, quit the magazine in protest.

Kooser remembers his mentor, who had turned fifty the year of his arrival, as

wiry and energetic, witty and charming. He had a slight lisp, an imperfection that I imagined he had compensated for by teaching himself to write beautifully. I remember wondering if perhaps I ought to try to develop a small flaw that I too could write my way out and around, not recognizing that I already was possessed by enough demons to keep me in poems for the rest of my life.

What I most clearly remember about Karl during that period were his eyes, bright and alert behind heavy glasses that magnified their size. He had a bemused, sidewise, almost birdlike glance that he reserved for occasions when someone said something stupid.

Although Shapiro is often characterized as difficult, Lee Lemon, a colleague in the English department and at the *Prairie Schooner*, says that "there were at least two Karl Shapiros, "the writer who could be quite savage, and the person who could be quite pleasant." He was, by many accounts, a thorough and inspiring teacher. His goal was, through class discussions and assignments, to provide students with a solid grounding in their poetic tradition and to help them discover what was important to them to write about.

Shapiro, after resigning from the *Prairie Schooner*, continued on at the university while looking for a new position, teaching more and enjoying life less. Not only was he frequently bored, but he had entered a department of New Critics, where, fellow faculty member Paul Olson recalls, "Brooks and Warren [authors of a major New Critics text] were everywhere." Shapiro, a prolific, vigorous, and often outspoken critic, also railed against the poetry of T. S. Eliot and Ezra Pound that had dominated the early part of twentieth-century poetry, calling it abstract, impersonal, and Eurocentric. The New Critics, inspired by Eliot and other Modernists, heralded the impersonal poem, one that could be analyzed in what seemed to many a scientific rather than literary manner. Born and educated mainly in the South where the movement was rooted, Shapiro felt the impact of New Criticism keenly and staked out his poetic grounds early on, following the lead of William Carlos Williams and W. H. Auden.

The literary heritage Shapiro was eager to pass along to Kooser and other aspiring poets was similar to Jumper's. Both mentors were well grounded in nineteenth-century poetry and considered the British Romantics, William Wordsworth, Lord Byron, John Keats, and Percy Bysshe Shelley, along with the American Transcendentalists, Ralph Waldo Emerson and Henry David Thoreau, a necessary foundation for any poet learning his or her trade. Also important to the two men was the poetry of Walt Whitman and Emily Dickinson (Jumper's favorite poet). For Shapiro, Whitman was the only poet of international stature of which America could boast.

In the classroom Shapiro relied on *Chief Modern Poets of England and America*, edited by Gerald Sanders, John Nelson, and M. L. Rosenthal, and poems submitted to the *Prairie Schooner* as his primary texts. Not only did his students receive a rich and systematic introduction to canonical authors, but they also received an introduction to contemporary poetry rarely available to young aspiring poets.

Shapiro's semester-long seminar on the prose and poetry of William Carlos Williams was a cornerstone of Kooser's development and is discussed in chapter 11. *Pictures from Brueghel and Other Poems* by William Carlos Williams, awarded the Pulitzer Prize in 1962, had impressed Kooser greatly when it appeared the year he graduated from Iowa State.

Kooser's program of study included seminars on Whitman, Dickinson, and Mark Twain, as well as a survey of American literature with Robert Hough. While the young poet found a Victorian literature course boring, the Willa Cather seminar with Bernice Slote, who followed Shapiro as editor of the *Prairie Schooner*, and Virginia Faulkner, editor-in-chief of the University of Nebraska Press, captured his interest. The scholars introduced students to Cather's novels, short stories, and essays, using artifacts to bring alive the time and context of her life and works. Cather's pastoral impulse, which reaffirms the relationship between nature and its inhabitants, resonated with Kooser.

During poetry workshops, Kooser says, "Karl was always very down to earth, but he was not a person to give specific criticism. . . . He was not a textual person." Unlike many workshops today, "we didn't sit in a circle. We sat in a classroom, which chairs all lined up, on the first floor here [Andrews Hall]. He did a modest amount of lecturing, things that would come to mind about contemporary poetry, and of course he was extremely well read; he knew everything about it. . . . His lectures were quite marvelous. I think one of the things he taught me," Kooser continues, "is that you can write about anything. That poem of his about the fly ["The Fly"] is an example: 'O hideous little bat, the size of snot'; nobody was doing that."

Kooser found inspiration outside the classroom as well. "Karl was," he recalls, "writing the cranky and explosive prose poems of *The Bourgeois Poet*, works whose form was dictated, he said, by the size and shape of a regular sheet of typing paper. They were the first prose poems I had ever read. I could feel the heat rolling off those manuscript pages. I was then living among the things and people that he was transforming into poems and it was a thrilling experience for a young writer."

The Bourgeois Poet, published in 1964, is a milestone in Shapiro's career, reflecting his democratic literary tastes, his turn toward the prose poem, and his continuing movement toward subjective experience. Plainspoken and direct, it is remarkable for Shapiro's command of the image.

By the end of the first semester, Kooser writes, he and his mentor were also friends. In the taverns and restaurants of the Bohemian Alps, Shapiro continued the exchange with Kooser that had started in the classroom. The senior poet's method of instruction was, as he describes it in his autobiographical novel, *Edsel*, "simply conversation, talking until I feel myself being carried away by my convictions or, what is better, by some new idea which gives birth to itself in my head while I am in full career." The Koosers, along with Shapiro and other friends, toured the rural hills and dales of Seward, Saunders, and Butler Counties, where he would eventually settle.

"About seventy miles in from the eastern edge of the state," Kooser writes, "is a north-south range of low hills known with a wink as the Bohemian Alps." Many of the small towns that have found their way into *Local Wonders*—Garland, Bruno, Bee, Dwight, and Prague, for example—were originally established as the railroad fanned west across the state. Some are still connected by tracks that remain in use to haul grain harvested from the rolling fields of corn, soybeans, and oats.

On weekends, Kooser writes, "we often took long drives through the country in my deeply mortgaged new [Chevrolet Corvair] convertible, taking the summer sun and drinking beer in the country bars." Diana Tressler, Kooser's former wife, remembers that often they would stop to walk the fields, pausing in the yards of abandoned farmhouses, barns, and sheds that dot the countryside, so Kooser could take a photograph or hunt for artifacts.

The Wisconsin glaciation that bypassed Teddy Kooser's Guttenberg in eastern Iowa spread across what became northeastern Nebraska. The ice mass retreated leaving gently rolling hills in its wake. An abundance of spring-fed creeks and rivers weave through the countryside, and all along the streams, oak and ash, willow and walnut trees are bountiful. Seward County, where Garland is located, is nestled in the Blue River valley through which the Big Blue flows. Along the roadside, early columbine can be spotted in April and the Blue phlox soon after. Rainfall in this part of the state, at thirty inches a year average, is plentiful, and compared to dryer counties to the west, vegetation can be dense. It is easy to imagine the Koosers stopping to admire the showy white lace of the wild plums or pausing to taste the sweet and seedy wild strawberries growing on the shady wooded slopes. Crumbling foundations of farmsteads still offer the passerby lilacs, corn lilies, and old-fashioned purple and yellow irises. Red-winged blackbirds, meadowlarks, woodpeckers, robins, jays, and hawks welcome visitors with their distinctive melodies.

Both Kooser and his mentor were impressed by the space between people and towns. "Where I was from, well, it was more like [Sherwood] Anderson's Winesburg, Ohio," Kooser says; "The plains were something different." Above the "great fact" of the land, as Cather describes it, was the arching sky, beneath, hidden as the treasure it is, the vast Ogallala Aquifer.

CHAPTER EIGHT

Journey to a Place of Work

Here in Nebraska, where we find ourselves
in love with leaving well enough alone,
in a city of little windows, little eyes,
art is as feared as cancer of the lung.

—from "Here in Nebraska"

Just as the countryside was coming into full bloom in spring 1964, Kooser's life took a dramatic turn. In April he won the prestigious Vreeland award for poetry, which included honorarium of $400, from the Department of English; the following month, he lost his graduate readership. Shapiro highly recommended Kooser for the award and predicted that his work would in time become well known. Even so, Kooser's grades were uneven, and his GPA proved too low to maintain financial support.

Intent on finishing his degree and completing his first collection of poems, Kooser knew that income from his wife's teaching job in Malcolm wasn't enough for the couple to live on. He looked to Shapiro for advice. If you really want to be a writer, his mentor counseled, get an eight-to-five job. "I thought, what the hell," Kooser recalls, "I'll go out for a few months and make some money and then I'll go back and enroll myself in graduate school."

Kooser answered an ad in the *Lincoln Journal* and was hired by an insurance company, Bankers Life Nebraska, as a "Correspondent," answering queries in the Policyholders Service Department. In July the poet wrote to Professor Wilber Gaffney, who was traveling in Europe that summer: "I have been working for Bankers in their life of Nebraska for a week. I'm a Correspondent, which means I handle all letters regarding policy changes: names, beneficiary, etc.... pays $400. I seem to like it so far.... Job is permanent for the moment." Poet Don Jones, teaching assistant in the English department at the time, remembers Kooser's "droll tales of medical histories, actuarial tables, etc. Tho he thought the job would be transitional, he was bemused by the example of Wallace Stevens—and of course retired as another insurance-company vice-president."

Kooser immediately felt comfortable at Bankers Life, he says, and the pay was good. Writing poetry, however, remained his primary occupation. The poet-businessman began his early-morning writing schedule, rising at 4:30 or 5:00 a.m., which he still holds to today.

Allen Ginsberg and Peter Orlovsky, crossing the continent in 1966 in their famous vw microbus, stopped in Lincoln. Ginsberg visited English classes, Kooser reports, and "read outrageous gay poetry, embarrassed the farm boys, horrified the farm girls, and generally disrupted most of eastern Nebraska." Later that evening Shapiro met Ginsberg, "chanting and tinkling his finger-cymbals," and his entourage at a party near campus. The gathering was, according to Kooser, "one of the highest concentrations of important poets Lincoln has ever known." Karl, he goes on, "seemed stiff and cautious." Shapiro's version of the Ginsberg visit can be found in *Edsel*, in which Kooser and Diana, fictionalized as Spoof and Helena Thomas, make an appearance.

By this time the couple had moved from A Street to a first-floor apartment at 2820 R Street, where Kooser set up an art studio and darkroom in the basement. He still devoted a large portion of his time to drawing, painting, and photography. As Kooser's essay "Small Rooms in Time," written many years later, will attest, his personal life had its own ups and downs.

Although studying English, visual artists were among his closest friends, including Lincoln native Stewart Hitch, who was studying for an MFA, Jon Gierlich, S. Clay Wilson, Don Williams, John Gary Brown, Bob Weaver, and Judi Heiser Gierlich. The group "talked about art all the time," Kooser says.

Kooser also became acquainted with Tom McLoughlin, professor of photography at the university, and his wife, Patty (later Lombardi), with whom he would become lifelong friends. Several years later he met landscape painters Keith Jacobshagen, who came to teach, and his student, well-known New York landscape painter Harry Orlyk.

The Sheldon gallery offered Kooser, his fellow students, and faculty access to one of the nation's top collections of nineteenth- and twentieth-century American art for a museum of its size. Among the painters represented was Edward Hopper, whose "Room in New York" would become a touchstone for Kooser. The Ashcan Eight, a group that included Hopper's teacher, Robert Henri, also well represented in the Sheldon, was favored by Kooser. *Robert Henri, 1865–1929–1965*, a retrospective marking the centennial of Henri's birth, was held in the autumn of 1965.

The poet's circle grew. Through Hitch, Kooser met Mij Engelhard (now Laging), Charlie Tisdale and his wife, Christie, who later introduced him to Burke Casari, a graduate student in sociology, and Laura Rhodes, who would marry Casari in the 1970s. Shapiro's older daughter, Kathleen, a classmate of Engelhard's at Southeast High School, and Paul Hemphill were also members of the group.

The 1960s were a particularly exciting time to study poetry at the university. "The interesting thing to me now," Kooser says, "is that when I came here there were so very many poets around." The companionship of local writers was especially important to Kooser as he made the transition to businessman. Lebsack's Tavern, within walking distance of the university, was a favorite rallying point where Kooser kept in touch with Wilbur Gaffney, a former professor at the university, and a variety of students, including Don Jones. Stewart Hitch dropped by from time to time. The group was joined by neighborhood regulars, including Lucille Davison, a milliner at Hovland Swanson, who had made hats for the writer Mari Sandoz.

Poet Don Welch, who taught at Kearney State College (now the University of Nebraska at Kearney) during the academic year, was in town during the summers working on his doctorate. Bill Kloefkorn, who would become Nebraska State Poet in 1982, was teaching at Nebraska Wesleyan University and had not long before turned to poetry writing after studying prosody with Shapiro. Jones was at work on his second collection, *Miss Liberty, Meet Crazy Horse*. Roy Scheele, who continued his Three Sheets chapbook series, kept in touch, although he was attending graduate school in another state.

Kooser's mentor was busy—and unhappy—as his account of this period in *Reports of My Death*, the second volume of his autobiography, and *Edsel*, describe. In addition to his loss of editorship and the expanded teaching load that had resulted, he was increasingly discontent in his marriage. He continued to teach at the University of Nebraska until 1966, when he moved to the University of Chicago.

Before he left Lincoln, however, Shapiro nominated two manuscripts to the University of Nebraska Press, *Medical Aid* by Don Jones and *Official Entry Blank* by Ted Kooser, launching his students' publishing careers and underscoring the importance of early publication to a developing poet.

Meanwhile midwestern and Plains poetry was entering its heyday, providing models for Kooser, who was still in the process of finding his own voice, as well as wider-reaching literary companionship.

Heartland: Poets of the Midwest (1967), edited by Lucien Stryk, was important to American poetry in general. Stryk observed in his introduction that poets from the region write from those "huge reservoirs of bypassed motions, ignored feelings, unexplained thoughts." He continues, "For a number of years now, a strong, varied poetry has been written in, and often about, midland America, a poetry which owes little or nothing to the example and achievement of those figures always associated with the region."

As examples Stryk included in his anthology work by twenty-nine (living) poets he admired, among them, Thomas McGrath, Lisel Mueller, Mary Oliver, Robert Bly, William Stafford, another early-morning writer of the world close at hand, Paul Engle, John Frederick Nims, Gwendolyn Brooks, along with excerpts from Shapiro's *The Bourgeois Poet* and poems by Bruce Cutler, whose first book, *The Year of the Green Wave* (1960), had inaugurated the University of Nebraska Press's First-Book Poetry Series.

Heartland was important for a number of reasons. The poets whose work was represented there had begun, individually, to make their impact on American poetry. Robert Bly's *Silence in the Snowy Fields* (1962), James Wright's *The Branch Will Not Break* (1963), Mary Oliver's *No Voyage, and Other Poems* (1963 and an expanded version in 1965), Thomas McGrath's *Letter to an Imaginary Friend* (1962), and Lisel Mueller's *Dependencies* (1965) are only a few examples of the explosion of midland poets who had begun publishing. Kansan William Stafford, a contemporary of Shapiro and McGrath whose influence on the next generation of Plains poets would be estimable, was beginning to bring Plains life to light in a series of books: *West of Your City* (1960), *Traveling through the Dark* (1962), which won the National Book Award in 1962, *The Rescued Year* (1966), and *Weather: Poems* (1969).

Collectively the *Heartland* poets heralded a major poetic force and direction rising up out of the midsection of our country. "It is my hope," Stryk wrote in his introduction, "that a clear sense of the region, in all its diversity, as well as its people, will emerge from the poetry in *Heartland*." Readers saw, "once and for all," that, indeed, "the midwest is made up of the stuff of poetry."

The pastoral impulse of many of these poets resonated with Kooser. As Cather's work attests, the American pastoral reaffirms the relationship between nature and its inhabitants. With deep roots back to Theocritus in Greece and to the Roman writer Virgil, the pastoral focuses on the lives of, as the name implies, "farmers, shepherds, and other country people" and their environment, including their familiar landscapes, and the animals and plants that share the seasons with them, as William Barillas describes it in *The*

Midwest Pastoral. Although the form has been modified over the years, certain themes and ideas remain consistent, including the poet's relationship with his or her reader, which Kooser will explore years later and make explicit in his "imaginary reader."

Kooser became publisher and editor, founding Windflower Press and *The Salt Creek Reader* in 1967 and the short-lived journal *The Blue Hotel* (1980–1981). Windflower, with its windmill colophon drawn by Kooser, began modestly with a series of broadsides, or "handouts" as they were called then, single-sheet poems by Kooser, Shapiro, Kloefkorn, and others. *The Salt Creek Reader*, inspired by John Bracker's *"Penny Poems,"* sold for one cent.

Named for Lincoln's small stream that feeds into the Little Salt Fork Marsh, providing an important resting and feeding area for migrating birds, *The Reader* provided poems, like salt, necessary to good health and essential to finding one's way.

Correspondence with Jones from 1967 shows Kooser's vision for the *Reader* as a reflection of place:

> I'm trying to keep TSCR [*The Salt Creek Reader*] completely calm. Is that a good word? Or should I say that I want it as whispery as abandoned windmills. Granted, Etter's poem isn't quite what I wanted, and Gustafson's not quite. Look at Denise Levertov's "The Victors" (From *O Taste and See*), Steinbeck's short story, "The Chrysanthemums," and maybe you can see the type of *tone* that I'm looking for. Or your mulberry tree poem. I want the imagery of the great plains, its language, its isolation. My volume cover, which won't come out until next year, after # 10, will carry the windmill and this small poem of mine:

> The windflower whirls upon its stem,
> silver and snow and scattering light,
> luring the sweet wet bee of the wind
> to enter and sweep the tin pollen away
> down the rusty cacophonous garden of hills.

His essay, "Small Rooms in Time," written many years later,

provides a window into his life. Within a year of joining Bankers
Life Nebraska, Kooser was promoted. Diana continued to drive to
Malcolm to teach high school until she became pregnant. Upstairs,
the Latvian women, Olga Ronsenstein and Auda Karpovik, cooked
their salt herring and tended their bright annuals along the drive.
After what seemed a long wait, the couple welcomed Jeffrey Charles
into the world on July 17, 1967. The following year, Kooser earned
his MA after four years of part-time study at night.

As "Small Rooms in Time" makes clear, the Kooser marriage
was strained: "the most ordinary unhappiness," he writes, "had
come to us—misunderstandings, miscommunications, a broken
marriage like thousands and thousands of others." Journal entries
from this time reflect Kooser's delight with his new son, his work as
an editor and publisher, parties with friends, and his unhappiness
on the job. In January 1969 he read proofs for *Official Entry Blank*
and struck "and Other Poems" from the title. "There is no poem in
the book called "Official Entry Blank," he writes to editor Virginia
Faulkner, "so the title as it now is [*Official Entry Blank and Other
Poems*], is incorrect. Even if the poem "Official Entry Form" were
to be changed . . . to suit the title, it would sound as if this poem is
the most important one in the book, which it certainly isn't." His
intention is, he continues, "that *Official Entry Blank*, by itself, would
refer to the collection as a whole—to the collection as a formal entry
into the competition between books of poems—and not to the first
poem ["Official Entry Form"]. . . . the use of this title should imply
that, as in an entry to a contest, the person entering has employed
everything in his bag of tricks in hope of success. This aspect reflects
the heterogeneous nature of the book."

In March, despite his memories of teaching at Madrid, the poet
followed up on a lead at Northern Iowa University, which would
take the Koosers closer to their families. Lincoln, however, felt like
home. "I honestly hate to discover myself nondescript somewhere
else," he wrote in his journal on the sixth, "perhaps I should talk to
Dudley Bailey [chair of the Department of English] about a job."
Kooser is clearly ambivalent. "For the record," Kooser confides

in his journal, "I'm scared to death, but guess I have been there before—I keep remembering how nervous I was when I taught at Madrid and hope that this won't start it all over again. I'm really not that bad off where I am—am I?"

Although Kooser was pleased by the cover proofs of *Official Entry Blank* he saw in April, he learned the collection would not be out until August. It must have seemed a very long wait indeed. He tended *Salt Creek Reader* and was always on the lookout for new writers. In a fan letter to Louise Glück on publication of *Firstborn*, "the finest collection I've seen in recent years," he tells her of his own upcoming book and invites her to send a poem for publication in the *Reader*." Denise Levertov promised a poem soon.

Kooser turned his attention to a new manuscript of found poems. In a draft preface he explains his intent: "The messages collected here have been excerpted from a large number of postcards written in the years 1900 through 1915, and their sentiments are representative of the majority of Americans living in the Great Plains during that time." Although the complete manuscript will not be published, many of these poems will appear in Kooser's second collection, *Local Habitation & a Name.* Several days later, Kooser is in the midst of plans for a story about Elmo, a young tree, for children.

Finally, after a three-year wait, Kooser held a copy of *Official Entry Blank* in his hands.

CHAPTER NINE

Official Entry Blank

Read anybody's first poem
and you'll see there was a model for it.

—*The Poetry Home Repair Manuel*

Dedicated to Will Jumper, "who taught me this," *Official Entry Blank* reflects Kooser's debt to his mentor at Iowa State University, under whose tutelage many of the poems were written. Its epigraph is taken from Leonardo da Vinci's notebook: "After the demonstration of all the parts of the limbs of man and of the other animals, you will represent the proper method of action of these limbs, that is, in rising after lying down, in moving, running and jumping in various attitudes."

Not only does Kooser draw attention to the visual arts, important to him since he was a boy, but he also offers an analogy that reflects on the origin, course, and goals of his poetry. Just as da Vinci's notebooks record the artist's study of the human body and his designs of mechanical models (of the heart, limbs, etc.), *Official Entry Blank* offers the poet's own articulations. While de Vinci drew his knowledge of the human form by mainly studying cadavers, Kooser has observed his own world, learning the principles of craft from his own masters, literary cadavers, if you will.

In the eighty poems Kooser's worldview emerges as does his regard for craft, his wry sense of humor, and his take on the literary life of the 1960s. A glance at the contents page immediately suggests the poet's awareness of the literary world, as well as his desire to take his place within it: "Genuine Poem, Found on a Blackboard in a Bowling Alley in Story City, Iowa," "For Karl Shapiro, Having Gone Back to the Sonnet," "Reaction to Haiku in Original Characters," "A Contribution to my Magazine," and "Walt Whitman."

In the initial poem, "Official Entry Form," Kooser, the fledgling poet/publisher, pokes fun of the rules and regulations of his profession. Following the proscriptive "standard procedure" all beginning poets must follow, the poet has filled out the entry blank, that is, faced all those blank pages and wrested them into a final manuscript that is now printed, bound, and distributed for a final reckoning by editors and readers.

To underscore Kooser's sense of play, and even his resistance to the existing order of things, he takes liberties with the sonnet form. This is the first of six fourteen-line poems scattered throughout the book. In addition, there are a half dozen twelve- and thirteen-line variants on the form that might be thought of as "Kooser sonnets." The traditional "turn," which Kooser sharpened with Shapiro, who also used it to great effect, is found after line eight.

Kooser also announces in this collection his emerging aesthetics, one that will remain relatively consistent throughout his writing career. Working through metaphor, Kooser offers an alternate view of the poetic process, subject, and poet's role to the well-known statement of aesthetic principles, Wallace Stevens's "Anecdote of the Jar," which appeared in his first book of poems, *Harmonium*, published in 1923. Stevens's poem was included in volume two of the text *Chief Modern Poets of England and America*, which Shapiro used in his poetry class at the university.

In "Anecdote of the Jar" the "poet" (the persona or "I" of the first line) positions a man-made object, the jar (the poem), on that hill in Tennessee. Stevens, another insurance man/poet, seems to privilege the human imagination; the placement of the jar upon the hill by the poet within the poem results in an ordering of an untamed nature.

In Kooser's account the poet's intention, object, and location, while superficially parallel to Stevens's anecdote, are quite different. A beer bottle is pitched into a ditch beside a burned-out, likely Nebraska, highway by a person only known by the action he or she has made. In Kooser's vision the poem seems a sort of artifact of life, natural in its own right, and like the proverbial cat, a miracle as it lands standing upright and straight, alive and "dazzled / in the sun."

Stevens's jar, like John Donne's classical well-wrought urn described in his poem "Canonization," Keats's Grecian urn, and the approaches privileged by New Critic Cleanth Brooks in his text *The Well-wrought Urn*, are replaced by the everyday disposable object found in the contemporary lives of reader and writer alike. Kooser's allegiance is apparent from the beginning; his language is clear, syntax is straightforward, place is identifiably rural, objects are ordinary, and the poet, who is more or less offstage, is someone we might know. The young author of *Official Entry Blank* is pledging his allegiance and taking his place, not alongside Eliot, Pound, or Stevens, or the impersonal, "high-brow" moderns that Shapiro decried, but with those who followed them—Frost, Williams, and Swenson. Implicit is Kooser's desire for reaching a general reading public, which will emerge later, pedagogically, as his "imaginary reader."

Kooser's politics are clear, although he will rarely be so overtly political in later work. "Scope," an elegy to Martin Luther King Jr., begins with the crosshatch of the rifle sights, alluding to Christ's death to redeem humankind. "Story Problem," composed with irony in heroic couplets, questions the logistics of war and the impersonal, statistical soldiers shipped off to Vietnam. "Birdsbeesbirdsbeesbirds-beesbirdsbees," as the reader might deduce from its title, addresses the failure of parents to instruct their children about sexuality, which renders, Kooser writes, John "impotent" and Jane "cold." In "The Anti-Mosquito Campaign" he addresses the deadliness of DDT to fish and birds and in "Country School," the effects of urbanization.

The poems of *Official Entry Blank* reveal a young man observing, grappling with, and at times protesting what he finds in his world. As Wilber Gaffney notes in a short review, Kooser's poems are "a kind of distillation of years of observation." He elaborates: "Before the wagons, the prairie was littered with buffalo bones, then, later, with broken wagon-wheels and the bones of wagons. Today it is littered here and there with the dry bones of abandoned houses and of 'groves' hopefully planted in years between droughts. But it still bears, and supports, people; and Mr. Kooser's concern is with the people who make this subsection of the nation, sharing it with wide earth and wide sky."

Although he has far to go, Kooser is beginning to discover the importance of his place to his poetry. His attention is frequently drawn to the details of everyday life, offering comparisons and subtle associations. "Walnut Saplings," newly planted along suburb streets, are "too spindly for boys / to shinny up" and reflect the spindly furniture, the Chippendale and French Provincial, found inside. The "Figure Seated at a Bar—half-in and half-out of thought," "shakes his head like an elephant," reminding the reader of Rodin's "The Thinker" recast, or more correctly recarved, his "elbows / white on the bar-top . . . trying / to lean on the brains in his knee."

The poet's interest in the lyric, a form of emotional intensity popular among contemporary poets, is clear. Highly personal, the lyric allows the writer, through revealing what is of emotional importance to him or her, to establish an intimate relationship with the reader. The ballads, letters, children's poems, epigrams, songs, and seasonal poems found throughout the volume are all subgenres of the lyric.

Kooser's keen interest in the dramatic monologue, written in a persona, is evident and will remain a favorite throughout his career. "A Letter from Aunt Belle" is Kooser at his best. The dramatic monologue appears to be a found poem—a piece of writing not originally intended to be a poem but considered so by the one who finds it—and it may be just that; it is also an extended metaphor, a conceit. The poem juxtaposes all that is life with the certainty of death, all material for the writer's pen, ending with the injunction, "Write."

Direct address immediately establishes an intimacy between the original letter writer—Aunt Belle (Belle McKibben was married to the poet's great-uncle Edward Kooser), the poet, and the reader. The archetypal familiarity of the letter form is enhanced by the writer's tone as she reports the news, makes connections to events and people, and, with pride, sends along a love and trust in our futures. The poet and the reader seem to be enjoined to care for those who survive and to "write," that is, to record what has taken place.

In "Abandoned Farmhouse" and other poems like it—"Country School," "Gas Station," and "Homestead," for example—Kooser is discovering and sharpening a technique that he will perfect in later poems, almost always lyrics. The poet offers the reader a sort of shared archetypal space, molded by "slivers and splashes of light," as it is described in "Milk Bottle," into which the reader can pour the particulars of his or her life.

In *The Poetry Home Repair Manual* Kooser writes about the continuing influence of Walter De La Mare's poem "The Listeners," how the mystery of the poem captured him as a boy and stayed with him over the years. In a similar way the frequently anthologized "Abandoned Farmhouse" stays with contemporary readers who are also engaged by the haunting rhythm and a summoning of archetypal fears. The more regular meter of the traditional ballad is replaced with an irregular but persistent rhythm. Language is evocative. The man was "big" and "tall" and "good." In the second stanza, the reader learns that his wife was a homemaker who saw to it that the bedroom walls were papered, the kitchen shelves covered with oilcloth and therefore easier to keep clean; deep cellars were filled with canned goods; their child played in the tractor tire filled with sand.

The date or time period described in the poem is not stated; oilcloth was popular during the 1930s through the 1950s, but the scene also recalls early settlement (Willa Cather's Ántonia, for example, "stood holding oilcloth bundles" when Jim Burden meets her; Ivor's oilcloth-covered table in his "little cave house"). Kooser's abandoned farm is far from town—down a narrow country road rather than one that was gravel, paved, or blacktopped. The poem's third stanza heightens the emotion, adding a sense of mysterious calamity, before the ending with its sense of envoy: "Something went wrong, says the empty house."

Kooser acknowledges that both Frost and Edward Arlington Robinson taught him to "use metrical verse with a rather informal . . . idiomatic language," used throughout nearly all the poems. Some of Kooser's titles "Home Town," "Homestead," and "Cold Pastoral," could pass for Frost's.

If he is aware of his peers in the literary community, he is also aware of his potential readers. "Man Opening a Book of Poems" reflects on the physical act of opening a book of poems and suggests a poet's worse nightmare. In contrast to the more traditional form of the book's initial poem, the final poem is free verse, with a block appearance that Kooser will favor throughout his career.

The poem's first line sends a surfeit of surprised small critters running in the bright light of the reader's imagination as he or she "bends and peers beneath it cautiously." The images are kinesthetic, full of motion, prompting a visceral reaction. Lines three through five surprise the reader, who learns that those creatures are—metaphorically—poems, and one of them, stopped dead in its tracks, is "waving its wet antennae to the light" and lifting "its mossy mouth," with a sort of literary kiss. We may be squeamish, unmoved, or accept the gift of the poem. Regardless, the reader lets "the page fall softly back on" the critter/poem and presses "down the cover with both hands," as though to crush it, an ominous conclusion to a first collection, if Kooser's humor weren't so wry.

The metaphor that joins insects under a rock with the poem on the page provides an excellent example of what Greg Kuzma sees as Kooser's "strange surrealism." The tension at the heart of the poem is based on the love/loathing response to the elements of the metaphor. The poem-insect, artifact of the poet's passion for language, "lifts its mossy mouth" to the reader to love and be loved—a relationship that Kooser will come back to again and again.

Not all reviewers were enthralled by the work. Holly Spence, writing in the *Lincoln Sunday Journal and Star*, found the poems "morbid" and the poet "obsessed with killing, death, and morbidity." Others saw hints of what was to come. A brief review in *Midwest Quarterly* notes that the collection "leaves the reader wanting to see what the poet will do when he finds his direction and sets to it."

Few of these poems will appear in *Sure Signs*, Kooser's first selected poems, eleven years later. As Dana Gioia, an early follower of Kooser's work, wrote, "Coming upon *Official Entry Blank* in 1969, one would have been hard-pressed either to predict Kooser's subsequent development or define his individually as a poet." As Kooser himself recognized, many of early poems were products of class assignments with Jumper. Images and metaphors are not consistently vivid. Missing from the collection is the strong narrative thread that pulls subsequent collections taut. Even so, *Official Entry Blank* is a window into Kooser's sensibilities and suggests directions that he would take in the future.

Kooser will revisit many of the descriptions, images, and metonymic devices with greater skill in later poems. Dated poems found in *Official Entry Blank* will be used to greater effect in *Winter Morning Walks*. Plum blossoms and red-tailed hawks and the mice they hunt will find their way into *Local Wonders*. The development of the metaphor throughout the poem as a conceit will become perfected in *Weather Central*'s "Etude." Hands, literal and figurative, will take on added meaning and import, as will old men and old women, yard sales, a variety of birds, especially after the poet's move from the city to his acreage in Seward County. The relentless passing of time and the loss and loneliness that result, Kooser's thematic preoccupations, are clearly present.

Roger Murray's review of *Official Entry Blank* from the *Denver Quarterly* the following year praises the collection's "sharp visual impact," observing that the impression Kooser's "portraits leave is that the people that they depict were there, but went way, leaving . . .

a certain ghostliness reminiscent of the painting of Wyeth or Hopper." When the poet sent the review along to Diana, from whom he was separated, he underlined the following: "Kooser's use of form indicates to me that he values it for its own sake and this tends to make it one-dimensional with some loss of control over meaning, so that whether it actually increases objectivity or not is another question." In the margin, Kooser notes, "exactly your perennial criticism." As later poems attest, this is an assessment that Kooser takes to heart. Although he will never give up form completely, rarely will he allow it to result in, to use Murray's words, "an ill-timed detachment."

The Kooser marriage, stressed for several years, teetered on through the autumn of 1969. "These are particularly difficult days for us," he records in his journal, hoping "to look back and laugh at this one day." His view of his own writing is colored by the turmoil he is experiencing. "I feel as if all the old poems are phoney," he writes, "and that I'm personally incapable of doing better—but perhaps to sit back and let all these violent emotions of the past few weeks steep into something genuine and true." Feeling increasingly trapped at work, Kooser includes a list of employment agencies, along with ideas for poems, books, teaching, and dreams in his journal. In October, after three semester of teaching night classes, he wrote the chair of the English department in hopes of obtaining a full-time position for the coming academic year; Greg Kuzma had just joined the faculty and prospects were bleak.

By this time the couple had moved to 1930 Garfield, but they lived there only a short time. Just before Christmas the Koosers separated. Diana, with Jeff, returned to Marshalltown, Iowa. Writing to a friend, Kooser says he spent Christmas day with his son before returning to Lincoln. "It is almost impossible to believe," he continues, "these things don't just always happen to others."

CHAPTER TEN

Running on Empty

One of the pleasures of painting is that it
doesn't have words to go along with it.

—Interview with Ted Kooser, in Shelly
Clark and Marjorie Saiser, *Road Trip*

Despite the publication of his first collection, Kooser was frequently discouraged as the new decade began. The poet missed family life and time with Jeff on a daily basis. Every other weekend, he drove over to Marshalltown, picked up his son, and continued on to his parents' home, where they stayed. The early 1970s would see the deaths of two beloved family members. On August 2, 1971, the poet's uncle Tubby, Herold Kooser, died suddenly of a heart attack. A year later, Kooser stood at the bedside of his grandfather as "helpless as flowers." John R. Moser died at ninety-eight on November 29, 1972, at the Good Neighbor Home in Manchester, Iowa, where he had shared a room with his son, Elvy, for three years. Moser was buried in the Guttenberg cemetery following services at St. Paul's Lutheran Church, where his grandson served as a pallbearer.

Added to his personal loss was an unhappy work life, where, he reflects, "I found myself buried at the bottom of everyone else, desperately writing my mean little poems and slipping them into the mail like messages in bottles." Working eight to five in the insurance business, Kooser often felt he was "dog-paddling in the abstract language with which nearly all business is conducted" even as it brought in a steady income and provided benefits. No matter how gratifying, no matter the wages and promotions, the job took time and sapped energy from his work as a writer and publisher.

"Abstraction is the nature of the insurance beast," he reflects. "An insurance policy," he continues, "is the record of a transaction involving risk, and what would be more abstract than risk? A policy is merely a stapled sheaf of paper, no handshake but the abstraction of an understanding between a person and an institution. In fact, I feel sometimes that the company is so far from the natural world of scent and odor and touch that it is like a section of empty cells in the honeycomb of life. Blindly, day after day, we dutiful workers feed the royal jelly of our lives into these hollow chambers."

Longtime friends Patty (later Lombardi) and Tom McLoughlin had moved to Toronto, and in early July Mij and Stewart Hitch sold their Mustang, bought a pickup, painted it a "John Deere Yeller," and prepared for their trek to New York City. Hitch printed business cards for the "Nebraska Haulers," Kooser hand-lettered "ACME" and "APEX" on alternate sideboards of their truck, and they too drove away.

There were brighter moments, although they may have seemed few and far between. Correspondence with friends and other writers seemed a sustaining force. Kooser, who had for many years dropped postcards and letters to writers he admired, continued the practice. "How much your poem 'Sorry' in *The New Republic* did for me the day I read it—It's a wonderful poem," he wrote Leonard Nathan, launching a friendship that would span decades. In July he announced in a letter to Steven Osterlund that he is "painting again! God how sweet it is!" In his journal Kooser notes why: "I despair in my poems. I am experienced in poetry: I am in all innocence in my painting. If I were to study painting, I would lose this joy as well."

Kooser, a part-time instructor in creative writing at the university in 1970, met poet Greg Kuzma, who had taken over the position

Shapiro vacated and had published two collections, *Sitting Around* and *Something at Last Visible*, during the year of his arrival. The poet, originally a predental major, had, like Kooser, traded in his slide rule for the pen. The two poets also shared an interest in publishing. Kuzma's Best Cellar Press was devoted to publishing the work of his contemporaries.

The year, however, ended on a gloomy note. Not long after Kooser's divorce became final, Kooser wrote to Don Jones about his recent lack of success in placing his poetry. "I'm having a bad run, lately (the last six months or so), of rejections—can't seem to place anything," he reported. "Had a batch back from *Poet & Critic* today, from my old friend [Richard] Gustafson to boot, saying I'd 'not only lost my finish but my polish.'" In the same letter, Kooser writes that he still had no response from Swallow Press to which he had sent the manuscript of his second collection. Nine months later he tells Jones that the "dry spell" persists, and he still has not heard back from Swallow.

Kooser continued to write and remained an active editor and publisher. In 1971 Windflower Press released Kooser's own slim chapbook, *Grass County*, including eight new poems accompanied by the poet's own pen and ink drawings. The horizontal cover of the small (4" x 6½") black-and-white booklet, dedicated to his son, Jeff, suggests the wide open skies of the grasslands; the ubiquitous windmill appears on the title page. Reviewer Hilda Gregory (who later returned to her birth name, Hilda Raz), future editor of the *Prairie Schooner*, describes its effect:

> The pages are long, narrow, and white with black lines making careful pictures of the brick and wood things of man that here and there rest on the back of the prairie: other windmills, marvelous in their variety; curving one-lane roads; small scratchings that make a town in the distance; the town restaurant-bar that defines and meets all human needs; a carnival sign pointing to nothing; a linear town cemetery. On each page are a few birds, wind-scattered and leaving. And, almost as an afterthought, the

poems, tucked into the drawings, typed and reduced to tiny rectangles turned sideways. It's an impressive melding.

Clearly, Kooser took to heart Shapiro's advice to write about the persons, places, and things of his life, and through his poetry and illustrations Kooser captures the language and expanse of the Great Plains. Kooser sensed that his work was beginning to loosen up. "I began to try and get my voice to be a little bit more idiomatic," he told the same interviewer. "The idiom is just not iambic. Now I'm writing in a kind of—sometimes—syllabic verse, sometimes accentual verse. I still feel the necessity to have some kind of form like that. I'm uncomfortable if I write a line that has too many heavy accents in it. There's no reason to be upset by that," he continues; "it should be organic. But it still bothers me. I've still got enough of that training in me and I feel that all the lines should be somewhat equal." Images gleaned from his travels through the Nebraska countryside and trips to Marshalltown and Cedar Rapids appear in "Driving Home," "The Geek," "Wild Pigs," "West Window," "Field Studies," "Tom Ball's Barn," "Notes on the Death of Nels Paulsen," and "The Sampson Church."

In *Grass Country*, as Dana Gioia notes, Kooser "found the proper subject and form for his poetry." Themes and images suggested in *Official Entry Blank* become sharper and distinctive. "Riding a winter sunset through the fields, / I want to put my arms around the hills," opens the collection. The lonely traveler is "Driving Home." The editor of *Poet & Critic* finds these poems "consistently elegiac," but what is important is that their persona finds comfort within nature where loss and death are part of the natural order. "I feel the sunset pulling up a quilt / out of the east," the poem concludes, to be tucked around car and driver.

As *Grass County* attests, Kooser's work was becoming increasingly and consistently visual. In an interview Kooser discusses the chapbook as well as the relationship between his literary and visual arts. "I do a little bit of drawing—that little pamphlet, *Grass County*, shows some examples of my drawings—and I do acrylic painting. I've done a couple that are a sort of mock-primitive—distorted perspectives of some of those small towns with lots of little buildings and houses. Now I'm starting a series of old store fronts, sort of photo-realist painting, but not done with that tremendous meticulous sense. I don't take quite so long on them. But they come off as being extremely realistic."

Kooser says he does not consider himself a serious visual artist; however, it is noteworthy he has painted consistently for nearly his whole life. "[In painting] You don't have to explain yourself in the same way you have to with a poem. You don't have to necessarily make sense with a painting. It has its own vocabulary, but it's a different kind of language."

Country life, like that of his Guttenberg relation, had always spoken to Kooser. Although it would be a decade before his dream turned into reality, just as spring was teasing the middle Plains, he began his search for his own place in the Bohemian Alps. The poet placed a "wanted to rent" ad in the newspaper, hoping to find a "quiet country home near Lincoln."

Kooser continued to see friends, including Laura Rhodes and Burke Casari, who had married. Patty McLoughlin (later Lombardi) had returned to live in Lincoln, and she resumed many of her earlier friendships. "Ted was wonderful to me when I returned," she recalls. "I was very poor and had two little kids and my family wasn't here. He was really my family; my kids think of him as family." A nurse, McLoughlin worked the 11–7 shift and occasionally called upon her friend to provide childcare and get the children ready for school the next morning.

"Ted often wrote a lot of the night," she says, "and I would come home and find a poem on my dining room table." On weekends Kooser often took her and her children, Sean and Maura, six months Jeff's senior, on drives, introducing a new generation to his Bohemian Alps. "One of the things we did in the summer times when my kids went to stay with their dad," Lombardi recalls, "was drive to Iowa." She and Diana had met in a nursing mothers' support group and had remained good friends throughout the years. "Ted would pick me up on a Friday afternoon when he got out of work and I got out at 3:30. . . . we would stop in Marshalltown to pick up Jeff and I would stay with Diana and then he would go on to his folks [in Cedar Rapids] where they would spend the weekend. Sunday afternoon he would bring Jeff back and pick me up and he would drive back."

By then Kooser had assembled a second collection of poems that he describes to Will Jumper as a "regional work, built around a town called Red Wing, Nebraska." He sent the manuscript, tentatively titled *The Sun Shines Bright on Pretty Red Wing*, which included his work from *Grass Country* and a selection of his "found" postcard poems, to Shapiro, who, while he thought the collection would profit from another title, responded favorably. Not only did Shapiro, now teaching at the University of California at Davis, write an introduction to the volume (eventually renamed *A Local Habitation & a Name*), but he urged his former student to send it to his editor at Random House. *The Heart-Shaped Box*, a volume of 133 messages from postcards, was already at Atheneum awaiting their decision. In his query letter to the publisher, Kooser explained he had chosen the title "because the postcards might be in such a box in someone's attic, and also because the messages are truly things of the heart."

Publishing was very much on Kooser's mind. In the late 1960s Wilber Gaffney had introduced Kooser to Glenna Luschei, another former student of Shapiro's, who was in town for a visit. Luschei, recently back from Colombia, where she published her first collection of poems, *Carta al Norte*, and newly settled in San Luis Obispo, had established Solo Press and began publishing the literary journal *Café Solo*. The two poets began a correspondence and poem exchange upon her return to California. Soon they were planning projects, including an anthology of Nebraska poets, for which Kooser began soliciting work. In the midst of this came Greg Kuzma's request to publish a small volume of Kooser's work.

For the moment, things were looking up, personally and professionally. Jeff would be spending some time in Lincoln with his father that summer, and in June Scribner's asked Kooser if they could take a look at his second collection. In July Viking also asked to see the manuscript. The anthology of Nebraska poetry was set aside, and he focused on his *Salt Creek Reader*, adding *New* to its title, changing it to a journal format, and renewing his efforts to attract quality work.

Inspired by Wilson and the underground comix movement in San Francisco, Kooser contributed a panel, "Silly Sally Scissors Says Let's Dress the Fans!," to *Comix Trip* edited by Scott Stewart and published in Lincoln in 1972. His pen and ink drawing features cutout figures, Arnold and "Princess" Jones, along with Nebraska Cornhusker attire, to dress the couple for game day. "Color them Red," the caption enjoins.

In October Viking rejected Kooser's second volume, as did Scribner's in early December, citing, the poet muses in his journal, the manuscript's "limited range." He continues, "I farm a little plot of things to say," he continues, "with not much frontage on the busy road." For a moment, Kooser contemplates searching for a full-time teaching position at the University of Colorado and readies his teaching credentials through ISU's Teaching Placement Division.

New Year's Eve finds Kooser babysitting, at "Patty's white kitchen table," while his friend was at work. As 1973 opens before him, he records three resolutions: "1. No drinking. 2. Exercise daily. 3. Write every day." *Twenty Poems*, Kooser's dark and haunting short volume published in the new year by Kuzma's Best Cellar Press, reflects the continuing sorrow and turmoil of the poet's life at the time. Dedicated to "Patty," the collection allows nature little redemptive value or even comfort as it did to the solitary driver of *Grass Country*. Here bridges lose their way and brains are grated along the sidewalk.

Remarried now, Patty Lombardi reflects on the book as well as the times during which it was written. *Twenty Poems* is, Lombardi says, "the darkest [collection] and that's why I like it. I love the poems in the book," "They Had Torn My Face Off at the Office," for example. "He rarely wrote about the office and its negative effect. . . . I like these dark poems because he has such a way of looking at things, even the dark side of things, which he doesn't often choose to write about."

Today a retired psychiatric nurse, Lombardi describes the collection as "about a bunch of us," Kooser's circle of friends that has remained relatively intact over the years. "There's a poem that's called 'Failed Suicide,'" Lombardi continues candidly, "and that was me. In 1973, I became really depressed; everything crashed. I mean the marriage, the finances, my father was dying. . . . I was so poor, it was impossible to go back as much as I wanted to be with him . . . and when the kids were away one summer, I tried to commit suicide, so that is why the poem was written and why the book is dedicated to me . . . although I have to tell you, he was angry with me, as people are with those who commit suicide."

Personal sorrows amplify each other throughout the collection. "Airmail from Mother" intensifies the sorrow of the poet's divorce, suggesting that news of it be withheld from the dying grandfather. "They had Torn Off My Face at the Office" uses biting language and surreal images to convey the intensity of the experience and the distortion of the human spirit that the work day demanded. "Cold, hard poems," Kooser described them years later. "Bankers Life was that kind of place, or so it seemed to a poet still in his twenties, wondering how he had wound up behind a gray metal desk wearing a necktie, answering letters about policy loans, beneficiaries, and bounced premium checks. How mundane that work and those offices seemed, how mundane *we* all seemed."

The incessant passage of time and the sorrow it brings are Kooser's persistent themes throughout this period; life never looked so bleak. "I was empty," he wrote mournfully.

Fortunately, change was just over the horizon.

Three

The Shepherd's New Song,
1970–1979

CHAPTER ELEVEN

A Local Habitation & a Name

Two truths approach each other. One comes from inside,
the other from outside, and where they meet,
we have a chance to catch sight of ourselves.

—Tomas Tranströmer, "Preludes (2)"

In March 1973 Kooser received welcome news from the West: Glenna Luschei, publisher of Solo Press, was interested in publishing his second collection of poems, along with Karl Shapiro's introduction to the volume. *A Local Habitation & a Name*, as Luschei recognized, is an extraordinary collection. While Kooser's first book, *Official Entry Blank*, with its variety of poetic techniques, forms, and attitudes, reflects the work of an apprentice learning his craft, his second reveals a poet who has found his way. Kooser is aware of his maturation as a poet. In a letter to Luschei, he writes, "This is really solid stuff, Glenna, and I'm excited as hell about it." A triptych of his personal and literary journey, it reflects a developing relationship with the natural environment, the byways and highways of Nebraska and Iowa. The poet's approach is uniform, his technical facility, sure and sustained, and as Kooser himself notes, *A Local Habitation & a Name* was "the first of my books to really begin to demonstrate a personal voice."

In choosing the poems to include, Kooser is intent on keeping the collection "strongly regional. I want it to be," he writes Luschei, "the best plains statement that I can make. This talk about considering a new Nebraska poet laureate makes me want to make it as appealing to the audience the discussion will create as it can be." He suggests trimming several poems that are not so obviously regional and including "the best regional poems" from *Official Entry Blank* to round out the manuscript.

Will C. Jumper, Kooser's college mentor, grounded the young poet in the craft of his art. American poets Edwin Arlington Robinson and Robert Frost were early models to whom Kooser first looked. Frost's impulse toward narrative and dramatic monologue; his astute, sometimes cunning, humor; a tendency toward blank verse; sensitivity to sound; and emotional undertow can be found throughout Kooser's work.

But it was study with Shapiro that had enabled Kooser to locate his own work and poetic aesthetic within the best of contemporary American poetry, always a topic of interest to the senior poet. Shapiro's own work had been stimulated and shaped by the work by William Carlos Williams, and he passed along his passion for the physician-poet from Rutherford, New Jersey. His first-year graduate seminar, which presented Williams's prose and poetry in a systematic way, allowed Kooser entry into Williams's theory of writing and aesthetics.

Almost thirty years later, Kooser addressed his debt to Williams in answer to a Poetry Society of American survey. "Though dozens of poets and hundreds of poems have shaped by writing," he wrote, "I am most deeply indebted to William Carlos Williams' notion of the 'local.'" As early as 1915 Williams had asserted that "the local is the only universal," a principle that would guide him throughout his long career.

Writing about one's place is not, Williams believed, to be confused with "regionalism," created by "artists who were imitators, copiers . . . [who express] the surface eccentricities of a particular locality." Williams was interested in "the impression created by the shape and color of it in the artist's 'sensual being—his whole body . . . his mind, his memory, his place." Rather than making a quest for the regional, Williams championed the *American* idiom, an essential aspect of Kooser's second volume.

Three other aspects of Williams's aesthetics are especially prominent in this collection. Like Kooser, Williams, for whom the image was crucial, painted from an early age. In *A Local Habitation & a Name*, Kooser's use of images becomes sharp and clear. "No ideas but in things," from Williams's poem "A Sort of Song," is perhaps one of the older poet's most quoted tenets. This is a lesson that Shapiro learned well from Williams and made a priority for his own students. Ideas and emotions are best expressed through, to quote Williams, "appearance: surfaces, sounds, smells, touch of the place in which I happen to be." One's locality, expressed by virtue of the artist's imagination through those surfaces and sounds, and so on, was the source of the universal experience that, Williams thought, "great art expresses."

Williams, as Kooser learned by the time he was working on the poems that comprise his second volume, was dedicated to the use of the American idiom to express the American experience. "We are Americans," Williams told a group of Briarcliff students, "a new race, speaking our own language." As the poet wrote in *Spring and All*, "When we name it, life exists."

A Local Habitation & a Name, Kooser's first mature work, sets in many important ways the tone for all the poet's work that will follow. For this reason, the collection warrants a close look.

By the time Luschei agreed to publish the collection, Kooser had addressed Shapiro's concern about the original title and renamed the book. Taken from William Shakespeare's comedy *Midsummer Night's Dream*, the new title is well suited to Kooser's, and Williams's, aesthetic position and artistic intent. Theseus, duke of Athens, observes in the play's final act that imagination is shared by the lunatic, who "sees more devils than vast hell can hold," the lover, who sees "Helen's beauty in a brow of Egypt," and the poet, whose

eye, in fine frenzy rolling,
Doth glance from heaven to earth, from earth to heaven;
And as imagination bodies forth
The forms of things unknown, the poet's pen
Turns them to shapes and gives to airy nothing
A local habitation and a name.

Through "appearance: surfaces, sounds, smells, touch of the place in which I happen to be," Kooser renders his experience in poetry ("When we name it, life exists"). Through "things"—abandoned buildings, graveyards, mice, cows, filling stations, tattooed women—he discovers along the roads he travels, the poet draws us into his world, literal and figurative, colored by the recent deaths of his maternal grandfather and his father's brother, as well as the end of his marriage and loss of his son's daily life to distance. He reports in a pause from his journey, writing from his desk at Bankers' Life, "wondering how he wound up behind a gray metal desk wearing a necktie, answering letters about policy loans, beneficiaries, and bounced premium checks." In doing so Kooser brings to light the patterns in life, those universals that go unnamed until they are rendered concrete by the artist's pen through particular events and places in the everyday world.

Midsummer Night's Dream, which has a complex plot including romantic mix-ups and misfortunes, a running commentary on the unequal social power of the sexes, three weddings, and a play within the play, may also be Kooser's commentary on his own sorrow and subsequently ironic view of marriage; the dedication to his collection reads "for Diana, anyway."

Composed of seventy-six poems, *A Local Habitation & a Name* is divided into two sections of unequal length. "Red Wing," containing fifty-five poems, is the book's thematic center, recording the poet's journey over the physical and emotional terrain of the late 1960s and early 1970s. Included are the eight poems of *Grass County*, plus six poems previously published in *Twenty Poems*, three reprinted from *Official Entry Blank*, fifteen found, postcard poems, and twenty-three uncollected poems. "Other Depots," section 2, with twenty-one poems, moves into the present and ends on a hopeful note for the future. "I put everything I cared about into that book," Kooser says.

"Red Wing," as section head, acts as metaphor and metonym, placing Kooser within his geographical and emotional milieu. The red-winged blackbird (*Agelaius phoneniceus*), a member of the same family (*icteridae*) as the meadowlark, the Nebraska state bird, is found throughout the Plains and much of the Midwest, including Lincoln, Nebraska, and Guttenberg, Iowa. The common and colorful North American songbird is a favorite of children, who look for its distinctive red shoulder patches and narrow yellow wing bars; its characteristic whistle, with a bit of practice, seems easily replicated. With the allusion to the red-winged blackbird, whose genus name (from the Greek *agelaios*) means "belonging to a flock," Kooser subtly calls attention to his inspiration and his emerging identity as a poet, a singer of the American idiom.

British poetry, especially after Coleridge and Keats, is often associated with birds, which are as rich with symbolic value as they are with song. The nightingale, for example, a song bird that sings during the night as well as the day, is found in John Keats's "Ode to a Nightingale," a meditation on the conflicted nature of human emotions. This theme resonates throughout *A Local Habitation & a Name* as the red-winged blackbird becomes the poet's muse as well as a symbol of his own song. The nightingale, however, is not found in North America where, on the Plains, the native meadowlark's song has been associated with that of the artist. Novelist Willa Cather, for example, sang the praises of the lark in her poem "Prairie Spring," which was published originally in *McClure's Magazine* and later served as an epigraph for her 1913 novel *O Pioneers!* The red-winged blackbird as poet is an image or symbol that Kooser will elucidate in *The Poetry Home Repair Manual* years later, quoting from his poem "A Poetry Reading."

Critic Helen Vendler observes that a poet does not describe the landscape "without entering it kinesthetically, feeling the motion of the crowded streams, humanizing the trees into noble pantomimists.

Landscape in poetry," she continues, "is always *projected outward from the writing self*" (italics Vendler's). On the surface Kooser seems to differ. In *The Poetry Home Repair Manual* he likens a poem's composition to being at a window, "looking out into the world. If the light that falls upon what lies beyond is very bright, you see the scene in vivid colors and there is only the faintest hint of your [the poet's] reflection in the glass. If the light beyond the window is faint, as at dusk, the speaker's reflection in the glass in much more prominent."

To write about the world outside the window, the poet brings up the light to give definition to what (the local) is held in view. To write about oneself, the poet brings up the lights inside. "The poem is," Kooser says, "the record of a moment at that window." Kooser's poems sometimes seem to only show the sunlight shining outside the house; by a shift of the feet, however, they, through metaphor and analogy, seem to reveal the poet as well. Kooser's traveler is on an "inward voyage" as well as one that takes him along I-80 and into the Bohemian Alps.

Critics looking back at Kooser's second collection have sometimes attributed Kooser's selective description of the landscape and people to a general description of landscape and its rural residents as unexciting, sometimes even tragic. In general, however, this is not the case. During the 1970s farm incomes rose rapidly; not until the early 1980s did the farm economy take a severe turn downward, both dramatic and tragic.

Red Wing, the fictional town in which stands the church-in-transformation that launches the collection, may be read as metonymic, a stand-in for the poet himself. "The Red Wing Church," the section's initial poem (originally titled "The Sampson Church" when it appeared in *Grass County)*, calls attention to the poet's home territory, colloquially referred to by locals as "God's Country." Based on a real structure in Garland that the poet saw on a road trip with Diana and Shapiro, the church is a landmark on the country roads that he has traveled since coming to the state in 1963.

The twenty-one-line lyric immediately draws the reader into the poet-observer's point of view as the journey begins and establishes the rate of perception and reflection. Voice is constant, observation close, allusion subtle. Its pastoral quality is reinforced by its conversational tone. The poem, an excellent example of the control the poet has gained over both his subject matter and his craft, merits attention.

Although loosely composed of blank verse, the local idiom the poet employs seems to drive the meter, directing our attention to the structure that is in the process of transformation:

> There's a tractor in the doorway of a church
> in Red Wing, Nebraska, in a coat of mud
> and straw that drags the floor.

The needs of rural life are making new use of the church. The viewer-poet, aware of the building's original function, may find parallels from the Bible. A "coat of mud" that covers the tractor recalls Joseph and his cloak of many colors. The plow's sprawl is reminiscent of beggars by the side of the road; straw brings to mind the nativity.

Lyric poems enact feelings, and frequently, as Vendler advises, they originate at a place of emotional disturbance. "When you encounter a poem of geography or regionality," she suggests, "ask yourself how it embodies a problem and how landscape has been 'lyricized'—that is, made a bearer of human feeling." There the reader will, more often than not, discover "two points of view in the poem. . . . These points of view represent an emotional, and even a moral, quarrel within the poet." In "The Red Wing Church," a religious structure is being transformed into a secular one, or more abstractly, an ideal is bowing to practical needs of the community.

Even if the reader knows nothing about the poet, a sense of melancholy, perhaps even distress, is conveyed; something once sacred is no longer so. The road the poet once traveled with family and friends he now travels alone. The poet himself is undergoing a transformation analogous to that of the church, from favored student to humdrum insurance underwriter and from husband and father to single parent who much of the year lives apart from his son.

The short sentence that begins line 6—"The steeple's gone."—causes the reader to stop with the poet-observer to look more closely at the balance of the line and the structure itself: "A black tar-paper scar / that lightning might have made replaces it." Lightning and healing (the "scar") are lingering associations to Bible imagery. But it is by human agency, the unidentified "they," that the structure has been transformed from a house of God to Homer Johnson's (shades of Howard Johnson's) barn, apparently serving the material rather than the spiritual.

The poem shifts again in the center of line 9; the poet asserts that the structure is "still a church" ("for Diana, anyway"), a holy place, although one in and of nature, located among the grasses and lilies of the country's fields where one might read hope in the birds' nests in late spring amid broken illusions of the human season that has just passed. "Good works of the Lord," the poet elaborates, "are all around," if one looks carefully for them, a notion once appreciated by Ralph Waldo Emerson. The steeple now stands in a garden up the alley where it has been transformed into a hen-house. "Fat leghorns gossip at its crowded door" recalls the parishioners, the flocks of bygone days, who frequently gather in front of the church doors after Sunday services. Church pews have been transformed into seats "on porches up and down the street." Even the stained-glass church windows have been reinstalled to cast their colors at the mayor's house.

The church bell that at one time rang out across the land calling the faithful, now from "atop the firehouse in the square," sounds the alarm for fire and calling for the firefighters (who surely are the community's faithful in their volunteer roles). The bell, pews, boxed signs, and so forth, no longer serve religious purposes; they have been put to practical use by rural residents, a sensible people who have long seen the value of recycling. The Lord's good works serve a useful purpose.

The poem's final line, the sentence "The cross is only God knows where," is an interestingly ambiguous one, to be taken literally and figuratively. The line's impact is heightened by the end rhyme "where" with "square" in the preceding line. (There is only one other end rhyme at work, the "ow" sound of lines 3, 12, and 16, which acts as a thread to tether the poem in place as the views change.) As a colloquial expression, the final line suggests a stymied conjecture. Literally, the cross cannot be located; who knows where it is or to what practical use it has been put.

As a symbol of the crucifixion, the cross connotes redemption as well as symbolizing death. Is the poet-traveler suggesting that the expected or traditional means to salvation, via the church or religion, no longer serves its purpose or that the relationship between heaven and earth is at least temporarily lost? The poet himself may well be feeling temporarily lost as well. The poem, however, is neither despairing nor antireligious; organized religion has been replaced by a nature's religion. Human activity takes on spiritual trappings here in God's country. Like images we find in Frost, another poet-traveler, Kooser's church/garage unites heaven and earth.

Our traveler, who will become the master of metaphor as his career continues, may also be offering an analogy to inform and clarify the entire collection that follows. For Frost, "poetry is metaphor," and as Sheldon W. Liebman explains, for the New England poet, it represented "'the height of all thinking'" because it replicated "the fundamental structure of the universe. The 'greatest' example of metaphor is, after all, the 'attempt to say matter in terms of spirit, or spirit in terms of matter' . . . : It reenacts the creation." As Kooser has reminded the reader in his allusion to *Midsummer Night's Dream*, "The poet's eye . . . / Doth glance from heaven to earth, from earth to heaven." For our red-winged poet-singer of the Plains, the Red Wing church is also, metaphorically speaking, an *ars poetica*.

"It is the imagination on which reality rides" that is at the core of nearly all of Williams's work. In a similar fashion Kooser stakes out his ground as a poet in "The Red Wing Church" and the poems that follow. By means of imagination, he speaks to and of the hallowed human labor and life of the countryside. He speaks in the American idiom of place, capturing the universal patterns of life and rendering their abstract nature in concrete terms, anchored in the senses, of his own local habitation and name.

A number of Kooser's frequently quoted poems come from this collection, including "Spring Plowing," "The Red Wing Church," "The Tattooed Lady," and "Driving Home." In writing about his own journey across the Plains and into the Bohemian Alps, the poet proves himself to be every bit the storyteller his father was. His habitation, literal and emotional, is populated by a rich array of men and women who've passed though, and some who have passed on, leaving their stories behind. All eight of the *Grass County* chapbook poems, vivid and quiet "still lifes" of place, appear throughout the "Red Wing" section, grounding the reader in the local landscape while speaking of human transience in a disinterested natural world of strong and mysterious forces.

Kooser captures a sense of detachment in "Tom Ball's Barn" reminiscent of "Abandoned Farmhouse," also included in the section, along with two other poems from *Official Entry Blank* ("A Letter from Aunt Belle" and "The Corpse of an Old Woman"). A reader learns of Tom Ball only through what has once belonged to him and survives after his death as told to us by the poet who has once again pulled his car to the side of the road to point out a landmark and tell its story.

Essentially a list poem of cause and effect, "Life's just one damn thing after another," as the local expression goes, "Tom Ball's Barn" is composed of a single sentence. The structure is the focal point for all that went wrong: the loan that "just wasn't big enough / to buy the paint, so the barn went bare and fell apart" after "twelve / nail-popping, splintering winters" when the mortgage (at 5.5 percent) was due, "three dry years, seven wet, / and two indifferent," the death of the banker who gave him the loan, the bank that is "deef" to the farmer's reason, and the "poor iron in the nails" that caused the barn—and Tom Ball's health—to collapse. The speed of the poem, a parody on the childhood rhyme "This Is the House That Jack Built," as critic Dana Gioia writes, "gives each fact a certain inevitability, as if mere eloquence were logic, so that at first glance the callous 'thus' in line 17 really does seem to explain Ball's death."

Kooser continues on, past the sideshow of a traveling carnival where the geek, a live chicken eater, takes a hamburger and port break, crossing a landscape that seems "full" of absence. Predators lurk along line fences. Creatures disappear or are threatened before our very eyes. Nature moves slowly and with deliberation; time is lethal. Like the farmer in "Notes on the Death of Nels Paulssen," the living can be suddenly reduced to "nail parings," hair, ashes, which leave no trace. The *Grass Country* poems, like the paintings of Edward Hopper, suggest the contemplative moment, the desolate melancholy, the empty road, long shadows and diffused light.

Immediately following "The Red Wing Church," Kooser positions the first of his "postcard poems," which comprise over one-fourth of the "Red Wing" section (they do not appear in section 2) and, acting as a kind of play within a play, provide its spine. Like Williams, who used "whatever I find in my view," Kooser utilizes messages from old postcards to point to universal patterns. "Halloo Sweetheart—," the card dated July 7, 1905 begins. Salvaged from an antique store run by Mrs. Bailey and her daughter, located at 7th and B (and long since gone), the postcard messages are both found poems and historical documents. They serve as another kind of still life that makes explicit patterns of relationship, milestones along the road through time. Kooser calls them a "thread," asking the reader to reflect upon those human patterns of thoughts, feelings, and concerns through time that allow one generation to recognize commonality with another.

The language on the cards provides, as philosopher Martin Heidegger might say, conversation through time, or in Williams's words, "The poem connects the past with the present. And thus we know we are alive for seeing particulars all around us, and being instructed by the poem that the past was no different, we get our sense of continuity and the world becomes real to us."

The "Red Wing" section ends with "Driving Home," from *Grass County*, one of a handful of poems that employs first person singular.

The winter drive at sunset across the snow-covered fields is exquisitely sensual, layering sharp visual and auditory images with tactile sensations as meaning is revealed. Hard times behind him, the poet is older and wiser, memories intact, tended and comforted by the countryside around him. Reminiscent of Robinson's "The Man against the Sky," the poet is cast against the winter landscape, moving slowly, wanting, it seems, to disappear into it.

Kooser's journey continues in section 2, "Other Depots," a section designed, he writes to Luschei, "just to show the reader that I do in fact have some range." Seven poems from *Twenty Poems* cast their dark shadow, including "They Had Torn Off My Face At the Office," "Words for a Man Who Never Missed," and "The Goldfish Floats to the Top of his Life," which extends Williams's well-known lament in "Asphodel, That Greeny Flower": "It is difficult / to get the news from poems / yet men die miserably every day / for what is found there." Although life has been at times daunting, the final four poems move beyond their grim neighbors, beginning with "Pocket Poem," the first of what will become Kooser's *Valentines*. "New Year's Day," the collection's final poem, offers a promise of dawn and the return of birds in the spring as the poet fashions a "feeding-place for the birds" from "castaway crates," recalling the crates that tumbled onto Highway 30 in the earlier section. "How they come!" he exclaims, as sparrows and jays, both common birds of the Plains, drop down from the trees to feast. The poet's work, feeder and poem, brims with hope.

CHAPTER TWELVE

Singing the Shepherd's Song

Who would have thought that the arc of the water
in a common drinking fountain could be so beautiful?

—"Out of the Ordinary"

"Yes, I *do* have a favorite young poet," influential reviewer and
anthologist William Cole began his *Saturday Review World* column
"Trade Winds," not long after *A Local Habitation & a Name* was
published in 1974. He's an "insurance underwriter in Lincoln, Neb.,
name of Ted Kooser," Cole continued, quoting from Shapiro's introduction that praised Kooser's "'gifts of honesty and lucidity, the
sharpness of focus, and that mysterious quality of voice.'. . . Yes,
indeed," Cole concluded, "It's a handsome book, and rich, rich. . . .
Priced at $2.95 and a quarter for handling. A steal at $3.20."

Cole, an admirer of Kooser's work since early in 1973, had gone
so far as to speak to an editor at Harper's on behalf of the poet's
collection; now, finally published, he could praise it in an influential
forum. Cole's notice brought the work national attention—and
sales, "a very unusual occurrence for a book of poems from a small,
independent press," notes Kooser, who dates his success as a poet
to the collection.

Closer to home, reviewers noticing the windmill on the cover (designed by Peter Langmack, Kooser's brother-in-law) and pen and ink drawing of a rural mailbox on the title page tended to describe the collection in regional terms.

Victor Contoski, writing for the *Great Lakes Review*, concludes his analysis with the assertion that "*A Local Habitation & a Name* is regional poetry in the finest sense. It's poetic impulses spring from the land and people of a particular section of the country; yet it is not provincial," he adds. Richard Gustafson, editor of *Poet & Critic*, published in Kooser's home town of Ames, calls attention to the book's design and physical appearance, which, he says, "enforce the rural stolidity and enduring yearnings of Kooser's midwest personas." George von Glahn defends the regional writer in his review of *Local Habitation*, which appeared in *Late Harvest*, an anthology of essays focusing on Midwest writers published in 1977: "In general it has been my experience that Kooser offers a rich and rewarding sense of 'place' for those who are willing to accept the modesty of Kooser's demands and have enough awareness not to be trapped in their own pretenses to sophistication."

In a *Dacotah Quarterly* review, however, Mark Vinz, while recognizing the importance of place to the poet's work, does not characterize it as exclusively regional writing. Vinz, echoing Shapiro's introduction, draws attention to the Edward Hopper–like qualities of "'clarity and purity'" that he finds in the poems and that "extend to the physical book" as well. Vinz describes Kooser's use of found poems, discussed below, as "a marvelous way of continually reasserting the unchanging human background of the collection." Kooser's poetry is not romantic, Vinz notes, with "none of the 'nature fakery' that crops up so often in Midwest-based poetry these days. (Life on a Nebraska farm or in the Minnesota woods is *not* a mystical experience, afterall.)"

The topic of literary regionalism colored many conversations during the late 1960s and throughout the 1970s, stimulating both poetry and critical thought. Lucian Stryk, sensitive to the tension between the universal and the regional, expanded the number of poets represented in *Heartland II*, his second anthology of midwestern writers, and addressed the topic in his introduction.

Kooser, whose work did not appear in volume one, is joined by other Nebraska-based poets Greg Kuzma, Michael Anania, and Rex Veeder in volume two. Also included are new, mostly male, voices, that include Stephen Dunn, Albert Goldbarth, Jim Harrison, Norbert Krapf, and Laurence Lieberman, many of whom Kooser had published in the *Salt Creek Reader*. Stryk, quoting another Plains native, William Stafford, seems to embrace what he sees as the special qualities of Plains writing within the wider context of universal understanding: "All events and experiences are local, somewhere. . . . paradoxically the more local the feeling in art, the more all people can share it; for that vivid encounter with the stuff of the world is our common ground."

In *The Midwestern Pastoral: Place and Landscape in Literature of the American Heartland* William Barillas argues that Kooser places himself in the pastoral tradition of British Romantics and the American Transcendentalists. Willa Cather, Jim Harrison, James Wright, Theodore Roethke, and other writers—pastoral or with a strong pastoral impulse—have been important to Kooser since the beginning. These writers, by modifying certain of the original literary conventions, have contemporized the pastoral.

Barillas notes eco-critic and scholar Glen A. Love's redefinition of the form, which "requires that contact with the green world be acknowledged as something more than a temporary excursion into simplicity. . . . A pastoral for the present and the future calls for a better science of nature, a greater understanding of its complexity, a more radical awareness of its primal energy and stability, and a more acute questioning of the values of the supposedly sophisticated society to which we are bound."

In Kooser's poetry beginning with *A Local Habitation & a Name*, there is little of the "sentimentality and false idealization of life in nature," which Barillas defines as part of the nostalgic tendency of the pastoral. Like the best of pastoral writing, it "acknowledges social complexities and conflicts inherent in the individual's striving for a meaningful life." As Barillas points out, the reader finds Jeffersonian republicanism as well as individualism, community, and nature. If not the yeoman farmer, the poet's literary persona is one of appreciation of the worker and the work as well as the desirability of community and stewardship. The edge, or counterforce, of the pastoral is never far removed.

Only in retrospect do the influences of a California-based poet, Leonard Nathan, and a Seward County painter, Reinhold P. Marxhausen, become evident in Kooser's second collection. Serendipity or synchronicity brought the work of both men to the poet's attention.

Reading through the *New Republic,* Kooser came upon the poem "Sorry" and dropped Nathan, a long-time friend of Will Jumper, a note of admiration, thereby launching a friendship of nearly forty years. Kooser writes, "We exchanged news of our families, news of our writing, and as the years passed, news of our health, in the manner of friends growing older, and, of course, we exchanged hundreds of poems in early drafts for whose success we had high hopes."

In a tribute to Nathan, written shortly after his death in 2007, Kooser noted his friend's "wise and generous counsel. I don't suppose there is a single poem in any of the books I've published since we met that doesn't show the genius of his helping hand. When he studied a poem," he recalled, "he weighed not only the total effect but the use of every word, of every line break and punctuation mark." Not since Jumper had Kooser had such a careful reader. "In Leonard I found not only a friend but somebody I could show work to for almost forty years, day in and day out." Kooser attributes much of his success to Nathan, whom he describes as "among the best and most intelligent writers of our age."

Marxhausen's work came to Kooser's attention at work. "Bankers Life Nebraska must have had one exceptional management consultant," the poet recounts in a speech at the Library of Congress to mark the conclusion of his first term as poet laureate. The artist was brought into the company, he explains, "to cheer us up, to show jaded long-timers and callow young people like the disgruntled author of 'They Had Torn Off My Face at the Office' that there was beauty all around us, even there, even in a boxy, concrete and glass executive office building stacked to the rafters with dull paperwork."

Marxhausen, who was teaching at Concordia College (now University), was a "delightful man, playful yet serious about art and its happy effects," a master of a number of forms, including painting, murals, sculptures, and photographs. At Bankers Life, he strolled through the insurance headquarters building photographing objects he found interesting—ashtrays, pencils in a cup, rubber bands, and letter trays—to produce a series of slides that were shown eventually to the company's four hundred employees in the company dining room. Through the slides—and later the color reproductions that were hung in the lobby and throughout the building—workers began to see "all the abstractions of their world . . . in a new way." Kooser reports,

> Marx appeared before an assembly of employees in the cafeteria and showed us what was all around us but what we had never stopped to notice. His slides were beautiful, rich, with color and mass and texture. Who would have thought, for example, that the arc of the water in a common drinking fountain could be so beautiful? We left our gray metal folding chairs feeling altogether happy and refreshed, as if sprinkled by a hose on a summer day. . . . That afternoon, with Reinhold Marxhausen's carousel slide projector clacking and creaking through image after image, was the high point of my years at that company. Pay attention, he was telling us. It will be worth your time. By the time I noticed those upside down banks [in the office windows of "At the Office Early"] I had begun to appreciate what was right under my nose, to celebrate the beauties and pleasures of the ordinary.

In 1973 Kooser joined Lincoln Benefit Life as a senior underwriter, a position that he held until 1980, working in the Federal Securities Building, where the company had recently moved, within walking distance of the university. There the poet occupied a corner office "with tall, dusty windows" where he sought the detail of life, in ways that were probably not so unlike those of other American insurance workers, poet Wallace Stevens and composer Charles Ives.

Kooser continued to work at his insurance desk by day and to write poetry at home in the early morning hours. After a short stay with friends following his separation, Kooser had moved into a stucco duplex at 1720½ C Street, where he lived until 1976, when he brought a house at 1447 Washington Street. Although he was teaching a night class at the university, he felt that his dream of an academic career was remote.

"I think what was happening during those formative years," Kooser reflects, "as evidenced in changes in my poetry, was that I was turning away from The Literary, with its steady forms toward a more local and particular poetry." As time passed, he continues, he "began to understand that my experience of living in Iowa and Nebraska were indeed legitimate subjects. I could find my own Grecian urns in the second-hand stores and in old sheds on abandoned farms."

By the 1970s Kooser had established himself as a publisher. The *Salt Creek Reader* included the poetry of, among many others, Roy Scheele, Gary Gildner, James Hoggard, and Marge Piercy. "I wanted the community of correspondence and publication," Kooser says. "Eventually, after I'd begun to publish my own work in magazines, and had struck up correspondence with other poets, like my friend Steven Osterlund, I felt that I could keep my place in the literary community without all the work and expense of publishing a magazine." The *New Salt Creek Reader*, as it became with the winter 1972–1973 issue when it went from a monthly postcard format to a quarterly, ceased publication in 1975, but Windflower Press remained busy: *Eleven Poems and an Interview* by Steven Osterlund in 1973, Kloefkorn's *Uncertain the Final Run to Winter* and a reprint of his *Alvin Turner as Farmer* in 1974. In 1975 Windflower published Nathan's chapbook, *Coup and Other Poems*, and the following year Osterlund's *Twenty Love Poems*. In 1977 Jumper's *From Time Remembered* was published under Kooser's Foothills Press Imprint.

Though an exchange of literary magazines, Robert Bly's the *Seventies*, for example, Kooser kept up with the latest literary news and made important contacts with his contemporaries. When Kooser quit smoking in 1970, he took up embroidery to keep his hands busy; among his projects was stitching *The Fifties* (the progenitor of *The Sixties* and *The Seventies*) logo on a blue denim shirt for Bly.

In 1976 Alley Press published two hundred numbered copies of a two-poem pamphlet, *Shooting a Farmhouse/So This Is Nebraska*, which are among Kooser's most popular poems. "Shooting a Farmhouse" was also one of fifteen poems included, along with an interview of Kooser by Arnold Hatcher, in the sixth volume of *Voyages to the Inland Sea*, edited by John Judson, who oversaw the Contemporary Midwestern Poetry series at the University of Wisconsin–La Crosse. In the preceding five years, Kooser's audience had grown substantially.

CHAPTER THIRTEEN

Not Coming to Be Barked At

Our lives are brief as dimes.

—From "In the Laundromat"

Kooser dedicated his third full-length collection, *Not Coming to Be Barked At*, to William Cole, the *Saturday Review* critic who had introduced *Local Habitation* to the national reading public two years earlier. Its title, taken from *The Kalevala*, a Finnish epic compiled in the nineteenth century, underscores, by analogy, Kooser's intent that his work be taken seriously by the literary establishment, as well as more general readers. As his short prefatory note explains, "The young hero, Lemminkäinen, pays a visit to the hostile people of North Farm. When he enters their great hall, they are astounded that their dogs do not bark at him. The gap-toothed mistress of North Farm asks Lemminkäinen how he has accomplished this feat, and he answers that he did not come there to be barked at."

Indeed, no one is barking here; the collection consists of intense, often understated poems that reflect the poet as he grapples with the ache of absence, the search for love, the persistent rush of time, and the certainty of death. While acknowledging life's pain and sorrow, Kooser records the small joys and large mysteries that it also offers. A careful craftsman, Kooser, in his exchanges with Leonard Nathan, has further refined his use of metaphor, sharpened his word choice, and heightened his use of rhythm to underscore meaning. His work continues to be less and less bound by traditional poetic forms. As he acknowledges, poems in *Not Coming to Be Barked At* "are very much like the poems that I would go on to write . . . that in a way I took on as my signature style."

The collection opens with "In the Laundromat," Kooser's droll epigram, heralding a major theme and symbol that will reoccur throughout the poems that follow: the fleeting quality of human life and its seasonal counterpart. The complete poem is as follows:

Our lives are brief as dimes—
a wash of odors
and a rinse of falling leaves.

The precision of language reflects Kooser's meticulousness. Connotation and allusion are deftly controlled for specific effect. Sound marries sense. The epigram, which poet Robert Bly has called "a versified idea," is a gift from the ancient Greeks, often witty and often ending with a twist. There is a wry humor in the organizing metaphor: brevity of life is compared with the coins necessary to operate the pay-as-you-go washing machines of the Laundromat. To use the Laundromat is, as the expression goes, to wash one's dirty linen in public. The corporeal quality of human life is underscored with "a wash of odors," and its swift passage, with a pun on the word "wash," by the loss of leaves each autumn.

Across the page the six-line "Old Soldiers' Home," marks, as Kooser has said, a significant development in his work. The initial comparison of a package with the soldiers' hands is as clear as it is extraordinary; the metaphor is extended into lines 3, 4, and 5; fingers open and close as a package might; images are easy to follow. Then Kooser asks us to leap into the mystery at the heart of the image as the old soldiers "unwrap the pale brown packages of their hands," look inside, and gaze "off across the grounds, / safe with the secret." Just what is the secret? We are left wondering. Life's sweetness and brevity? The answer, as Williams might have argued, must remain unspoken.

One reading of the poem might conclude that "memory," one of the defining characteristics of being human, is the secret. The old soldiers can, as they gaze across the ground, "cross" temporarily from the present at the home to their memories of themselves as younger men. The poem itself as an extended metaphor is built on the "crossing" of comparison as fingers "cross" to the package; the distance they cross keeps the secret a secret. The old soldiers, as they gaze into the past, also cross to the future as they look across the grounds, "holding" their world and identity safely within. However the reader may think about the "secret," a leap has been prepared for and made; the poem, rather than ending, remains open.

Bly provides an interesting way to look at how a metaphor works. He defines its leap as "the ability to associate fast. In a great ancient or modern poem the considerable distance between the associations, the distance the spark has to leap, gives the lines their bottomless feeling, their space, and the speed of the association increases the excitement"—and the real joy—"of the poetry."

The apparent surreal edge of Kooser's work is associated with that leap. The Swedish poet Tomas Tranströmer and Spanish poet Federico Garcia Lorca, according to Bly, effectively employ the leap in their work, but in general, Bly writes, "the grudge American critics and university teachers have had against surrealism" prevented American poets from embracing the technique wholeheartedly. Lorca's essay, "Theory and Function of the Duende," Bly notes, addresses the "kind of elation" when an association to death is present in the metaphor. The poet who can make that heightened leap or "wild association" with that "head of emotion," as Bly describes it, does so, as Kooser does in "Old Soldiers' Home," with "the shadow of death in the room." The mystery of this brief life, why the dogs did not bark when Lemminkäinen enters the great hall of the hostile North Farm residents, is at the heart of this collection.

Kooser effectively uses the familiar as a jumping-off point; the result is both sorrow and joy. "Greatest of all attempts to say one thing in terms of another," Frost believed, "is the philosophical attempt to say matter in terms of spirit, or sprit in terms of matter, to make the final unity." These "metaphor-centered poems," as Kooser calls them, "are of a type I have explored in my own work over and over." Like Frost and Emerson before him, he sees metaphor as a way to make those "marvelous connections" to "reach through the opaque surface of the world and give us a glimpse of an order beyond."

With *Not Coming to Be Barked At*, Kooser continues his journey. One of the joys of an extended metaphor is watching it unfold before our eyes as it did in "Old Soldier's Home." Often the comparison is one of personification. "In An Old Apple Orchard," the wind is compared with an old man. Details of the wind-as-old-man are revealed one by one; the leaps are incremental: the trees feel the "soft tug of his gloves / for a hundred years," then the "old fool / thinks he's young," until he "goes off / late in the day / toward the town" and comes back tipsy, that is, "reeling with bees," and in the final lines, when the reader finds him (and the wind) rolling around in the long grass in his sleep.

In "Fort Robinson," the comparison is as subtle as it is dark, as the poet recalls a summer road trip with his young son. Employing first-person singular, unusual for Kooser, the poem recounts their visit to Fort Robinson (now part of the Nebraska park system), where Crazy Horse, leader of the Oglala Lakota, surrendered in spring of 1877 and was killed. Two years after Crazy Horse's death, as the poem alludes, Dull Knife, the great chief of the northern Cheyenne, and a band of his people were held captive in unheated Fort Robinson barracks, where they received little food. Starving, they escaped and headed toward Pine Ridge Reservation, where they arrived eighteen days later.

When Kooser and his son arrive at the fort a century later, the grounds crew is "poking the young birds / down from their nests and beating them to death / as they hopped around in the grass." By poem's end, "My little boy hid in the back and cried," and the reader sees that parent and child are associated with the chick and magpie mother. The boy's identification with the birds under attack parallels the story of Dull Knife and his people and sends Kooser and his son into "those ragged buttes / the Cheyenne climbed that winter, fleeing."

In a 1977 review for the *Lincoln Journal and Star*, poet Mordecai Marcus writes that "Kooser loves the fields, the cemeteries and the dwelling places of rural people on the Great Plains." At the same time, while appreciating the "persisting vitality of these places," Marcus says, Kooser is able "to empathize calmly with destructiveness that he hates." These polar aspects, which Kooser highlighted earlier in his two-poem pamphlet for Alley Press, inform the collection.

These poems, "Shooting a Farmhouse" and "So This Is Nebraska," are examples of how far Kooser's work has developed over just a few years. The first poem is elegiac, a tribute to Kooser's mastery of diction and detail, while the second, an idyllic poem, showcases his use of the metaphoric "leap."

By Kooser standards, both are long poems, thirty lines and twenty-eight lines, respectively. "Shooting a Farmhouse" depicts a guerilla war waged on a way of life, symbolized by an old farmhouse, initially with its old couple inside. The opening three lines show signs of a quiet aggression that escalates as time passes and the stanza progresses. The "first few wounds" inflicted on the mailbox, by line 3, become .22 bullet holes associated with the truck that "rumbles past in the dust." "In a month," line 5 begins, "you can see sky / through the tail of the windmill" through a good-sized hole, the result of "target practice." Ominously the attic windows "grow black and uneasy." The final lines of the stanza record casualties: "When the last hen is found shot in the yard," the old couple is gone.

One might be tempted to offer this stanza, and the poem as a whole, as an example of what Kooser calls "the writing of impersonal observation" if it were not for his meticulous noun choice. The power of a word's connotation is the "follow through" that expands the metaphor.

Kooser explains his attention to diction and metaphor:

I have a theory that every word or figure a poet drops into a poem, along with all the implications of that word, stays with the reader, and requires his or her reckoning, all the way to the end. So that if in the first few lines the poet says something looks like a melon, that melon, green and hard and heavy, stays right there in the reader's mind all the way down the poem. It is always best if that melon or something about melons has a subsequent use, or if it somehow fits into the overall scheme of the imagery. If enough disparate things spill into the poem, along with all their implications, then the poem becomes as cluttered as a flea market. The way I try to control this in my own work is to be sure that every image is interlocked into an overall imagistic scheme, so that everything builds toward the final effect . . . it is best to leave out a metaphor and go for direct statement unless that metaphor can be directly woven into the imagistic fabric of the whole poem. A metaphor put in for its own inventive or beautiful sake just doesn't add to the poem unless it feels like an organic part of the overall direction. In fact, it's a liability.

Stanza 2 begins, "In November. A Land-Rover," providing a temporal shift to hunting season. The four-wheel drive, all-terrain vehicle is an upscale British-made multipurpose vehicle often associated with city dwellers rather than locals. The Rover and its occupants take on a paramilitary tone; it is "Like a tank," "flattens the gate," and pulls into the yard where "Hunters spill out." Their challenging posture is suggested by conflating two colloquial expressions, to throw down one's hat and to throw down the gauntlet, as they "throw down their pheasants like hats." The hunters vandalize property. They "shoot from the hip," the poet continues, with irony: not at all the cowboys from boyhood matinees, they are full of false bravado when faced with the likes of an abandoned farmhouse.

It is sunset in stanza 3, by which time the trespassers have "kicked down the door" and blasted holes in the plaster and "piss[ed] on the floors." A "soft blush of light" in the second line contrasts their desecration. Not until evening falls, beer and shells spent, do the hunters "drive sadly away, / the blare of their radio fading." The use of the adverb "sadly" modifies their drive, suggesting the hunters' frames of mind as they return from their day of killing (pheasants and a farmhouse) to return to their workaday worlds. We as readers are also sad at what we have just witnessed. Quiet returns to the farmhouse, and as the requiem concludes, a sigh can be heard as the breeze moves through the shelterbelt.

By contrast, "So This is Nebraska" is paean in praise of the Bohemian Alps and the joy the region can bestow. According to Homer, Paean was the physician to the gods of ancient Greece, and in pairing the celebratory song with the elegy when they were first published, Kooser appears to be offering the countryside a healing antidote for the kinds of destruction witnessed in "Shooting a Farmhouse." The slow first line of the poem introduces the metaphor that will be developed as the stanza, a quatrain, picks up speed:

> The gravel road rides with a slow gallop
> over the fields, the telephone lines
> streaming behind, its billow of dust
> full of the sparks of redwing blackbirds.

Metaphors abound, the leap increasing. Comparisons of "things" with human beings afford a kind of intimacy with a countryside that takes on an almost familial character. The "loosening barns" are established as "those dear old ladies," and then the metaphor is exquisitely extended and terms interchanged: "their [the barn's] little windows / dulled by cataracts of hay and cobwebs, / hide broken tractors under their skirts." Although this is an archetypal image, it is also one that a driver in Seward County and many counties throughout the Plains states and Midwest is likely to encounter. Other drivers with their air conditioners at full tilt forfeit the experience of "driving along / with your hand out squeezing the air," but the meadowlarks, cedars, and hollyhocks still greet passersby.

The vintage pickup, a widely recognized figure in Kooser's work (and cover illustration for the *Local Wonders* paperback edition), is found in stanza 4, inviting the reader into the poet's neighborhood:

Behind a shelterbelt of cedars,
top-deep in hollyhocks, pollen and bees,
a pickup kicks its fenders off
and settles back to read the clouds.

The poet extends the comparison (pickup and person) into the stanza that follows, and by emphasizing the second person, "You feel like that," invites us to identify personally with the pickup. His careful tempo and diction move us into the simile in the fifth stanza and identification with the pickup at the side of the road: "you feel like letting / your tires go flat, like letting the mice / build a nest in your muffler, like being / no more than a truck in the weeds."

By now the poet has invited the reader so deeply into the fabric of the metaphor that the leap between the terms compared can widen, and we will follow with ease. By stanza 6 the reader has "become" the old pickup in the weeds, "clucking with chickens or sticky with honey / or holding a skinny old man in your lap." The transformation is astounding, and so is the poet's ability, through control of the pronoun "you" in the last line of the seventh stanza, to leave the metaphor behind and return the reader to the road.

"The proper response to a work of art is joy, even hilarity," Kooser frequently quotes Shapiro as saying, and beginning with its fourth stanza, "So This Is Nebraska" evokes such joy that the reader emotionally follows the poet from "you feel like // waving," to, in the final stanza, "stopping the car / and dancing around on the road." His final image, the wave and then glide of the hand "lark-like over the wheat, over the houses," suggests that the poem may also be read as an *ars poetica*. The poet waves at the world as he passes through it; he is waving to the reader. Here is our world; pay attention, see the beauty around us.

In many of the volume's poems, the poet seems to be alone as he is driving and observing his surroundings. The content page speaks to loneliness, mortality, and sometimes sorrow: "In a Country Cemetery," "Sitting All Evening Alone in the Kitchen," "Late February," "Leave of Absence," "An Empty Place," "The Death of a Dentist,"

"A Dry Winter Letter to Friends," "Obit for John Berryman," and "For An Old Love."

Kooser's chapter "Fine-Tuning Metaphors and Similes" in *The Poetry Home Repair Manual* is one of the best explications of the workings of metaphor and simile and how a poet might follow the comparison as a means of discovery. Many of the poems in *Not Coming to Be Barked At,* in particular in these two longer poems where the development of the metaphor can be seen over a number of stanzas, follow the pattern Kooser sets out in that chapter. The process or journey of the metaphor is, he writes, "a little like stepping through a mirror. The poem begins in the real world, steps through the devise of the comparison, which is like a transparent force-field, and looks back through from the otherworldly side. Then, at the end, the poem starts to step back through the mirror and pauses midway, one leg on one side and one on the other."

The collection concludes with "Year's End," returning to seasonality of human life, a theme first sounded with "In the Laundromat." It must be with irony that Kooser alludes to his place of work as the seasons close their files "on each of us, the heavy drawers / full of certificates rolling back / into tree trunks, a few old papers / flocking away." Even as "someone we loved / has fallen from our thoughts," life goes on, joy eventually returns: we fall in love again.

CHAPTER FOURTEEN

"Walking Home to You"

Just so are you and I gathered at 5:00,
your bicycle left by the porch, the wind
still ringing in it, and my shoes by the bed,
still warm from walking home to you.

—From "Five P.M."

As "Year's End" predicted, love was on the horizon, although as 1976 opened, it was not clearly in sight. Literary successes, however, continued. Kooser won the Prairie Schooner Prize in poetry; then in June he was notified by the National Endowment for the Arts that he was one of 165 writers across the United States to be awarded a 1976–1977 NEA creative writing fellowship of $6,000.

Following the publication of *Not Coming to Be Barked At*, Kooser closed on a house at 1447 Washington Street. Built in the early 1900s, the two-story white frame home was in need of restoration. Journal entries of this time are filled with reports of fumigation and renovation, beginning with the first floor so that he could at least move in while he finished repairing and repainting. On August 23, three and a half weeks after purchase, the poet looked forward to moving in the next day.

In early November Kooser, on his way to a dinner party, noticed a neighborhood woman out walking. Kathleen Rutledge was on her way to B&R IGA for groceries. "It was a very cold day," Rutledge recalls, "when he pulled over and said 'Would you tie my bow tie?' I got into his car and took off my gloves to tie this tie—it was really a ribbon—and then he went off to have dinner with another girlfriend." That night Kooser writes in his journal of the party he had attended and the end of a relationship with another woman. At the bottom of the page, without comment, he prints: KATHY RUTLEDGE.

Several days later Kooser called to tell Rutledge he had found her gloves in his car and to invite her to his house to retrieve them. Rutledge, he remembers, was "going pretty steady with a guy at the time," and shortly after she picked up her gloves, he began writing poems and leaving them in her mailbox in an attempt to woo her. "I have at last met Kathy Rutledge," he notes in his journal on November 12, "and we have spent a little time getting acquainted. I am fascinated by her."

Rutledge remembers being completely charmed by Kooser and his Washington Street home. "I was a twenty-year-old woman going back to college with a part-time job as a van driver and living in this little apartment. He was nine years older, working with the insurance company, an underwriter or something, and had this very nice house that he was renovating. I walked in," Rutledge recalls, "and there was all this art and books, objects that he had collected—he collected all sorts of things. He served me apple juice in this huge sort of goblet. It was a fairy-tale house."

The two soon discovered that not only had Rutledge lived in Ames, where her father, Richard Fischer, taught ROTC in the 1950s, but her house on the corner of 16th and Stafford had been on the young Kooser's paper route. Although living in Iowa, Rutledge, a native Nebraskan, returned with her parents every summer to visit friends and relatives in the Sandhills. The family often stayed in Valentine at the home of Rutledge's grandmother.

Rutledge retained a "soft spot" in her heart for her birth state, and when it was time for college, she applied to the University of

Nebraska in Lincoln, her father's alma mater, where he played half-back for the Huskers in 1936. She went on to earn her bachelor's degree in English. Following graduation, Rutledge, who had married a graduate student in philosophy, held a variety of jobs before working at Cristo Rey, a group home for boys on South 14th Street. When the school closed and her marriage ended, Rutledge enrolled in the graduate program in journalism at the university.

Kooser's journal reflects the ups and downs of their early courtship. They see Cocteau's *Orpheus* at the Sheldon Museum of Art and Merle Haggard at the newly opened Devaney Sports Center. Friend Patty Lombardi remembers a note that Kooser left for her one morning following babysitting, saying that he was dating Rutledge and that the relationship was important to him. Lombardi, who says that they had seen each other through a number of romances, knew that this relationship was different from the beginning. "She was funny and very, very smart," Lombardi says of their first meeting. "She knows him better than anyone."

By March Kooser invited Rutledge to Iowa to meet Jeff, Diana, and her family in Marshalltown and then they traveled on to Cedar Rapids to visit his parents. Shortly after, Rutledge began her career at the *Lincoln Journal* as the newspaper's "death and weather" clerk, writing obituaries and weather notes for page one. She worked in various capacities and eventually served as statehouse reporter for over a dozen years before moving into editorial work. The summer before their marriage, Rutledge, Kooser, and Jeff, who turned ten that July, visited her parents in Colorado Springs and traveled on to the Anasazi cave dwellings in southwest Colorado.

The couple married on Saturday, September 24, 1977, in Burke and Laura Casari's Lincoln backyard with Patty Lombardi acting as "best man." The ceremony was presided over by Reverend Louis DeGrazia before twenty-five to thirty friends and relatives. Rutledge wore a simple white dress with white embroidery; the groom wore a new, more conservative suit. There was, Rutledge recalls, a "hippy feeling to the wedding." Prior to their vows, the couple spoke of their commitment. Acknowledging their previous marriages, and wrestling with "my feminist diatribes that marriage is traditionally for the convenience of the man, and doubts about whether two such strong-willed persons as we are could weather the conflicts that are sure to come," Rutledge explained, "we were impelled by our love for each other, our hopes for the future, and our desire to clasp hands with the past by embracing the tradition of marriage." Kooser also spoke of their prior marriages, thanking "our previous spouses for their help in maturing us and teaching us the humility that we feel before the complex and wonderful concept of marriage."

The couple celebrated with a party for over two hundred friends several weeks later at the Washington Street house where Rutledge had come to retrieve her gloves a year earlier and where they would spend the first eight years of their marriage.

Kooser traced the course of love in *Old Marriage and New*, a chapbook of thirteen short poems, published in a limited edition by Cold Mountain Press in 1978. "I've given away / my grandfather's gun," Kooser writes in "Healing," the emotional fulcrum of the book, "but kept his cane. / I guess I'll stick it out." Only two poems from the chapbook appear in Kooser's collected poems, *Sure Signs*. Shadows of the failed marriage linger, but if there is a loss of innocence, there is also an exquisite joy in the fruition of a second love.

Love at times had been a bumpy ride for Kooser, and *Hatcher*, the first book published after his second marriage, reflects the trials and tribulations of a "poet, raconteur, bon vivant." Courting a reluctant woman several years earlier, Kooser turned to the U.S. Postal Service for an ally. "I had all these old German magazines with steel engravings in them. I would take a piece of cardboard and glue it on there and then I'd put a little voice balloon, saying something about the possibility of getting together."

After mailing her over a half-dozen cards, it was Kooser who got the message: her interest lay elsewhere. But he was still captivated by the literary potential of the technique, and he collected his "enhanced engravings." Kooser used what remained of his fellowship money from the National Endowment for the Arts to publish the slim volume under the Windflower imprint in 1978. Dedicated to his friends, listed on the copyright page, the poet includes a wry apology to the NEA judges "for the surprise that this book may be to each of them. I am sure," he continues, "that the panel members expected me to write and publish more of the poetry for which they had commended me."

Hatcher is surely a departure in form and content from the poet's usual work. An anonymous and enthusiastic review in the student newspaper, *Daily Nebraskan*, begins, "Lincoln's claim to fame may very well include the masculine shaped state capital building, UNL's health center being unofficially rated in the top five percent and Ted Kooser." The plot of the "illustrated novella," the review continues, "mocks the early 19th century romantic poets: Shelly, Byron, and Keats. Hatcher, the main character, is lewder than Tom Jones and Kooser's exaggeration of the romantic's life makes enjoyable reading."

Today we might look at *Hatcher* as a graphic novel, 106 pages that tell the story of a traveler known by his last—or first—name, as seen through the eyes of his lovers, husbands of lovers, priests, children, and townspeople. Hatcher is part troubadour and poet, and all Don Juan, the archetypal lover who never met a woman he did not feel the urge to seduce. Hatcher's women continue to love him and marvel at his sexual prowess long after he has gone. Lord Byron, whose unfinished poetic epic *Don Juan* is by some considered his masterpiece, casts the title character as a sort of innocent victim, twisted by Catholic clerics who tried, unsuccessfully, to repress natural sexual urges. Kooser alludes to this in the opening page; an illustration, a lithograph, depicts what looks to be nineteenth-century Italian clerics seated around a table overlooking the countryside.

Hatcher is reported to be an accomplished lover, but not all portraits are complimentary. A field girl reflects, he was "forever the fool of love. I have never known a man so maddened by the erotic. When he was in pursuit of a woman, his entire day was given over to muttering, plotting, and dreaming, and in the feverish preparation of love-gifts, be they flowers that he had run deep into the forest to select or poems that he carefully pared from the coarse wood of the vulgate. I have seen copies of his manuscripts showing the little bloodstains that his finger-tips made as he nipped at his nails with his broken teeth." When Hatcher departs, he is as mysterious as when he arrived.

Reviewer Hugh Luke tells of Kooser's retrieval of the 1870s lithographs from the Lincoln Goodwill. *Über Land und Meer*, the source of most of the engravings, was an illustrated German-language magazine published in Stuttgart from 1859 to 1923. The weekly, either brought to Nebraska by immigrants or received by subscription, included short stories and novels as well as nonfiction pieces that appealed to its largely bourgeois audience. The poet saw their appeal immediately, but it wasn't until he received the fellowship that he was able to complete *Hatcher* and fund a run of five hundred copies.

Kooser, promoted to assistant vice president, underwriting the year *Hatcher* appeared, continued to lead a busy literary life. In 1979 Windflower Press published a four-hundred-copy edition of the 68-page *Cottonwood County*, poems by Kloefkorn and Kooser. He promoted his press, read his work at the Sheldon Museum of Art and at the university, and reviewed poetry books from time to time for the *Lincoln Journal Star*.

As the 1970s drew to a close, Kooser lost two family members; first, his father, Theodore Briggs Kooser, died of leukemia on New Year's Eve, 1979. Kooser recalls in a letter to California poet Lee McCarthy, he was driving to Cedar Rapids, Iowa, called back on the last day of the year "because my father was dying." He continues, "I was driving the 300 miles across Iowa in bitter cold. When I got to Des Moines, I tuned in WOI radio in Ames, my home town, a very good public radio station. There is a man who reads books, Doug Brown, and he was at the minute I turned in reading some poems. By coincidence he read my poem 'Christmas Eve,' which is about my father and me sitting down on Christmas Eve for a talk. . . . I knew the minute Doug Brown read that poem that my father had died."

Just after the new year Kooser wrote a moving tribute that makes clear the depth of his father's legacy to the poet his son became: "At the ends of our summer vacations at the home of my mother's parents in Guttenburg, Iowa, our father would pick a large bouquet of tiger lilies, and with my sister and me skipping along on either side of him, the three of us walked up the gravel lane that led to the cemetery overlooking the board and sparkling Mississippi. There is a very old tombstone in that lovely place—the quaint statue of a seated maiden. Her head is bowed above her empty arms. There, in the cradle of those frail arms, our father would arrange his lilies. He didn't know whose grave this was, nor what this maiden's special loss had been. But to place that bouquet of brilliant flowers there was our father's remarkable province in life, a sense of the wonder and beauty of continuity. And in walking away from that grave, that lovely moment, with our small hands in his, we felt in everything about us that blend of mystery and love that, smiling down at us, we call 'tradition.'"

Elvy, Kooser's maternal uncle, died the following month. Kooser memorializes both men in his essay "Lights on a Ground of Darkness" and in *Local Wonders*.

Kooser, who won a second *Prairie Schooner* poetry award in fall 1979, had much for which to be thankful as the decade drew to a close. Ed Ochester, poet, editor of the Pittsburgh Poetry Series, and long-time admirer of Kooser's work, invited him to assemble a book of his best work. Karl Shapiro, who read the manuscript, *Sure Signs: New and Selected Poems*, for Ochester, urged publication. "There is little in contemporary poetry that can compare with it in excellence," Shapiro wrote. "I find myself surprised at its freshness, the purity of the writing, its open-eyed honesty, its humor and kindliness, its strength of character, its overwhelming sense of place, and so much more."

Four

American Scripture,
1980–1994

CHAPTER FIFTEEN

Sure Signs

"A long hard winter ahead
for sure," my neighbor says,
reeling a cobweb onto
a broom in his garden.

—From "Sure Signs"

Sure Signs: New and Selected Poems, published in 1980, suggests that
the copy of Adolf Harnack's *Outlines of the History of Dogma* Kooser
carried around to impress his college classmates may have actually
had some effect on his thinking. Harnack, a humanist and considered by some a heretic, rejected the major doctrines of organized
Christianity and offered instead an unorthodox interpretation
of the Bible; he believed that religion should be lived rather than
systematized.

Although he has never described himself as a religious man,
Kooser credits poetry with helping him catch sight of a universal
order that he believes lies beyond the surface of the world. "If I
understand what he wrote, Ralph Waldo Emerson suggested,"
Kooser explains in *The Poetry Home Repair Manual*, "that there
might be a plane of common unity among all things and occurrences
that he called the Oversoul, and that all things touch each other on

and along the plane." Kooser believes that poets, through metaphor, reveal those connections, informing and enriching human life.

By *Sure Signs* Kooser is clearly a poet looking to the natural world to provide lessons on how to live one's daily life. He is at home in his parish. Like Thea Kronborg, another of Cather's artists, from her novel *Song of the Lark*, he finds physical, emotional, and spiritual nourishment in the land. "Under the human world," as Cather reminds her readers, "there is a geologic world . . . which [is] indifferent to man." By reading signs, indifferent though the geologic world and, by extension, nature may be, Kooser sees the order behind life's apparent chaos. Metaphor makes that connection manifest.

The collection's title is a nod to George von Glahn, to whom the poem "Sure Signs" is dedicated. Von Glahn, in his review of *A Local Habitation & a Name*, wrote that Kooser "lives the role of the passionate and awake searcher for signs to announce or proclaim, 'the power of nature.'"

"You get to know a thing or two," the seventy-year-old neighbor tells the narrator of the title poem, a pastoral dialog. Seven decades of experience have taught him to listen to the crickets, abundant in the year of the poem, who sound their weather forecast "like strings of sleigh bells" in the night. The bounty of cobwebs in the garden supports the crickets' forecast: "A long hard winter ahead / *for sure*" (italics mine), he says, emphasizing their certainty, reeling them in with the end of his broom. Reading of signs is a direct result of a felt connection with an observation of the creatures around him; they are his neighbors, companions, and teachers. But human beings have to go looking for signs, fishing for them, the metaphor suggests, bait the line and go to where the clues are biting. The biblical imagery (the old man, fish, and garden), though light-handed, resonates throughout.

The poet acts as the reader's neighbor, sweeping the countryside for treasures and casting his own lines as he writes poems for which the reader brooms. The unremitting passage of time, a continuing, perhaps essential, theme in any Kooser work, is sounded as the poem draws to a close. The neighbor (wearing reading glasses to better see the signs) has seen many seasons and many men come and go over the years; he checks to see if the narrator is still there. Such is the ephemeral nature of life.

"Sure Signs" tells us how to read the book and what to look for in the poet's poetry. Kooser, the son of a storyteller who crocheted hats during his retirement and a conscientious accountant of household expenditures who stitched her family's clothing, presents readers with the dense fabric of his experiences, threaded by images, the shadows cast by juxtaposition, content, and metaphor, by which readers may, if only they allow, gain the wisdom that his neighborhood and its inhabitants have to offer.

Sure Signs, the collection, is a repository of epistles and parables that Kooser has caught and reeled in over the years. The twenty-five poems collected for the first time are very much akin in tone and content to their previously collected siblings. The majority (seventy-three) of the poems have appeared in *A Local Habitation & a Name* (thirty-one) and *Not Coming to Be Barked At* (thirty). Only three poems survive from *Official Entry Blank* along with two from *Old Marriage and New*.

Although several critics have pointed out that the poems are arranged neither by date written nor date published, they are not without order. As William Carlos Williams noted, in poetry the form "IS the meaning." Kooser carries this dictum to the arrangement of *Sure Signs*, where the poems spread out before the reader like the long horizontal roads that stretch across the gentle roll of the Plains drawing us in and on to the small town, city, and country life Kooser sees. New poems are integrated with previously published poems to reveal, by analogy, the narrative line of the poet's own life, assembled with the eye of the magazine editor he is.

"Selecting a Reader" opens *Sure Signs*, signaling a shift in the poet's intended audience from the literary establishment ("Official Entry Form" opened his first book) to someone closer to home. The imagined reader is from his neighborhood. "Beautiful," searching, and "careful," she is already interested in poetry, enough to enter a bookstore and see what's on the shelf. She too is looking for signs.

Her description suggest concern; the sun has apparently given way to rain, figuratively, literally, or both, and her raincoat, "an old one, dirty / from not having enough for the cleaners," needs attention.

"She will take out her glasses," Kooser imagines, to see more clearly, setting up the parallel with the old man in "Sure Signs." Since it is "the loneliest moment of an afternoon," she may be searching for comfort or for company. It may be she is looking for motivation to complete all those mundane chores of life. Kooser's word choice is precise: "she will thumb / over my poems," suggesting attention and comprehension. Although she replaces the book on the shelf and says to herself, "For that kind of money, I can get / my raincoat cleaned," she has in some way been changed. When she entered the store she was wearing a raincoat that she couldn't afford to have cleaned; when she leaves, she is all the richer for the experience, rich enough now to clean her raincoat as, the poet assures, "she will."

Like the artifacts from his country sojourns, like the cookie jars he collects from antique stores and garage sales, Kooser's poems are repositories of the wisdom of the land in which he dwells. He, like Cather, is writing for his neighbors in the world ("parish"); like Lentil, he is bringing music and great riches to his community of readers.

Kooser reveals his philosophy regarding the importance of his imaginary reader. In *The Poetry Home Repair Manual*, he quotes critic Sven Birkerts, who notes how the reader and writer are joined by the experience of reading: "Reading . . . is not simply an inscribing of the author's personal subjectivity upon a reader's receptivity. Rather, it is the collaborative bringing forth of an entire world, a world complete with a meaning structure. For hearing completes itself in listening, and listening happens only where there is some subjective basis for recognition. The work is not merely the bridge between author and reader; it is an enabling entity. The text is a pretext."

"Selecting a Reader" identifies Kooser's imagined reader with whom readers of the collection's initial poem identify, and by this identification are brought to an "imaginative readiness" for the poems that follow.

"First Snow," immediately following, grounds the reader in physical place, as Kooser's poems frequently do. A winter kitchen is "a kindergarten / steamy with stories." The "old black dog" comes in "with the first few snowflakes on his back / and falls asleep." Dog and snow are greeted with excitement. The use of "our" and "each of us" suggests a couple at home. "This is the night," the poem continues, when "one of us gets to say, as if it were news, / that no two snowflakes are ever alike." This subtle and unexpected allusion to Williams's poem "Asphodel, That Greeny Flower," underscores the ability of poems to inform and transform. His execution of the sonnet is so smooth that the form of "First Snow" is easy to overlook.

Across the page, in "An Old Photograph," Kooser presents the story of another couple after forty years of marriage. The poet imagines their preparation for the photograph, rising at daybreak and dressing by the stove, "Lydia wearing black wool with a collar of lace / Nils his worn suit." Signs within the photograph, itself a sign, tell the reader about the couple, "already like brother / and sister—small, lusterless eyes, / large ears, the same serious line / to the mouth." Theirs is a life sentence, posed and enduring, "thirty years to go," unlike the convivial couple on the preceding page. Or is this a cautionary tale? "The Old Photograph" invites a look back to "First Snow," opposite, to reconsider the movement of the old dog from the kitchen to the "heart" of the home. Will this couple's love also grow cold? The dramatic effect of "The Old Photograph" is as fascinating as it is unsettling. A stern warning of the toll life can take.

The poems that follow touch one against the other, rubbing shoulders through metaphor or with the knees of image, drawing us into an intimacy with the world and its patterns. "Sitting All Evening Alone in the Kitchen," paired with "Sure Signs," stitches together images of two kinds of readings, "the dull book of a dead moth" and "crickets and cobwebs." Signs of time passing are evident in both poems: the tide can be heard gurgling out in "Sitting All Evening Alone in the Kitchen," while the informer of "Sure Signs" is seventy and in need of glasses. One of the most interesting juxtapositions is that of light and dark, presence and absence, sets of images that will continue to play and intensify throughout Kooser's future work.

Throughout *Sure Signs*, poems from previous collections take on additional meaning when paired with other new neighbors, "Old Soldiers" Home," for example, with "Self-portrait at Thirty-nine." The relentlessness of time shows up again and again, often by juxtaposition, as in "At the Bus Stop Next to the Funeral Home" (new) and "Visiting Mountains."

Kooser's facility with capturing the inhabitants of the workaday world continues. Who can forget "The Salesman" (a new poem) in his "pond-scum green" double-knit suit and "his vinyl shoes, / shiny and white as little Karmann Ghias / from the body shop" who has made his way down our street too. We recognize the "Brillo pad / of graying hair" at his neck, the cross and chain that tosses there, when we opened our door. The poem and its spread companion, "The Constellation Orion," are two very different, but related, emotional encounters.

"Shooting a Farmhouse" and "Beer Bottle" are paired midway through the collection, juxtaposing wanton human destruction and a miraculous artifact of human carelessness or disregard. Love poems resonate more deeply when placed side by side, as in the case of "Looking for You, Barbara" and "Pocket Poem." Both the "Abandoned Farmhouse" and "The Blind Always Come as Such a Surprise" raise and read together magnify questions that are not easily answered. Kooser immediately connects, by simile, "bruises or shadows," signs of illness giving way to death the poet reads under his grandfather's skin, "in My Grandfather Dying" to "shapes / skaters find frozen in rivers—leaves caught in flight, or maybe the hand of a man reaching up / out of the darkness for help," heightening the naturalness of change and even death. Across the page the Red Wing Church gives way to secular uses, and when we reach its final line, "only God knows where," we are sent back to the grandson who witnesses another sort of transformation in his grandfather's death.

The volume concludes with two new poems, "Walking to Work,"

knitted to the preceding poem by ambulation and destination, and "Sunday Morning," an *ars poetica* that further explores the here and now, in conversation with Wallace Stevens's well-known poem by the same name.

"Today," begins "Walking to Work," calling our attention to the moment in which we live. The poet is off to work again, and despite his destination,

> the obsidian
> ice on the sidewalk
> with its milk white bubbles
> popping under my shoes
> . . . pleases me.

Under the "black ice," as it is colloquially named, rarely celebrated, and often feared, a joyful crackling lies. The recognizable observation of the sidewalk, sight and sound, is acute. Then Kooser transforms the "lump of old snow / with a trail," into a simile, "like a comet." This too is a sign, a harbinger of someone so joyful in love that he or she has kicked the lump of old snow "all the way to the corner." The poem's compression, eleven lines composed of forty-eight words, and its irregular measures, its plosive "p" sound adds to the poem's own vibrant jaunt down the page. Even in a world of chance and bad weather, love, like spring, is in the air.

"Now" and "Here" are the warp and weft of "Sunday Morning," on the page opposite. The beginning words of the first and third sentences orient the reader quickly to the poem's celebration of the world in which the poet lives:

> Now it is June again, one of those
> leafy Sundays drifting through the galaxies
> of maple seeds. Somewhere, a mourning dove
> touches her keyboard twice, a lonely F,
> and then falls silent. Here in the house
> the Sunday papers lie in whitecaps
> over the living-room floor.

One again, the reader is introduced to the scene via sound and sight. The celestial image of the comet in the preceding poem is complimented and extended by the image of "galaxies" of whirling maple seeds through which this Sunday drifts. The forlorn call of the mourning dove can be heard "somewhere" in the distance, but here the floor is covered with whitecaps bobbing with the week's news. Then Kooser in his characteristic way extends the water metaphor and touches on the celestial one that in lesser hands would send the poem carrying leaden weight to the very bottom of the sea.

Small rectangular photographs of smiling June brides float on the living room floor, showing themselves first, like reflections in window panes, as sky and starlit cloud. The photographer's light, that nuptial moon, illuminates them. Despite the mourning dove's lonely call, the subtle reminders of the possibility of "pane"/pain in this heavenly morning, and the thorns of the sweet-smelling locust tree, love prevails!

Sunday, the day of rest and family activities, Sabbath and day of worship for many, is a day devoted to many aspects of love. Lurching weekday cars are transformed into "smooth canoes . . . soft with families." The church bell "strides through the green perfume / of locust trees" tolling "thankfulness" rather than marking the passage of time or of burial.

Kooser's mindfulness of Stevens's "Sunday Morning," which also celebrates the here and now, is clear in word and image. Stevens' poem, however, raises questions—Why should beauty die? for example—which seems irrelevant or nonexistent in Kooser's world. The celebration of existence, whether or not there is life after death or even a God at all, is firsthand and immediate.

Nowhere are the two poems more different than in closure. Stevens's ends with the downward flight of birds into night, linking beauty and death. Stevens seems to accept transient beauty and death in a way that does not occur to Kooser in his "Sunday Morning," which ends with the return of the mourning dove and her plaintive call from the third and fourth lines, who, "to her astonishment, / blunders upon a distant call in answer." No matter what, if anything, may follow and no matter the accompanying pain, Kooser's poem seems to suggest, love, relationship, and the sounds and sights around us, connected in a marvelous way, are to be enjoyed and celebrated through poetry and in life.

Sure Signs was awarded the Society of Midland Authors Poetry Prize in 1980. In a letter to Kooser, Karl Shapiro praises *Sure Signs* as a "complete and mature work of poetry. . . . I find myself surprised at its freshness, the purity of the writing, its open-eyed honesty, its humor and kindliness, its strength of character, its overwhelming sense of place. . . . I see it as a lasting work, comparable to the best of the *Spoon River* or Frost in his richest vein."

Dana Gioia compares it to a box of chocolates: "I kept intending to put the book down to finish later, but kept sneaking one more poem until there was none left."

Positive reviews were many. And while one may argue with Peter Stitt in the *Georgia Review*, who describes Kooser as "a more or less average citizen of a more or less average small city," it is true, as he also notes, that the poet's work grows from his interest "in the land, which endures, and in the people, whose lives and concerns—however individual and unique—are still somehow typical, repeating cycles begun long ago, which endure."

Dana Gioia's review of a dozen poets that appeared in the *Hudson Review* refers to *Sure Signs* as "A first-rate collection," with poems that "have surprising twists that one never settles into that sort of drowsy half-attention." They are, he goes on to say, "readable . . . alternately so delightful and mysterious and always so unassuming."

Charles Molesworth, perhaps overwhelmed by the need to review seven new collections in limited inches, finds Kooser's work, as well as the work of those other poets—Louise Glück, Gregory Orr, Charles Simic, Alfred Corn, David St. John, and Marilyn Hacker—wanting. Kooser, whose images the reviewer sometimes finds "fresh and keen" and at times, he says, "humdrum and clumsy," is in good company. Mary Kinzie, reviewing eight books at a clip for the *American Poetry Review*, has some of the same reservations as Molesworth. Even so, she notes Kooser's strengths as well: in "Sunday Morning," for example, where the expression of the brides "touches the observer with the warm reflex of their hopefulness."

Compression and connotation are hallmarks of Kooser's work and keys to the richness and evocative nature of his metaphors. As Stitt points out, even "one of Kooser's slightest poems, 'Sitting All Evening Alone in the Kitchen,'" illustrates the poet's facility to capture and hold the reader's interest as he builds his metaphor.

Revision is the key to the success of poem after poem in *Sure Signs*. It should be no surprise that Kooser follows Shapiro's aesthetic theory, "result without a trace / of the cause, end without means, what without why," in his poem, "Magician," from *V-Letter*.

Gilbert Allen in a review of *Sun Signs* for *Southern Humanities Review* notes that "Kooser knows his craft." Noting his "controlled and appropriate diction" and "felicitous line-breaks," Allen concludes that Kooser "always seems to know what he wants to say and exactly how he wants to say it."

Kooser discussed his method of composition, which has changed little over the years, in an interview published shortly before *Sure Signs*. "I usually begin a poem in longhand," he tells Robin Tawney,

> and write half a dozen lines and then I go to the typewriter and type that up, see how it looks and then I take it out of the typewriter and make a longhand addition to it, then go back and retype the whole thing all the way down. I'm continually adding on lines and throwing out ones. So I might, in a poem of twenty lines, have typed it ten or fifteen times by the time that I've gotten it where I want it. But I always write from the top down. I keep proceeding through the poem from the top down. Mainly I'm interested in the poem flowing from the top and so that's why I have to keep reading it again from the top so that it all moves together.

"I do extensive revision," he told poet Marge Saiser, in a later interview, comparing writing to painting. "For the small poem of twelve or fourteen lines," he offers, "there might be thirty or forty versions by the time I'm done. My revisions are toward a kind of clarity and freedom so that . . . it appears the poem came off the brush like a stroke of watercolor without any effort whatsoever."

Sure Signs is a stunning collection of artifacts, the poems themselves and the places and aspects of life that they bring to light. As Matthew C. Brennan summarizes, "Just as Frost used New England for his metaphors, Kooser uses landscapes and portraits of the Plains states and their people as vehicles for expressing experiences and feelings (especially loss, decay, and loneliness) that are universal." When Kooser's seventy-year-old neighbor predicts, "A long hard winter ahead / for sure," the reader, no matter where he or she might live, listens, sure to learn "a thing or two."

CHAPTER SIXTEEN

Common Ground

What writers on the Great Plains share is the Great Plains.

—Interview with Ted Kooser, in Mark Sanders
and J. V. Brummels, *On Common Ground*

As Kooser looked for new topics and other signs, his insurance career advanced steadily at Lincoln Benefit Life; in 1981 he was appointed second vice president, new business. The compilation and publication of *The Windflower Home Almanac of Poetry*, a 141-page anthology edited by Kooser, was one of his largest press projects, bringing together 180 poems from a variety of writers, well known and unknown. Favorite Nebraska poets—Roy Scheele, Shirley Buettner, Mordecai Marcus, Don Welch, and William Kloefkorn—rub shoulders with Plains neighbors, Thomas McGrath, Linda Hogan, Mark Vinz, Linda Hasselstrom, and William Stafford, as well as with those from afar, Theodore Weiss, Marge Piercy, Carole Oles, and Henry Taylor. Long infatuated by the eclectic nature of home almanacs, Kooser set out to collect poems that described the human seasons within the context of nature's larger seasonal display.

Almanacs have long been popular in North America. *The Book of the Seasons*, published in 1881 by William Hewitt, was, according to Laurence Buell, one of the first books on nature that Thoreau read. Benjamin Franklin's *Poor Richard's Almanak*, published from 1732 to 1759—one of the first magazines of its kind in the American colonies—was a best seller. Poems, puzzles, proverbs, and household hints accompanied weather forecasts. Kooser's cover for *The Windflower Home Almanac of Poetry* pays tribute to the 1851 cover of the longest continuously published (1792 to today) almanac, *Old Farmer's Almanac*, where charts of the tides and planting tables make a single source for essential information.

Kooser's cover, featuring the almanac's characteristic ornate scroll work, also includes an atypical illustration: covered wagons and men on horseback. Windflower's windmill colophon is located midcover along with the proclamation "ILLUSTRATED." Indeed it is. Laced throughout the hand-sized, 4" x 7", saddle-stitched book are original pen and ink drawings, clip art, and advertisements from early farmer's almanacs. Both visual and literary effects are striking, and all one needs to get through a year of planting and pestilence, heartbreak, and reward—all for, as the cover notes and William Cole must have appreciated—$2.00 a copy.

Like its antecedents, *The Windflower Home Almanac of Poetry* includes "recipes": "Making Applesauce" by Kathy Mangan, "Jellied Moose Nose" by Don Welch, how to clean, cook, and dispose of the bones of a "Trout" by Ronald Wallace, prairie drinks, "Herbal Teas" by Ramona Weeks, and "Wild Sarsaparilla" by Susan Hauser. Joseph Hutchison's one-line poem, "Artichoke," still a favorite of Kooser's, quietly sits across the page from a chubby cherub-like baby on a garland of buds and birds.

Poems that mark weather, seasons, and the equinox provide the book's natural rhythm. A sketch of "types of stinkers" shares a spread with "Freeway Blackberries" by Al Masarik and Robert Hedin's "Great Bear." Henry Taylor's heart-wrenching "Burning a Horse" runs alongside an ad for Oaklawn, "The Great Nursery of Percheron Horses. 200 Imported Blood Mares, Choicest Families. Large Numbers all ages, both sexes, In Stock." "Everything you need to live and grow / is here if you / can give up wanting more," a poem by Patricia Henley begins. *The Windflower Home Almanac* won the

1980 *Library Journal*'s award for one of the best books from small presses; it is as wise and delightful today as it was three decades ago.

Kooser also launched a new literary journal, the *Blue Hotel*, in 1980, named after a short story by Stephen Crane published in 1899. Crane traveled west during the winter of 1894–1896 as a reporter for the Bacheller, Johnson & Bacheller news syndicate to investigate the effects of the drought and crop failures on the Plains. A blizzard swept across the state during his time in Lincoln, serving as inspiration for his short story, which critics and local readers, with a combination of pride and persistence, still try to unravel.

Crane's model for the blue hotel, painted by its proprietor Pat Scully "a light blue, a shade that is on the legs of a kind of heron, causing the bird to declare its position against any background," was the Sam Lawrence Hotel. Located at 1042 P Street, where the Embassy Suites stands now, the hotel had been right around the corner from Lebsack's, where Kooser, Gaffney, and friends met for drinks and conversation. The first issue of the new journal includes an interview of poet/editor Brewster Ghiselin, appreciations of Ghiselin's work by Nathan and John Schow, a musing on an eclectic sampling of literary personages by Wilbur Gaffney, along with poems and reviews.

The following year the *Blue Hotel* anthologized a group of distinguished Scandinavian writers. Edited by Norwegian writer Niel Ingwersen of the University of Wisconsin–Madison, *Seventeen Danish Poets in Translation* appeared as a combined issue, numbers 2 and 3 of the journal. Long impressed by Swedish poet Tomas Tranströmer's work, Kooser discovered in Norwegian Rolf Jacobsen the clean lines and attention to phenomenological detail that were reminiscent of his own. Low sales brought the *Blue Hotel* to an end after this second issue.

Kooser was also involved with the large community of Nebraska poets. He and Susan Strayer Deal served as cohosts of the August 1981 Tin Camp Writers' Picnic, held at the Tin Camp Ranch near Sutherland in the Sandhills. According to Mark Sanders, poet and publisher of Sandhills Press who attended the event, about twenty Nebraska writers camped that weekend, most from Kearney or Lincoln. "We ate hot dogs, chips, drank beer, soft drinks, sipped pan-boiled coffee over an open fire," Sanders reflects. "Ted sold Tin Camp Writers Picnic and Windflower Press T-shirts: 'Support the arts, take a poet to lunch.'" Sanders continues, "At night, when the locusts sang, we stood around the bonfire and read samples of our own poetry."

Two years later, the event attracted nearly fifty poets and musicians to Davis's OLO Ranch. "For the fifth straight day the temperature was over 100 degrees," Fran Kaye, former editor of the *Great Plains Quarterly*, reported, "the corn on the edge of the pivot circles stood brown and shriveled." Fiddlers fiddled, poets read, and then singing filled the night air.

Kooser also traveled promoting his poetry and Windflower Press. In 1981 he met his early champion, critic William Cole, in New York before traveling on to read in Ithaca and Rochester. The following year he headed west, visiting Carol and Leonard Nathan and reading at Berkeley and seeing Karl Shapiro at the University of California, Davis and Glenna Luschei in San Luis Obispo.

Back in Lincoln, he set to work on a series of dramatic monologues in which nature took charge, inspired perhaps by the blizzard of Crane's "The Blue Hotel" and based on the deadly Blizzard of 1888. The poems, each in the voice of a survivor, tell the story of one of the Plains' most deadly storms; between 230 and 500 lost their lives.

The Blizzard Voices was performed as a one-act eight-character play in the early 1980s by the Community Playhouse Gallery Theater, directed by Patricia Dickerson. Terry Flatt, reviewing the play for the local paper, described its language as "full of power, humor, tenderness, sadness, and horror."

In 1983 the first book-length critical work featuring Nebraska-based poets—Kloefkorn, Kooser, Kuzma, and Welch—*On Common Ground*, edited by Mark Sanders and J. V. Brummels, was published by Sandhills Press. While, according to the foreword, the "coincidence of habitat" drove the selection of these particular four poets, all male, Sanders notes the distinctive voice of each represents a common ground no matter where one lives. The importance of this early volume focused on Nebraska poets and their work cannot be overstated.

While the pastoral qualities of each poet are not directly addressed, the topic of regionalism comes up once again early in the Sanders interview as well as in the two critical pieces that are included, "Words and Raincoats: Verbal and Nonverbal Communication" by Victor Contoski and "Explaining Ted Kooser" by Dana Gioia. Kooser was quick to take issue with "boosterism," what he believed much of the "talk about regionalism and sense of place" was. "What writers on the Great Plains share is the Great Plains," Kooser continued:

> the same summers and winters. . . . People have known for years that the best way to involve a reader in what he's reading is to introduce concrete imagery, and when you live in a place you draw your imagery from what's around you. You can't draw from experiences you haven't had. Bill Kloefkorn and Don Welch and I have lived nearly all our lives in Nebraska, Kansas, and Iowa, so when we go to our experiences we have nothing else to draw from. Greg Kuzma has lived here, but he's also lived in the east, and he draws from both regions. . . . What's important to me is whether the poetry that gets written is any good. Where it got written doesn't make much difference.

In another interview that year Kooser talks about his recent travel to both coasts, noting that New York City was "incredibly rich . . . so full of life and excitement. Everything that's possible is there someplace." Kooser, who got "a glimpse of the Atlantic," got a longer look at the Pacific. In the same article, while admitting that he sometimes thought "it would be nice to live somewhere else sometime," he professes that he was happy living in Nebraska, which he found nurturing for writers and other artists. Kooser was content: "When I go out for Sunday drives I can go 35 miles from Lincoln and really feel fulfilled, that I'd really seen some country. I don't need to go to the ends of the earth to travel. I guess I'm a little more interested in going places now than I used to be—feeling more confident. I could very well have been a person that would stay in his home town all his life. Get a job there, raise a family there and die there, and never feel I'd ever missed anything."

As Gioia notes in his overview, "Explaining Ted Kooser" (subsequently collected in his book *Can Poetry Matter?*), "Ted Kooser is a genuinely popular poet" writing "naturally for a nonliterary public." Praising his "common speech" and conversational syntax, Gioia noted the "unexpected moments of illumination" that Kooser draws "from the seemingly threadbare details of everyday life. . . . He has transformed the common idiom and experience into fresh and distinctive poetry."

By the time Kooser was forty-four, his poetry was nationally visible and appeared in many distinguished magazines, including "The Fan in the Window," published in the September 19, 1983, issue of the *New Yorker* and widely anthologized. That same year Kooser ran across Lewis Hyde's *The Gift: Imagination and the Erotic Life of Property*, inspiring him "to give something back" to his community. He became a member of the Nebraska Arts Council and the Lincoln Library Board and served as president of the Nebraska Literary Heritage Foundation.

When Kooser received a second National Endowment of the Arts fellowship for $12,500 in 1984, he was able to do more than dream about moving to the Bohemian Alps; he and Rutledge purchased an old farmstead, outside of Garland, just west of the home of good friends Dace and Steve Burdic. They set to work renovating and enlarging the old farmhouse, converting the outbuildings into work and reading areas, planting a garden, raising hens for fresh eggs, and exploring the hills around their home while maintaining busy professional and social lives.

The year 1984 was also significant in that it marked the end of Kooser's drinking. As he later told Saiser, "When I used to drink, I would write when I was loaded, write these things that I thought were brilliant. The next morning I couldn't read them or make any sense out of them." He added, "I realized that drinking took up so much time. . . . I've come to think of writing as an athletic endeavor. You've got to be, particularly as you get older, in good physical shape."

Recalling his history with alcohol, he says, "We didn't drink in high school, but when I got into the fraternity at Iowa State that's what frat life was all about. You can see I was pretty thin in photographs of the time. And when we came to Lincoln, I was real anxious all the time and drank. Diana encouraged me to get some help. I was drinking a lot, doing things I shouldn't be doing. When you're drinking a lot you don't make good decisions."

Quitting seemed sudden, but, Kooser says, "I had known for a long time I drank too much. I was getting older and older; the hangovers were harder to get past. Kathy also expressed concern for my health. I never got into any legal trouble, nor did I need treatment to help me quit. I just got up one morning after a late night out and decided I was going to stop then and there. I have attended AA meetings off and on over the years."

Kooser kept to his schedule, getting up at 5:30 to write until 7:00, when he headed for Lincoln Benefit Life, a half-hour's drive away. The poet made peace with his insurance work. "I think it [making his living writing poetry] would spoil writing for me," he told Ina Aronow, a staff writer for the *Omaha World Herald*. His job at LBL, he said, gave him "a sense of order," blocking out time and giving "him regular work hours. . . . I like participating in the decisions of the company and coming up with ideas that will advance it." But he adds that he "would not be at ease with myself if I were merely holding down a job. I have a real need to stand apart by being an artist, which is being an observer of the social order." In a *Magazine of the Midlands* feature by Aronow highlighting Kooser's poetry and drawings, the poet also talks about the central importance of metaphor to his work. "I begin with a metaphor," he says, "and then build a real tight skin on it like a balloon that is about to burst, and then I stop there."

CHAPTER SEVENTEEN

One World at a Time

The question is not what you look at—but
how you look and whether you see.

—Henry David Thoreau, *Journal*, August 5, 1851

One World at a Time, published in 1985, is dedicated to Leonard Nathan, master of the short poem. Of the fifty-one poems, only "Father" runs over a page long; most are under twenty lines. In poems written before settling into rural surroundings, Kooser frequently meditates on human-made artifacts found in cities or along the highways that link them. Above all, Kooser's fifth full-length collection is a paean to the here and now, to interconnectedness, and to pattern.

For the first time it is clear that the ideas of Alexander von Humboldt, by way of the American Transcendentalists Emerson and Thoreau, serve as philosophical underpinnings to much of Kooser's work. Like his friend Emerson, Thoreau looked for that "radical correspondence of visible things and human thought." Best known for *Walden*, the condensed account of his two years living beside Emerson's pond, Thoreau saw the seasons as analogous to human development. For him, the essence of being human was found in full engagement in the natural world in which we live. He focused on the knowable, and when asked as he lay dying of tuberculosis whether he had glimpsed the hereafter, Thoreau responded, "One world at a time." By choosing this title, Kooser makes overt his literary inheritance and directs our attention to individual life lived deliberately, to close observation of the surrounding natural world, to the joys with which the attentive are rewarded, and the subject matter that he has chosen for his major artistic focus.

Like Frost, who was himself influenced by Emerson and Thoreau, Kooser sets out to observe nature, that "open book with lessons on every page awaiting the sensible reader." Filled with lights and dark places, *One World at a Time* might well have been named *Delights & Shadows*. Nearly every page offers stars, streetlamps, sunlight, basement light bulbs, moonlight, and sunset balanced by shadow, night-black wings, "folds of blackness," nightfall, and darkness. For Frost, however, human beings are able to (and desire to) grasp scraps of heaven.

Kooser, two years older than Thoreau at his death, had been touched by human seasons. His father had passed away, along with both sets of grandparents and his uncle Elvy. There were other profound changes: the disappointment of losing his university readership, entry into the workaday world, divorce, a long-distance relationship with his son, as well as the springtime of his second marriage and move to his own acreage with its version of Walden Pond.

In 1982 Leonard Nathan, professor of rhetoric at the University of California, Berkeley, convinced Kooser, a reluctant plane traveler, to journey west. "Flying at Night," which opens *One World at a Time* (and will become the title of the poet's second selected works, published in 2005), immediately establishes the tie of flight to Nathan and the light/star motif that shines throughout the book.

Striking is the use of the first-person plural pronoun "us" in the first line, employed to express the archetypal as well as the personal. Kooser invites his imagined reader along with the rest of humankind into the experience of flight. The two sentences of the first line—"Above us, stars. Beneath us, constellations"—immediately and places "us," human beings, in the caesura, that place of pause and leap, "the in-between," that time-full place, where the transfer of the metaphor and transformation takes place. "As above, so below," a saying attributed to early alchemists and astrologers, could well be the bumper sticker of the metaphorical poet. This is Emerson's "cosmic harmony." Stars above, electrical "constellations" below; literally we are between heaven and earth, between unknown space and the concrete world, lights above and lights below. Kooser quickly reminds us that despite the disparity of the known and unknown, there are similar patterns: "Five billion miles away, a galaxy dies / like a snowflake falling on water." Both disappear before our eyes. Throughout the poem short sentences and phrases reveal relative positions; long sentences and the long lines of ten and eleven syllables connect them.

Line 3 ends with another short directional phrase, "Below us," calling our attention down to earth, and the balance of the sentence, longest of the poem (over three lines), continues to establish the corresponding relationship. Kooser, alluding to Frost's "tenant farmer," imagines someone, like the old neighbor in *Sun Signs* who lives so close to the natural world that he feels a connection, "the chill" of the dying galaxy, and "snaps on his yard light, drawing his sheds and barns / back into the little system of his care." The poem ends with a couplet that, by simile, melds heaven and earth, city and country: "All night, the cities, like shimmering novas, / tug with bright streets at lonely lights like his." Connection, like gravity, tugs at us all. The poet as tenant farmer does not himself illuminate the dark but directs us to illumination.

While the seasons pass before our eyes, the first section of *One World at a Time* continues to point to that time and place "between." "A Fencerow in Early March" arrests the moment so it may be grasped. "Just now, if I look back down / the cool street of the past, I can see / streetlamps, one for each year," the poem opens; memories are the bright but futile leverage against time and the enormous "cold darkness around it."

Mortality flickers in the shadows. In poems from earlier

collections, "Selecting a Reader," for example, a young woman puts on her glasses to read poetry in the bookstore; in "Sure Signs," the seventy-year-old neighbor looks over his glasses to share the secret message of the world. In *One World at a Time*'s "In the Basement of the Goodwill Store," the observer/poet finds "an old man" who is "trying on glasses" from a box of discarded eyewear that, one assumes, have lost their usefulness for their original owners.

The themes of human connection and disconnection, in the present and through time, are often considered within the same poem. Midway in part 1, "Tillage Marks" meditates on the passing of one generation into the next. Each leaves its mark on that "flat stone, / too heavy for one man alone" as he plows. Each of us is the solitary farmer snapping on the light, as in "Flying at Night," scraping life's plow against the fieldstone.

This world—field, land, rock—endures; human beings, however, are transient. Just across the page, "In January, 1962," the ground is literally being prepared for the final resting place of the poet's grandmother; a "scratched" stone will soon mark her grave. Connection and transience are amplified in "Good-Bye." Two sentences make up this farewell between the "you" and the narrator, standing on the porch, the domestic stage for coming and going. "Your" hand is, Kooser writes, "dusted with the chalk from the past," continuing the "marking" image of earlier poems.

Kooser takes the reader on the road in section 2. The poems are, in the words of the poet Wendell Berry, "local life aware of itself" rather than proponents of the narrow regionalism employed by a chamber of commerce brochure. The initial poem, "The Giant Slide," introduces a Plains' artifact, an icon, suggested by its capitalization in the first line of the poem: "Beside the highway, the Giant Slide." The meter is a relaxed, irregular pentameter. From the highway, reminiscent of Highway 30, the abandoned slide "with its rusty undulations lifts / out of the weeds." Like the Red Wing Church of *Local Habitation*, it stands as a roadside shrine to the past while it provides a foothold in the present, for the reader as well as for the "Blue morning glories" that "climb halfway up the stairs, bright clusters / of laughter." The cries of the children exhilarated by the downward pull of the slide have "gone east," blown "on a wind that will never stop blowing," a reminder of this place on the planet where weather "blows down from the Rockies and over the plains." We, like those "bright leaves," children who played and laughed and screamed in this world, will also, in time, be gone. Time is the wind that never stops blowing.

"A Roadside Shrine in Kansas" offers a homemade shrine, a plaster Virgin sheltered by the curve of a bathtub sunk upended into the ground. As Kooser draws us closer, the poem takes an Edenic or Thoreauvian turn. Kneeling before the porcelain grotto, "through / the rusty drain hole"—literally the cross hatch of the drain's grid strainer—we "can see / in the shimmering distance, / God," divine *and* human, the poet's farmer tending his fields, in this case, walking the beans.

Poems themselves serve as memorials in section 2, tributes to contemporaries, writers who died in the early 1980s. "Walking at Noon near the Burlington Depot in Lincoln, Nebraska" commemorates poet James Wright, who died in 1980. Wright, like Kooser, moved from the conventional form and meter of his earlier work to free verse. There are other similarities. Steve Hahn writes, "I often see his [Wright's] ghost in the background [of Kooser's work] . . . not only in the sense of social issues, but I think Ted works with images in much the same way that Wright did." Both poets are known for their clarity, music, and engagement with the world at hand. Although both poets looked to the natural world for nurturance and instruction, frequently Wright's poetry, more overtly than Kooser's, illuminates, and sometimes provides a social commentary on, the lives of the working class. Wright's work often reflects a level of alienation not found in Kooser's.

Wright's long titles, as in one of his most widely anthologized poems—"Lying in a Hammock on William Duffy's Farm in Pine Island, Minnesota"—are reflected in Kooser's tribute. Each of its five stanzas reflects an urban phenomenology, in contrast to the rural description of the Wright poem, which opens "Over my head,

I see the bronze butterfly / Asleep on the black trunk, / Blowing like a leaf in green shadow." Kooser's butterfly will come later in the elegy, in a very different context. In both poems the poet observer takes in the world around him. Wright's narrator, "I," is the chief organizing figure, while in the Kooser poem the narrator's presence, though just as central, is less overt. Although there is no personal pronoun "I" to direct our attention, the pacing of the speaker as he walks near the Burlington Depot directs our course. The short lines that follow—only five, six, and seven syllables long—move us quickly along the streets of the Haymarket, a Lincoln industrial area that dates from 1867, when market days were held along the banks of Salt Creek.

Kooser's walk begins at the "rat-gray dock" of the old Candy Building, two blocks north of O Street, on 8th Street. Urban details are as sharp as Wright's rural descriptions from his hammock. Streets are populated by factory workers, who "in caps and aprons / as white as divinity / sit on their heels and smoke." Down the block, "two pickets in lettered vests / call back and forth." In stanza three, "A girl sits in her car / . . . and plays her radio," leading to the "one tattered butterfly," flattened "on the grill of a semi / smelling of heat and distance." The symbol of transformation, like the poet, is dead; the reflection of the empty grocery cart, the predominate image of the final stanza, sounds his absence, "in a blackened window, a little / piano recital of chrome," an elegy of metaphor "for someone to whom all things / were full of sadness."

Music and motion stop and the light goes dark in "The Ride," written in memory of John Gardner, who died in 1982 as a result of a motorcycle accident, near Susquehanna, Pennsylvania. Best known for his novel *Grendel*, a retelling of the story of Beowulf, and *On Moral Fiction*, a book of literary criticism, Gardner, in theme and metaphor, investigated light and shadow, as reflected in his book titles *October Light*, *The Sunlight Dialogues*, and *Stillness and Shadows*.

Kooser's thirteen-line poem, recalling "The Giant Slide" that opened the section, captures layers of movement and ultimate stillness—Gardner's, ours, the Ferris wheel, and the earth. Long lines and the pronoun immediately pull "us" into the poem's kines-thetic: "High in the night, we rock, we rock in the stars / while the Ferris wheel stops to let someone off." While writing about a more abstract notion, the circle of life, Kooser chooses and then trans-forms memories of the American experience that readers would likely share, such as the Ferris wheel ride. High up the basket rocks "in the starlight," the music below has stopped, and the motor of the Ferris wheel pops, recalling the pop of the motorcycle. "The midway goes dark," the last line begins, and like the shutting down of the park itself, the lights go off "booth to booth, as he passes," literally and metaphorically.

The poet returns to the phenomenology of his daily life in the collection's third and final section, which Hahn characterizes as a move into "more of a psychic territory. The objects in these poems," he continues, "are still familiar ones" but are seen in an "unfamiliar, darkening light." By 1985 when *One World at a Time* was published, Kooser had been in insurance for twenty-one years and now served as second vice president at Lincoln Benefit Life. As we learn in "At the Office Early," he now occupies an office with windows. The section's lead poem, which moves easily between present, past, and future, is, as Hahn writes, a "statement on economics and class structure." It begins by marrying the phenomena of nature with the observable objects of office life before it turns unexpectedly surreal without losing its anchor in the real.

The section continues with other losses, couched in natural terms, sometimes celestial, sometimes meteorological, sometimes sea-sonal, sometimes familial, and always associated with the swift passage of time. Strikingly visual images transform before Kooser's eyes. The attempt to "say," to locate the past in the present, to reach back across time, to mediate against loss is always present, always valued. "A Letter" anticipates his later poems to his parents as it weaves together many of these themes. There are family stories and there are community, even national, stories, and often they are braided together.

Kooser draws on *The Wizard of Oz* by L. Frank Baum to describe our attempt to know what lies "beyond," literally and figuratively. The sun, the moon, and the stars in the sky are joined by "The Voyager II Satellite," that cold "tin man," whose "glitter of distant worlds / is like snow on his coat." In Baum's story the Tin Man has no heart. Launched in 1977, the space probe known as Voyager 2 set out to explore the distant planets of our solar system. Pictures of the probe show an erector set of limbs akimbo, which the poet characterizes as arms that "he" spreads "to catch / the white, elusive dandelion fuzz / of starlight."

Voyager 2 also functions as an analogy. Tin Man/space probe is both like the dove Noah released to see if there was land on which to settle and the scapegoat loaded up with sins and set out into the desert to perish with them. It is a "dreamy beast / of peace and science," who, as we watch from earth, "grows smaller, smaller" as it falls "so gracefully / into the great blank face / of God." Perhaps God is the great wizard, perhaps the pretender that the Tin Man, Dorothy, and their companions uncover when they finally reach Oz. From the perspective of earth, this other world of universe and heaven is unknowable. This is the lesson of Frost's farmer who set fire to his house for insurance money in order to buy a telescope, Gerber writes, quoting Frost's "The Star-Splitter." "We've looked and looked," the poem continues, "but after all where are we?" For Frost, bound by life on earth, looking at the sky doesn't matter in the end, doesn't show him what he "hungers after." Kooser's interest, his hunger, when all is said and done, is, as was Thoreau's, in the world immediately before him.

Kooser's use of synecdoche, a comparison of a part of something used to refer to the whole of it, reminds the reader that the great fact, death, is both certain and unknown. "The Heart Patient" "watches the doorway, the darkness / beyond the dead ferns in the window." "The Urine Specimen," herald of illness or heath, notes vulnerability. In "Geronimo's Mirror" the flash of the famous Apache warrior's mirror in the mountains, like the poem, is a warning to all of us: No one comes out of this life alive.

As the collection comes to an end with "Porch Swing in September," the poet returns to the archetypal porch of his earlier poem "Good-Bye." Autumn approaches; it is time to bring in the cushions. The small brown spider "has hung out her web / on a line between porch post and chain / so that no one may swing without breaking it," another of those sure signs that says "it's time that the swinging were done with." Long associated with the creative act, the spider reminds us of the three fates of Greek mythology, whose task it is to spin, measure, and cut the thread of life. Dew, natural condensation of the night's moisture, reflects the world all around as did the raindrops that held the banking world of the section's initial poem and as does the poet's poems.

By *One World at a Time*, Kooser has integrated a web of influences, Frost, as well as Thoreau and Emerson; however, in doing so, he has also established himself as a unique poet with a distinctive voice. Although Shapiro praised Williams and disparaged Eliot and Pound, Shapiro and Kooser are the literary inheritors of all three poets. Eliot's use of the colloquial sometimes goes unnoticed. As Eliot's "The Influence of Landscape upon the Poet" makes clear, although his "personal landscape is a composite," it is no less important to his work than Williams's Patterson or Kooser's Bohemian Alps. Prufrock's settings, "half deserted streets" and "cheap hotels," come out of the physical environment of his life just as Kooser's do. Prufrock, as critic Christopher Beach reminds us, was "a complete departure from the genteel tradition of American poetry." Frost's tenant farmer and Kooser's old man with glasses may well be Prufrock's cousins. Eliot, Beach argues, discovered the "short dramatic scene" of the symbolists that Leonard Nathan perfected. The call to deep image, belief in the "direct treatment of a thing," lean and careful diction, and musical phrasing, hallmarks of Pound's influence on the traditional lyric, are all lessons Kooser and his mentor made their own. Kooser's close observation of this world so that others may notice is yet another variation on Pound's well-known belief that "artists are the antennae of the race."

Now that the dust from various literary debates has settled, Eliot's move toward the meditative mood can be found in the poets who came after him, including Wright and Kooser. This is the mood that the poet emphasized in the arrangement of his work in *Sure Signs*, and it is a hallmark of *One World at a Time*. What is perhaps most original in Kooser's work, as we shall see, is depth of metaphor.

CHAPTER EIGHTEEN

Weather Central

Someday, with the work of the wind,
this will be gone—the hollow school,

its hollow in the changing hills,
the fallen door with its shiny black knob.

—From "An Abandoned Stone Schoolhouse
in the Nebraska Sandhills"

Five years after the Lincoln Community Playhouse Gallery Theatre produced *The Blizzard Voices*, Kooser's original text, with illustrations by Michigan artist Tom Pohrt, was published by Bieler Press. The skip-rope rhymes and sections from George Greenleaf Whittier's poem "Snowbound" added to the play, according to Kooser, for familiarity and length were eliminated.

The Blizzard of 1888, which has captured the imagination of many Plains residents over the years, is also the subject of Jeanne Reynal's large mosaic that hangs in the north bay of the Nebraska State Capitol foyer. Commissioned for the state's centennial in 1967, the mosaic is composed of shards of Venetian glass depicting a country teacher and her young charges tied together with clothesline rope as they make their way into wind and heavy snow to eventual safety.

"All of my life," Kooser writes in the introduction to the 2006 edition, "I have been talking with people about their experiences of the great storm." Kooser dedicated the book to his uncle, Elvy Moser, who would have heard family stories about the storm as it swept into the Turkey River valley.

The subject matter was compelling for other reasons as well. Memory, imagination, the futile human attempt to stay the insistent passage of time, all important themes in the poet's earlier work, find voice in a classic story of the power of nature. "The poems that follow," he continues in the introduction, "are isolated voices heard in that blinding snowstorm we know as the passage of time." For inspiration he turned to recollections of members of the Blizzard Club, survivors still alive in 1947. Compiled by W. H. O'Gara, *In All Its Fury* includes weather information, newspaper reports, and tallies of the losses of game birds and livestock, as well as human accounts of human survival and death, and songs written to commemorate the event. The poems that resulted, Kooser writes, were not taken from O'Gara's narrative, but rather were "trimmed and shaped and imagined by me. I took the straws snagged on the fence and froze my own stories around them."

The winter of 1887–1888 started off cold and remained cold until Thursday, January 12, 1888, when a warm front fanned up from the Gulf of Mexico and moved west across the Plains. Morning temperatures in Nebraska rose from below zero into the thirties; men and women took the opportunity to head to town for supplies or to shed their coats and roll up their sleeves to take on outdoor tasks put off due to cold and snowy weather. Women stripped their beds and aired their bedding. Children set off to school.

In the early afternoon a massive Arctic cold front blasted down from Canada and across Dakota Territory, bringing freezing temperatures and stinging winds, zero visibility, ice, and snow. Winds rose to sixty to seventy miles per hour; heavy cloud cover and falling snow turned day into night. Valentine, where the temperature was recorded at thirty degrees above zero at six o'clock in the morning, saw a thirty-six-degree drop by two o'clock. By nine o'clock that night the temperature stood at fourteen below zero. "Odd weather for January," *The Blizzard Voices* reports, "a low line of clouds in the north; / too warm, too easy."

The storm hit Lincoln around three in the afternoon. Ten minutes later, it hit Crete, about twenty miles to the southwest, where Signal Corp Private C. D. Burnley reported that "the temperature fell 18 F degrees in less than three minutes. The snow drifted badly; travel was dangerous."

The poet returned to the dramatic monologue that he has used from time to time since *Official Entry Blank*. Often thought of as a relic of the Victorian period, the form was brought to prominence by Robert Browning's 1842 *Dramatic Lyrics*. Turn-of-the-century poet E. A. Robinson popularized both the monologue and the sonnet, writing of the troubled lives of the residents of his fictional Tilbury Town. Chicago Renaissance poet Edgar Lee Masters is best known for *The Spoon River Anthology*, a collection of 244 monologues of the dead who speak from their graves in the also fictional Spoon River, Illinois, cemetery. Frost is the modern master of the monologue; Kooser couldn't have had better models.

Kooser's ear remained tuned to the flavor and cadence of colloquial speech. "Corn was at twelve cents a bushel," he writes, "a good deal cheaper than coal, / so we fed our stoves with corn / and, sometimes, with twists of hay or cowchips." His speakers tell of death and survival. Robinson's Tilbury Town and Master's Spoon River specters, and even to a large extent Frost's "people," are a more cynical lot than Kooser's. While Master's deceased, for example, often show themselves as hypocritical and morally corrupt, Kooser's survivors are ordinary men and women who tell their stories a in straightforward manner, with little moralizing or embellishment. Thirty-six speakers, identified as "A Woman's Voice" or "A Man's Voice," tell their stories; *The Blizzard Voices* is a collective chronicle of the often harsh and unwelcoming Plains.

Kooser's interest in and exploration of the Plains continued. In 1989 Windflower published a second poetry anthology, *As Far As I*

Can See: Contemporary Writing of the Middle Plains edited by Charles L. Woodard, with illustrations by Robert L. Hanna.

By the mid-1980s, Kooser had begun to accompany Rutledge to Cherry County in the Nebraska Sandhills to visit friends and relatives. The sparsely populated "great American desert," as early explorer Zebulon Pike labeled the region, covers over a quarter of the state. Despite the area's dry and sandy character, the rolling dunes, left behind by the retreating glaciers of the last ice age, sit atop the Plains' Ogallala Aquifer, which provides a substantial number of shallow lakes, some permanent in nature and some that come and go depending on water level and rainfall. Relatively stable dunes, available water, and plentiful native grasses of the region, native home to bison, have proven a boon to cattle ranchers for over one hundred years.

The passage of time became even more prominent in Kooser's work as the poet found inspiration in his forays to the northern part of the state. Death of loved ones also came at close intervals: "Uncle Charlie," his father's brother, Derral, in 1988; his mother's sister, Mabel, in 1990; and his mentor at Iowa State, Will Jumper, in 1993. Time, in Kooser's hands, is a not at all an abstract concept, which is perhaps why literary critics may often overlook the "ideas" or "intellectual constructs" in the poet's work. Matter transforms within the poems just as lakes shine suddenly from Sandhills dunes.

In the heart of Cherry County, Valentine, Nebraska, was the touchstone in Rutledge's young life. Her grandmother's home provided a constant in a life of military travel. Kooser set out to investigate the vast sandy topography, finding among other treasures the abandoned stone schoolhouse and a lost forge of *Weather Central*. Kooser and Rutledge began refurbishing the old Stetter/Fischer home, but because of the distance from Garland, the family finally sold the house in the mid-1990s. Both led busy professional lives that made demands on their time. In 1993 Rutledge was promoted to editorial page editor; two years later, following the merger of the *Lincoln Star* and the *Lincoln Journal*, she was named city editor of the *Lincoln Journal Star*.

The 1994 publication of *Weather Central* marked Kooser's tenth year as a resident of the Bohemian Alps. Home and outbuildings renovated, the poet gave up raising chickens but continued to garden and to explore the countryside. His seventh collection is a mirror not only of the poet's natural surrounding but serves as a self-portrait of the poet as artist, businessman, and lover in his fifty-fourth year.

Two years earlier the poet's tribute to the metaphor was in the form of a chapbook, *Etudes*, published by Bit's Press. Each of the five poems—"Etude," "Snakeskin," "Shoes," "Spider Eggs," and "Five Finger Exercise"—is a conceit, based on the development of a metaphor, and is included in *Weather Central*.

"Etude," the collection's preface poem, is an exquisite illustration of Kooser's mature facility with the metaphor:

> I have been watching a Great Blue Heron
> fish in the cattails, easing ahead
> with the stealth of a lover composing a letter,
> the hungry words looping and blue
> as they coil and uncoil, as they kiss and sting.
>
> Let's say that he holds down an everyday job
> in an office. His blue suit blends in.
> Long days swim beneath the glass top
> of his desk, each one alike. On the lip
> of each morning, a bubble trembles.
>
> No one has seen him there, writing a letter
> to a woman he loves. His pencil is poised
> in the air like the beak of a bird.
> He would speak the whole world if he could,
> toss it and swallow it live.

The title describes the poem as a study, in this case of the heron but also of the metaphor, a figure of speech underscoring essential connections and relationships, according to Aristotle, "the greatest thing by far." With "Etude," Kooser establishes the volume's major subjects (correspondence within nature and the role of the poet) and themes (the inescapable passing of time and the preservation of memory through art), while creating an intimate relationship with his reader. Because of the poem's important function and its complex use of metaphor, it will be examined here in some detail.

The great blue heron (*Ardea herodias*), the *tenor* of the developing metaphor, is a visitor in late March to Nebraska, where it breeds and frequently stays for the summer. The graceful wader is easily recognized by its plumage, which ranges from black to dark blue to gray, its tan or brownish S-shaped neck, and small, rather elegant head, covered with fine white feathers. The heron searches for fish in the water or marsh, as the poem suggests, by stretching its head out before it and then striding forward, its long yellow beak poised for action.

Kooser, with his choice of the present perfect progressive tense ("I have been watching") establishes an ongoing activity as a correspondence between poet and heron. The "I," presumably the poet, is continuing to watch as the heron is continuing to ease. The second verb, "easing," however, can be read two ways. Because of its placement and the parallel construction of "watching" and "easing," the sense of the sentence can be read as "I have been . . . easing"; the activity of poet and heron can be taken as a common one, establishing the *tenor* as heron and poet (or poet's imagination) as *vehicle*. The bird is being observed as it also watches for fish "in the cattails, easing ahead / with the stealth of a lover composing a letter."

But the poet has also gone to (or found himself in) the marshes (both literal and of the mind) to see what delights can be found there and has discovered the heron, the metaphor, and the possibility of a poem. He, the poet, can be seen as "fishing," searching for the words, metaphors, and other figures of speech—easing ahead, sorting through those available, those hidden in the cattails of mind or memory—with which to describe (to capture or, in this case, to spear, as the heron does) the scene before him, the meaning he makes, the experience he captures, articulating both the finding and the making within the poem. This takes poetic stealth to be sure.

Kooser's letter writing recalls Emily Dickinson's well-known poem, which begins, "This is my letter to the world, / That never wrote to me, / The simple news that Nature told, / With tender majesty." Poems have always been, as Kooser has often professed, love letters—first for his high school sweetheart, now for his readers. When interviewed about his conversational tone, Kooser clarifies: "My poems are not spoken to a reader walking beside me, but one at some distance, as if he or she were being approached by a letter I'd written." Within the poem, the heron is now poet/lover; "hungry words" suggest the poet's passion for both poetry and his desire for affection. The words are those of the lover as they continue to accommodate the hunger of the heron for fish. The searching movements of the heron are described as they "coil and uncoil," movements of the bird's neck as the bird steps ahead looking for fish and movements of the pen across the page; both can "kiss and sting."

Kooser has compared his morning writing process to "doodling that occasionally becomes more complex." This "Etude" is that something, which he elaborates on in his interview: "it's as if you were playing the piano, and in the middle of it a little melody started up." He is seeing and sounding the music of the natural world and the patterns it suggests, a view similar to Emerson's, in his long poems "Woodnotes" and "Woodnotes II," for example.

Kooser directly involves his reader by beginning the second stanza with a suggestion directed to the reader: "Let's say." Heron is poet, is lover, and now is transformed into a businessman: "His blue suit blends in." Kooser moves further into the transformative space between the elements of the metaphor with the ease of his heron in water. By using the colloquial address, rapid though the association may be, mutuality is accepted with ease. The heron is now the blue-suited office worker, preparing the way for the reader to accept "long days," in line 8, as fish. The glass top of the desk also exists as water's surface where bubbles tremble. The desk belongs to the lover, the businessman, and the poet as it remains the heron's fishing ground. Hunger is a common motivation of all four.

As Kooser confesses in *Journey to a Place of Work*, "While I am writing memoranda for my company, dog-paddling in the abstract language with which all business is conducted, I crave solid, concrete nouns like *oak* and *salt* and *carrot*. I hunger for verbs like *jump* and *shout*." Poems and fish are to be discovered in the bubbles below. "Writing can be exhilarating work," he says. "While you sit quietly scribbling into your notebook, memories and associations rise like bubbles out of the thick mud of the mind."

Stanza three opens reminding the reader of the stealth and loneliness of the heron and the poet/lover/businessman: "No one has seen him there." The reader's attention has been directed primarily to the multiple *vehicles* when Kooser snaps us back to the heron's bright yellow beak, "the pencil poised / in the air." The image leads the reader back to reconsider "the lip / of each morning [where] a bubble trembles," that Genesis-like moment when the poet stands ready to create order from the apparent chaos of daily life. Within the act of writing, the poet grasps the world (and makes it new), the businessman/lover reaches out for his love, and the heron spears the fish it has been patiently watching for since stanza one. At this moment *tenor* and *vehicle*, the hungry heron/businessman/lover/poet, are engaged in a sort of creative ecstasy. This is the liveliness conveyed by the metaphor that so impressed Aristotle. "Etude," from this perspective, while it describes the artistic discipline, also describes our intense pleasure as we read, making the leap within "that space between" afforded by the metaphor, allowing another sort of transformation, participation in the creative act itself.

Kooser enacts the metaphor, using by *tenor* and *vehicle* to demonstrate its essential attributes, including the crossing of the space between the components themselves. Through the enactment, we witness and participate in the correspondence that Emerson and Thoreau saw in the world.

In the postscript of a letter to Carol Bly dated September 29, 1999, Kooser writes,

> If it [the metaphor] is suddenly revealed to me through the process of writing that a stack of cannon balls looks like a bunch of grapes (sorry for such a dreary example!), I feel a kind of exhilaration

because there is the suggestion of universal order, something like what I recall Emerson writing about with his idea of the Oversoul (it's been years since I read it). In other words, if I suddenly recognize that the cannon balls share something with the grapes, then perhaps the tree I see out the window shares something with something else and suddenly, in a marvelous rush, *all* things appear to be related to another when there seemed to be nothing but disorder before. And, of course, if "The Big Bang" is correct, all things have come from one source and may thus be related. Metaphor can be seen to be a miraculous insight into that grand order.

Nathan introduced Kooser to George Steiner's *Real Presences*, "a stunning book," the poet says, "in which he attempts to suggest there is a universal order through the devices of language, the way language works." The parallel and complementary "Cosmic Consciousness" was a lynch-pin of Karl Shapiro's view of North America's poetic tradition.

"Life poetry," Bernice Slote called it, is "the poetry which starts in the sun [and] makes two great affirmations: connection and creation," both reflected in "Etude." Shapiro's essay, "Cosmic Consciousness," traces the resurgence of "life-poetry" to cosmic consciousness, which he defines as "the capacity of the individual consciousness to experience a sense of total unity with all Nature, or the universe, or some degree of that experience." Different than human consciousness, which wants to see itself as "distinct from all objects and beings in the universe," cosmic consciousness provides a "sense of identification with the universe, an intellectual enlightenment of illumination which may last only briefly but . . . places the individual on a new plane of existence."

This was an idea formulated and promulgated by Richard M. Bucke, a Canadian psychiatrist, Whitman's friend and advocate in *Man's Moral Nature* (1879), *Walt Whitman* (1883), and *Cosmic Consciousness: A Study in the Evolution of the Human Mind* (1901). Shapiro notes that Bucke lists both Emerson and Thoreau as "imperfect instances of cosmic consciousness."

Life-poetry and its foundation in cosmic consciousness are made manifest by Kooser's metaphor. While it may be true, as critic Matthew C. Brennan suggests, that Kooser's revelations are "rarely sublime," this correspondence is at the very heart of his notion of being-in-the-world and of the creative act itself. Kooser's "One World," this "between," is fertile ground, "Central," as the collection title states. His home is "between" the coasts, the geographic center of the continent, "fly-over state" for travelers on United Airlines and "pass-through state" for transporters of commodities and passengers on I-80. Weather, a central concern, is, or seems to its residents, unpredictable, with extremes in temperature as apparently divergent as *tenor* and *vehicle*.

Martin Heidegger, in *Poetry, Language, Thought*, describes the "in-between": "In the midst of beings as a whole an open place occurs. There is a clearing, a lighting. The thought of in reference to what is, to beings, this clearing is in a greater degree than are beings. This open center is therefore not surrounded by what is; rather, the lighting center itself encircles all that is, like the Nothing which we scarcely know. . . . Only this clearing grants and guarantees to us humans a passage to those beings that we ourselves are not, and access to the being we ourselves are."

The *auseinandersetzen*, as the "in-between" is known to German Existentialists, is where being comes into the world. It is a time-ful place, where summer and spring meet and converse, where presence and absence rub shoulders, where past and present commiserate, where one species transforms into another, where one sense informs another. It is the place Bly describes, where leaps are made "from the conscious to the unconscious and back again" and transformation occurs.

Kooser's world—microcosm *and* macrocosm—is revealed in "Etude" and throughout the seven sections of *Weather Central*. The poet creates and interacts with the landscape around and within him. Metaphors and images in one poem often provide foundations for those to come. Music, literal and figurative, plays throughout.

Section 1 takes the reader into the heart of seasonal nature, spring through autumn, in and around the poet's home; the second and longest focuses on city life. Sections 3 and 4 are on the road, visiting sites and other citizens of the Plains. The country of love and relationship, the significance of the ordinary, and the art of everyday life provide the focus of section 5, while section 6 addresses loss of loved ones, significance of memory, and increasing awareness of time passing. The collection concludes with its title poem, "Weather Central," a reminder of the fragility of life.

Birds, moving between earth and sky, frequently serve as Kooser's muse and at times stand in for the poet, birdsong for the poem. "Poem before Breakfast" is a conceit based on the songbird-poet comparison. Placed early in the first section, the poet calls readers to his subject matter, nature, while he provides insight into his own process as a poet.

The red-winged blackbird stands in for the young poet Kooser had been in "A Poetry Reading." He explains the symbol as the younger poet, whose impulse he recognizes from his own experiences, when the "idea of being a poet . . . matters most. It's those sexy black wings and red shoulders. / You sang for yourself but all of them listened to you." When the heron shows up in stanza two, he carries all the qualities—wading bird, poet/seer, lover, and businessman—found in "Etude" to the podium, providing poignancy and pathos.

Kooser's relationship with his reader is paramount. "A poem is the invited guest of its reader," he writes in his *Manual*. Like the space that must be crossed between *tenor* and *vehicle* in the successful metaphor, the distance between poet and reader must also be carefully crossed. As Shelley writes, "A poet is nightingale . . . his auditors are as men entranced by the melody of an unseen musician, who feel they are moved and softened, yet know not whence or why."

Nowhere is the distance so consistently crossed to ensure collaboration than in *Weather Central*; it is accomplished in three often interrelated ways, previewed in the preface poem. First, by use of recognizable detail Kooser ensures reader participation. Second, by his portrayal of a familiar poetic persona we feel at home, open to conversation. Lastly, he uses direct address to form a participatory relationship. "No one is going to read your poem," he warns, "just because it's there."

"A devoted chronicler of the Midwest," David Baker writes, Kooser is "so careful, so meticulous, that even his most modest poems ring with pleasing recognitions." "In Late Spring," which inaugurates section 1, for example, opens with rich, evocative description beginning with the F-4 jet fighter crossing overhead. The visual depiction detailed in line 2 as it makes "a long approach" includes the plane's rate of speed and its angle of descent. The poet then points out the jet's shadow "flapping along" on the ground below. By line three, the jet can be heard "howling in over the tree-tops," and in line 5 coyotes in the backwoods cry in response. Kooser is careful to introduce and then amplify the physical qualities of the image.

The shadow, "like the skin of a sheep," suggests an undercurrent of violence as soon as it is placed in close proximity to the coyotes and dogs. When the jet passes and the coyotes fall silent, the quiet, as readers will recognize, "rings a little, the way an empty pan / rings when you wipe it dry," an echo that resounds beyond the Plains.

"And then it is / Sunday again, a summer Sunday afternoon"; the reader accompanies the poet back into the heart of the day, the Sabbath, day of rest after a week of world creation, at home amid the texture of his surroundings, where, beyond his window, "the Russian Olives / sigh foolishly" and "bluegills nibble the clouds" reflected on the pond behind the house. With a pun, Kooser joins his own earlier subvocal reading to "bee-song." Description is tactile: "perfect porcelain bells," the peonies stand "in piles of old papers," last year's leaves and stalks are "bald-headed" now. Mutuality of simile and personification points to the familiarity of detail: ferns have "shy ears," the horsefly "twirls his mustache" and brushes dust from his sleeves, the tulip wears lipstick as spring dashes by on her way toward summer, her "run-down broken toe shoes / . . . trailing green ribbons of silk." Kooser's poem recalls, updates, and Americanizes Blake's "To Spring," in which "the hills tell each other, and the listening / Valleys hear; all our longing eyes are turned / Up to thy bright pavilions."

Not until stanza 4 does Kooser use first-person singular: "I have been reading for hours, or intending to read, / . . . I have forgotten my place in the world." By carefully choosing the precise moment of embodiment, the poet forges alliances with the reader that suggest intimacy or complicity. The relatively late introduction of the "I" enables Kooser to build on the relationship he has established already with his phenomenological precision and involvement in the preceding stanzas. By this time the reader is already committed to a journey. An intimacy has been established, so much so that it seems the reader has also heard Steve Burdic and his daughter call to one another. When the speaker announces that "the world knows my place and stands and holds a chair / for me," the reader is poised to listen to what the balance of the collection has to say about that—*our*—world.

Kooser's being-in-the-world illuminates the reader's own. The poet has drawn the reader into the "between" with him. When he announces, "I have forgotten my place in the world," the reader, similarly engaged by the rich and evocative physical world, recognizes the feeling, a feeling the reader never entirely shakes as the poem moves to conclusion. By implication the world knows the reader's place too and reveals itself to others as it does to Kooser.

The journey continues as he enters the space shared by him and the horsefly. Connection to the natural world is intimate. When he participates with the horsefly in his twirling of his mustache, readers, in a sense, twirl their own; they too brush pollen from their sleeves. Then the poem turns: "But the world knows my place and stands and holds a chair / for me, here on these acres near Garland, Nebraska. / This April, in good health, I entered my fifty-fourth year." He is midcountry and midlife, a "between" place and time he is willing to share. The Midlands, the geographic "in-between," is a place with space for transformation to occur—not only within the poem but also within the reader's understanding of her or his own life. Whether driving along a road, as in "A Heart of Gold," or at his desk or in his yard in Garland, Nebraska, Kooser has involved the reader in the geography of being in the world (*Dasein* to the Existentialists).

Weather Central provides a geographical and historical triptych in part 2. Mostly urban, the seventeen poems display the hard and critical edge sometimes overlooked in Kooser's work. Metaphors draw the reader into intimate engagement that is sometimes uncomfortable.

There are, however, hints of other worlds, other gestures that resonate between the known world of the here and now and a possible place beyond. In "A Sound in the Night," a ticking electric fence sounds in the night capturing the attention of a mouse, a coyote, and even the poet's deceased father, who reaches across the darkness for his wife's hands. "The Sweeper," which closes section 6, contains a memory, or perhaps an image from a dream, of Kooser's father transforming a broom into the paddle of a gondola.

Kooser's familiar theme resurfaces throughout the collection like lakes in the Sandhills. The poet reminds us of the seasonality of life, spring through autumn, excluding the bitter cold of winter. A death knell sounds in the distance. A woman at the end of a pier signals into the dark in "Fireflies." "Nine white Pekins," of "The Time of Their Lives," seem to laugh with one another as they eat windfalls under the apple tree joyously unaware of their fate at the hands of a "young farm wife / easy with killing."

Chronologic and mythic time, the "stuff of transformation" in many Kooser poems, is interrelated. The poet's father with his broom, in "The Sweeper," can be read as both literal and archetypal as the father/gondola-paddler moves along the river of his/all life/Life. The circle of life occurs and reoccurs throughout *Weather Central*. Past and present and future merge, separate, and join again in "For Jeff." But perhaps nowhere is the theme of time more clearly or directly stated by Kooser than in "An Abandoned Stone Schoolhouse in the Nebraska Sandhills," which stands at the midpoint of the collection. The blocks of sandstone that remain are "always ready to go."

From the chaos of *Weather Central*'s beginning, we have arrived at book's end, with a map designed, above all else, to proffer at least momentary if delusional order. It begins:

Each evening at six-fifteen, the weatherman
turns a shoulder to us, extends his hand,
and talking softly as a groom, cautiously
smoothes and strokes the massive, dappled flank
of the continent, . . .

The time is as precise and as regular as clockwork as the weatherman takes his place, midcountry, on the TV screen. He, like the poet, is, for the moment, apparently in control, though he needs to be cautious. The poet's ability to order and fix, it is suggested, is as precarious as the weatherman's ability to map, predict, and present weather conditions. What both do, through a variety of signs and symbols, is to show the reader/viewer how things look at this moment and hazard a guess at the near future. Projections and predictions here on the Plains, despite Doppler, are still risky. So sensitive is the object—horse, weatherman, life itself—that "with a horsefly's touch / he [weatherman literally but also poet] brushes a mountain range and sets a shudder / running just under the skin."

What the poet offers is, perhaps paradoxically, both inevitability and possibility. As the editors of *Twentieth Century American Poetry*, Dana Gioia among them, write, Kooser's Ames, Iowa, "in his best poems becomes as universal as Constantine Cavafy's Alexandria." Mutuality provides the space and means of transcending the confines of our own skins, our own section of the continent, our own continent and hemisphere, to make a leap into relationship and community, into the dead center of the richness of Life. This is Kooser's gift to readers no matter where they live.

16. Ted and Diana Kooser, Karl Shapiro, Ed and Connie Jancke at the Bee Tavern in the Bohemian Alps.

17. Ted with tripod and camera for photographing Bohemian Alps, 1964.

18. Salt Creek Original Christmas card with Windflower Press colophon decorated for the holidays.

19. Jeff Kooser and his dad in 1970.

20. Ted reading in the tub at the Washington Street house.

21. Jeff on the road with his dad to Fort Robinson.

22. Ted Kooser and Kathleen Rutledge cutting the cake after the wedding ceremony in the back yard of Laura and Burke Casari.

23. The young insurance executive going to work at Lincoln Benefit Life 1983.

24. In 2004 Kooser was named poet laureate, beginning two years of extensive travel.

25. Columbia University president Lee. C. Bollinger presents Ted Kooser with the Pulitzer Prize for his 2004 collection of poems, *Delights & Shadows*.

26. Jeff, Margaret, Ted Kooser, and Kathleen Rutledge at the groundbreaking for Kooser Elementary School, Lincoln NE.

27. Ted Kooser in his art studio in Dwight, Nebraska.

28. Long-time friends Jim Harrison and Ted Kooser.

29. The poet at his Garland studio at work in Uncle Tubby's chair.

Five

"Feeling the Speed,"
1995–Today

CHAPTER NINETEEN

"Lights on a Ground of Darkness"

The iris in my garden will soon bloom.

—From "Lights on a Ground of Darkness"

Kooser quickly went on to publish two chapbooks in limited edition by fine arts presses: *A Book of Things* by Lyra Press in 1995 and *A Decade of Valentines* with Bonnie O'Connell, director of Abattoir editions at the University of Nebraska at Omaha in 1996. However, the loss of loved ones, the fleeting nature of time, and the desire to preserve life and times through imagination, memory, and poetry, major themes of *Weather Central*, continued to weigh on the poet's mind.

Reminders of mortality seemed to be around every corner. On December 15, 1997, when his first grandchild was born, Kooser's mother's health was showing signs of decline. He traveled to Illinois in early 1998 to visit his son and new granddaughter. "I am quite taken with Margaret Emily Kooser, now up to 6# 2 oz." he wrote the Nathans. He continued, "I held her for an hour Saturday night and she put her tiny hand in my chin whiskers and showed me her eyes, which are blue-black, like the night sky.

"When she [Margaret] is her father's age, I will be my mother's age (exactly), and when she is my age, her father will be my mother's age. . . . Sometimes it is thrilling, isn't it, feeling the speed."

Feeling that speed made his desire for more writing time urgent; as early as 1986 he corresponded with Karl Shapiro about the possibility of early retirement. In a letter to a friend announcing his granddaughter's birth, Kooser noted his anticipation of early retirement from Lincoln Benefit Life to "write and paint and read and cook and garden for the rest of my life." Without retirement, he wrote to another friend, "I doubt if I'll have another book for years yet."

Spurred on by his mother's failing health Kooser worked steadily through the winter on the final draft of his family memoir, "Lights on a Ground of Darkness: An Evocation of a Place and Time," so that his mother, who was in increasingly frail health, would have an opportunity to read it. Set in 1949 when the poet was ten, the essay tells of the importance of summer vacations with his grandparents, John and Elizabeth Moser, and his extended family in the Mississippi River valley. Although it tells a sort of creation story in which the awareness of the boy broadens and deepens, Clayton County is no Garden of Eden before the fall; at the same time he seeks to preserve the time and people, he acknowledges the ephemeral quality of time and the profound loss that accompanies its passage. Only memory and art, he realizes, can preserve the past and keep its treasures safe. This youthful lesson informs virtually every word he will write in the future.

Kooser immediately establishes the essay's tone with an epigraph from the autobiography of Scottish poet Edwin Muir (1887–1959), the son of a farmer, who rooted his own poetry in the countryside of Orkney Islands. Muir attempts to capture the essence of his childhood in much the same manner as Kooser, writing about the place that was so important to him as well as the people who seemed to grow from the landscape itself.

"There is no road back into its country," Kooser quotes Muir, "only the imagination can venture upon it." Yet, recollection has its limitations. According to Muir, "our memories of a place, no matter how fond we were of it, are little more than a confusion of lights on a ground of darkness." Like Wordsworth, who traced in *The Prelude* the history of his imagination to key moments of his childhood he calls "spots of time," Muir and Kooser look to their pasts to locate the origins of theirs. The title, "Lights on a Ground of Darkness," recalls many poems that touch upon the use of memory and the imagination—"The Night Light," "The Ride," "At Nightfall," "Just Now"—to stay the encroachment of what Frost referred to as the "enormous Outer Black."

Kooser begins in Guttenberg, Iowa, where the river's presence, marked by the wheeling of gulls overhead and the sounds of barges heading south, was inescapable. History and familial stories are folded into the fabric of the essay as the homes of aunts and uncles are folded into the neighboring hills. Through his mother's family, the boy learns to appreciate beauty in the life of all things, to find comfort in community and in the "timeless perfume" of nature.

The essay is a compilation of dappling lights written in an associative and conversational form. Drawing together threads of many years and many stories, it sounds like a tuning fork struck against our own childhoods. As Muir wrote, "no autobiography can begin with a man's birth, that we extend far beyond any boundary line which we can set for ourselves in the past or the future, and that the life of every man is an endlessly repeated performance of the life of man."

"I was worried it would make her sad," Kooser reports, explaining the significance of showing the essay to his mother, "and yet I wanted her to see it, too. So a couple of weeks ago I ran off a copy in 18 point type so that she could read it and left it with her. Mother has since told me that she liked it, and I was so relieved I wept. I have always felt that this might be the most important writing I would ever do, because the people meant so much to me."

By this time Kooser's mother had sold the family home in Cedar Rapids and moved into an assisted living complex. Her heart was enlarged, "her lungs were down to 10 percent capacity, and she was tethered full time to an oxygen machine." Kooser's letters trace his mother's move to hospice care and her growing fragility. After she died, March 23, 1998, he summed up her strengths in a letter to Reverend Lloyd Brockmeyer, who was to perform the memorial service in Cedar Rapids:

> Mother maintained a keen intelligence until she died. She kept a close eye on current affairs and enjoyed watching all the news shows on television and reading the newspapers. Politically, she was neither a true Republican nor true Democrat but rather a progressive, part of the old and now lost liberal wing of the Republican party. She believed in government and its ability to solve social problems and also in the obligation of wealthy people to share their good fortune with the poor. She was highly principled and never in her long life lied or deceived or cheated anyone. When she was still able to get around she would drive across town to save a nickel on a purchase but if she had found a satchel full of money on the street she would have gone to great lengths to return it to the owner. She had a stern sense of right and wrong and there was no room in the middle.

When "Lights on a Ground of Darkness" was published later in the year, Kooser formally dedicated the work to her, adding a preface poem "Mother," to be later collected in *Delights & Shadows*.

"The iris in my garden will soon bloom," he writes as he brings his tribute to a close. It is "forever young," having "no stories to sadden it, to weigh it down." The iris, like the essay, like many poems that commemorate people and places he holds dear, "offers its beauty and fragrance as if nothing has changed, as if no one were gone." His grandfather, "tolerant of Republicans only until they get evangelistic," lives on. Sitting back in his swivel chair, feet up on the roll-top desk, smoking his pipe, Grandpa Moser is rooted in our imagination as he was rooted in his young grandson's imagination on those long summer afternoons and evenings.

During an interview years later Kooser talks about the significance of his family and the loss he still feels: "I've never gotten over that loss of parents, and family, and grandparents; it's sort of my theme, I think. I think about those people. I don't think a day goes by, that I don't, at some point, line them up in my mind like

I'm running an inspection and walk along and check in with them, just momentarily. Uncle Pete Noyes is here. Ira Friedlein is here. I suppose it's a deliberate thing at some level that I do this; I want to remember them. Of course it's a way to keep them alive."

Kooser's thoughts were also on the future. "I am 361 days from retirement," he wrote to his son, Jeff, on May 4, six weeks following his mother's death, the day before his twenty-fifth anniversary with Lincoln Benefit Life. In a letter to friends the following day, he notes that he had spoken with the company president, and "I'm going to be out of here in (probably) two months!" Kooser e-mailed his son good news two weeks later: "I can't officially retire till April, 1999, but I can take unpaid leave up to that point without impairing my retirement benefits."

On Monday June 1 Kooser drove from Garland into Lincoln. On either side of Highway 34 the fields were "lush and green" from abundant spring rains. "The temperature," he continues in *Local Wonders*, "was in the low seventies, . . . a perfect early summer, with enough moisture for the farmers and not too much heat for the rest of us." An hour later, at a routine dental checkup, Kooser asked the dentist to take a close look at a tender spot at the back of his mouth. "He wrapped a piece of gauze around my tongue," Kooser reports, "gently pulled it out, and, with his gloved finger, felt the area. It took him a couple of minutes, and I guessed he was thinking of what to say. 'Well,' he said, looking serious, '*something*'s going on back there.'"

"Just when I had this retirement all set up and was feeling that the world was perfect," he wrote the Nathans the day before his visit to the oral pathologist at the University Dental Collage, "I was awake half the night thinking about radical tongue surgery and radiation and dying of oral cancer like Freud." The examination proved inconclusive; a biopsy was recommended. The oral surgeon was hopeful, and Kooser, with aid of painkillers, was able to get some sleep that night. The next day, the pathologist reported squamous cell carcinoma.

"Coal in my tongue," Kooser recorded in his notebook, "how long had it lain there, / waiting to burn me alive?" Despite the best efforts of the cautious weatherman, the order of the universe appeared in jeopardy, preempting retirement plans and his mother's memorial service. Even early morning walks were suspended. On June 6 he reported his bad news in a letter to Debra Winger and her husband, Arliss Howard. Kooser had become friends with the actress in 1983 when she came to Lincoln to film *Terms of Endearment*. "I have a malignant growth (squamous cell carcinoma) on the back of my tongue," he began,

> and I'm going to the university med center in Omaha on Monday afternoon for a surgical consultation. I was referred there by the oral pathologist who biopsied the lesion on Thursday. The general idea is to remove the growth and some lymph tissue in my neck to see if the tumor has spread.
>
> I am badly frightened, as you might expect. This has come at me just at a time when I was the happiest I've ever been, living with a woman I love more than any other I have ever loved, preparing to retire from my job, looking forward to writing and painting for the rest of a long life. I am bitter that I gave so many years to the insurance company, thinking to secure a long and happy retirement, when it seems I secured nothing at all.

Kooser's pathologist scheduled an appointment the following Monday with William Lydiatt, a Sloan-Kettering trained otolaryngologist who practiced at the University of Nebraska Medical Center in Omaha.

On Saturday Kooser and Rutledge spent two hours with Frank Brown, a therapist with whom both had worked before. Brown instructed Kooser in relaxation exercises and self-hypnosis. "Whenever I felt anxious or panicky," he recalls, "I was to proceed through a series of pleasant, orderly, imaginary scenarios." He chose his view from the Mississippi Valley Overlook, located on highway 54 where traffic begins its descent into his grandparents' home just south of Guttenberg, where time seems to stand still even as the river flows on. He imagined river and bluffs, boats and barges, and "smells of the cedars and hardwoods that grow near the overlook, of the ragweed down the side of the bluff, and of the warm limestone gravel upon which I imagined I was standing. . . . I came to rely on this scene for the next six months."

On June 17 surgeons removed a tumor from Kooser's tongue and discovered cancer in three adjacent lymph nodes in his neck beneath his left ear. Lydiatt told Kooser the news in his hospital room and recommended radiation. "Then, when his clutch of young residents had moved into the hall, [he] stayed behind for a moment: 'I don't know what kind of a spiritual life you have, Mr. Kooser, but you are about to enter one of the great life-affirming experiences.'"

As Rutledge drove him home following surgery, Kooser remembers about fifty turkey vultures "waiting" on fence posts and in the grasses. He says he felt as though he "might as well get out and lie down at the side of the road." He watched them move about, opening and closing their black wings. "For the time being," he imagined them thinking, "we're waiting. Just working our wings a little and slowly turning our heads and showing off the red fists of our heads and our bright yellow eyes that can see right straight through human hope."

On July 11, a month after surgery, Kooser received another blow; his mother's long-time friend, Ruth Sticklfort Kregel, his own "Aunt Sticky," died at the age of ninety-two. (He commemorates her in the poem "Flow Blue China" published in *Delights & Shadows*.)

By this time his tongue and neck incisions were healed up, and although his neck was still numb, Kooser began radiation treatments at Lincoln General Hospital. He explained the effects of radiation in a letter to his office colleagues. "Next time you see me," he writes, "I'll probably appear thinner, without a beard and maybe with some new bald spots. But I'll be pretty much the same old Ted, though with a new and keener appreciation for life and, of course, for each of you."

Supported by his wife and friends, Kooser visited the Mississippi Valley Overlook in his imagination, read, and wrote letters. A pro- digious correspondent, Kooser has long-time relationships with a wide variety of writers and other friends.

Although he was depressed, by September 15 radiation treatments were completed, and Kooser reported to friends that "I am beginning to read and write and even to laugh once in a while. . . . the world looks good to me as autumn begins to show." His sick leave was about to run out, so he decided to take a leave without pay until April 30 of the following year when he would turn sixty and could officially retire. As his joie de vivre returned so did his daily walks.

In a letter to Jim Harrison two days later, Kooser's observation about his friend's manner of walking and talking may already suggest the origin of the form his next work, *Winter Morning Walks*, would take. After several paragraphs about the migration of Monarchs going on around him, Kooser continues: "Though you are at times driven to exhaustion on the shiny silk highway or, as you call it, Glitzville, you have more of the butterfly in you than I do. I like especially *the way you stop walking to say something*" (italics mine).

"Then as autumn began to fade and winter came on," Kooser records in his preface to *Winter Morning Walks: One Hundred Postcards to Jim Harrison*, "my health began to improve." By October 2 the poet writes to Harrison that he feels well enough to walk two miles at a brisk pace. "Yesterday, for the first time since I got sick," he continues, "I sat at my desk for a while and looked over some old and perhaps unpublishable poems, moved some files around on my laptop, etc. Felt like a real poet for a few minutes." By the fifteenth he posted a new poem, "An October Evening," to Leonard and Carol Nathan, which opens

On the barn door,
an unlocked padlock,

and in the hole
where the hasp snaps in

some tiny creature
has spun a cocoon

so thin and gray
I thought at first

the lock had somehow
filled with dust.

With its cocoon finding refuge in the barn door lock, the poem suggests Kooser was approaching another door that would lead him back to his art. Transformation was in the air. "I think my biggest breakthrough," he writes two days earlier to Carol Bly, whose own radiation treatment was nearly completed, "has been a better ability to live for the day rather than to worry myself sick about recuperating or death. . . . So today, I have been sitting by a wood fire in my 'library'—an outbuilding full of books—enjoying the first snow falling over our little pond. And I tell myself, 'I am going to die someday, but I'm not going to die today, and probably not tomorrow or the week to follow, or the week after that.' . . . A kind of mantra." In early November, on the flip side of a postcard to Harrison, Kooser pasted the first dated poem and carried it to his mailbox for pickup.

CHAPTER TWENTY

Winter Morning Walks

I am afoot with my vision . . . I tramp a perpetual journey.

—Walt Whitman, *Song of Myself*

Journey narratives have been central to storytelling since our earliest ancestors sallied forth from camp in search of roots and berries and returned to the clan with harrowing and heartening accounts of life's perils and possibilities. In North America oral accounts and written records reflect patterns of journey, dislocation, and settlement as European invaders pressed west.

Like stacked stones found in the deserts, painted symbols on cliff sides, and leather maps drawn by explorers, varied writings—from *The Journals of the Lewis and Clark Expedition* to Erica Jong's *Fear of Flying* and from Thomas McGrath's *Letter to an Imaginary Friend* to Joy Harjo's *Woman Who Fell from the Sky*—are like letters home, telling not only where others have gone but pointing to the promise of travel.

Throughout Kooser's poetic career, journey and observation have been central to his work. *Winter Morning Walks: One Hundred Postcards to Jim Harrison*, published by Carnegie Mellon University Press in 2000, Kooser's record of treatment and healing, continues and renews this tradition; it is the archetypal journey of Everyman summoned by the Reaper himself.

Like much peripatetic literature, Kooser's collection is an accumulative experience, and its overall effect lies in its rhythmic pace, meditative tone, attention to detail, and wealth of associations that gathers with each venture out of doors. Kooser, for whom metaphor is central, offers a book-length conceit, a continuing conversation with and about place, time, and mortality, as personal as it is universal.

The poet has favored postcards as a means of communication, using them to solicit poems for his press, send personal greetings, as well as incorporating them into *Local Habitation*, printing them as part of the *Salt Creek Reader* series, and mailing them as valentines. Alongside seemingly accurate descriptions of animals, trees, and other aspects of the poet's natural world, the postcard poems often include subtle allegorical aspects, frequently presented in metaphor, by which the poet animates his emotional world. These contribute to a fable-like quality that grows in intensity throughout the lyric poems of *Winter Morning Walks*. Because of Kooser's conversational tone and because personification is so seamlessly imbedded in literal renderings, the reader often overlooks this magical quality: a lilac tree is likened to the great aunt who remembers all the birthdays; the eyes of the turkey vultures can see through human hope; mice spend pleasant mornings in their nests; the quarry is the dusty lap of time; the trees, full of wind, just have to keep talking. This is the poet's world.

The preface poem that launches Kooser's walk heralds the volume's lyrical style, plain-spoken language, and attention to the particular as it provides an example of the poet's facility with metaphor. Kooser offers a breadth of associations within the confines of a relatively short poem as he sets up the trajectory of the poems that follow:

The quarry road tumbles toward me
out of the early morning darkness,

lustrous with frost, an unrolled bolt
of softly glowing fabric, interwoven
with tiny glass beads on silver thread,
the cloth spilled out and then lovingly
smoothed by my father's hand
as he stands behind his wooden counter
(dark as these fields) at Tilden's Store
so many years ago. "Here," he says smiling,
"you can make something special with this."

Kooser's speaker begins without ceremony and in an intimate
tone that compels us to follow as layers of meanings and compound
allusions accrue in a manner reminiscent of Willa Cather. Just as
a reader of *The Song of the Lark* can find her way around Cather's
Red Cloud, Kooser's reader can recognize the poet's early morning landscape by the familiar terms of neighborhood. The road
that first tumbles toward him is colloquially known as the "quarry
road." "Quarry" defines a place from which stone is mined, but it
may also define the object of a chase, as the poet had been pursued
by cancer.

The physical place, the road emerging "out of the early morning
darkness," transforms by metaphoric leap to the "unrolled bolt"
of fabric that his father will smooth. Through association, fabric
becomes "fabric of life" from which each successive generation
is cut; the road becomes a path of memory and meditation from
which art will be fashioned.

The preface poem and the ninety-nine daily walk poems that follow are filled with those dazzling sparks that "light up the sky" for
which his work is admired. Word choice is critical as he weaves his
comparisons. The road shares qualities with the fabric by means of
metaphor; for example, the "glowing" is the light of Tilden's Store
and the early morning light. Those interwoven "glass beads on
silver thread" suggest and are suggested by the points of melting
frost that appear to be threaded on the roadside barbed wire fence.

A cluster of shared images from the fabric of our Western tradition adds a depth and resonance that reverberate beyond apparent meaning. The most immediate and "visible" allusion is to the three Fates who determine the "course of human life." They are described as "daughters of night—to indicate the darkness and obscurity of human destiny," Clotho spins the "thread of life," Lachesis "fixes its length," and Atropos cuts it off. Tomas Tranströmer, a poet Kooser admires, notes in his poem "Black Postcards": "In the middle of life it happens that death comes / to take your measurements."

The silver thread and fabric may also allude to Book Five of *Paterson* in which Williams, by analogy, describes the first four books in terms of the Unicorn tapestry, "silk and wool shot with silver threads," that depicts the capture of the mythical beast who represents the poet's imagination. *The Tempest* sounds in the background: "And, like the baseless fabric of this vision," Shakespeare wrote, "We are such stuff / As dreams are made on; and our little life / Is rounded with a sleep." Allusions to the Bible, though more distant—the rending of fabric, the genealogical listings of the human line, the stone tablets, and the "Our Father"—inform the reading of this poem as well as many of those that follow.

As Kooser establishes the recognizable external place of his walk, he summons the reader's participation by calling on, or up, his or her own images of early morning and of parental relationship: the frosted road itself, the dark fabric of the way, the "tiny glass beads on silver thread," and, of course, the recollections of our own parents, whose gestures we have come to know them by, in our own familiar world. He invites us into the fabric of our own lives, to remember our own journeys and the sensual quality of our own parent's hands. At the same time, he keeps our eyes fixed on his literal flesh-and-blood father, the faith he has had in him, and his own journey.

Kooser writes about his father's hands in "Lights on a Ground of Shadows," noting that they were "at their best when smoothing fabric for display—the left one holding a piece of cloth unrolled from a bolt while the right lovingly eased and teased the wrinkles from it, his fingers spread and their tips lightly touching the cloth as if under them were something grand and alive like the flank of a horse. I can feel the little swirls of brocade beneath the ball of his thumb."

"Make something special with this," the poem ends with the memory of his father's request; this is, Kooser wrote to his friend Jeff Gundy, "exactly what I have been trying to do with my life for as long as I can remember."

By the time the walk poems begin, Kooser has provided the lay of the land with the prose preface, outlining his medical history and the genesis of the collection, and the preface poem, setting the stage from which and on which the journey will take place. Two views are presented: the daily physical walk in the here and now and an allegorical walk, using sustained metaphor and fabulist elements by which his world offers companionship and community. Kooser's former professor, Bernice Slote, argues in her essay, "The Kingdom of Art," that Willa Cather "*thought* allegorically (or symbolically)" and wrote with "a style of mingled allusiveness and symbolism over a groundwork of fixed, related metaphors," traits observed in *Winter Morning Walks*. "Broken allegory," Slote's term for describing the effect, accurately describes Kooser's as well. The solitary soul who sets forth on this modern-day pilgrimage is similar to Christian, the hero of Cather's much-loved *Pilgrim's Progress* by John Bunyan.

Walk and metaphor or "broken allegory" consists of a daily audit of the world. With only several exceptions, each short poem, from two to twenty-one lines long, begins with the date and a brief weather report, beginning November 9, when it is "Rainy and cold" through March 20, "The vernal equinox." Time and weather, the structure suggests, march along, and seasons change, unmoved by the solitary figure who witnesses them.

Once the physical and temporal overview is established, Kooser's engagement—physical, literal, and metaphorical—with his environment can begin. Kooser brings the knowledge of his diagnosis and treatment, his uncertainty about the future, his memories, thoughts, and feelings of daily life, his knowledge of the road along which he has lived and walked for many years.

Two levels of activity or "reality" are apparent, parallel those of Bunyan's pilgrim who, taking a break from "walking through the wilderness of this world," took a nap and dreamed of "a man clothed with rags, standing in a certain place, with his face from his own house, a book in his hand, and a great burden upon his back," a description that in many ways fits the protagonist of *Winter Morning Walks*. Kooser, by consistently beginning with the date and weather report, affords a steady, predictable pace or measure throughout the collection, and the same time, through the irregular and sometimes nearly unscannable rhythm, suggests another level of concern on the part of his "small man in coat and cap, / tying his shoe," as he is described in "November 13." Day by day Kooser answers his father's injunction, to "make something good out of this."

In the composition of the *Winter Morning Walks* poems, Kooser is as careful a poet as he has always been. They are not, he says, "spontaneous outbursts" that followed without revision after each walk. After he worked on each poem for several hours each morning, some "went through 30 and 40 revisions before I got them exactly the way I wanted."

Although not haiku, many of the poems, especially the early ones, are, with their seasonal references, caesuras, and crystalline images, reminiscent of the form. Not in the metrics or sound units of the haiku, they often do alternate short and long lines (his favorite appears to be ten syllables) resembling a sort of call and answer of the English-language form.

"The poem needs insulators," Shapiro writes in *Reports of My Death*, "which is why they look the way most poems do: surrounded with white space, lying in patterns, sounding in patterns. Typography is serious business, margins and indentations like silk and rubber wrappings, like skin and flesh that cradle veins and let them do their job."

As an editor with significant graphics experience, Kooser is keenly aware of the use of "white space" to direct attention and often to underscore meaning; two distinct aspects of each day's walk are highlighted: date and weather. Time is privileged.

"Anapest is the kind of speech I want to speak," Kooser has written, and surely there is a preoccupation with the anapest foot. But the poetic foot, like the poet's footing, varies throughout the collection, giving way to spondee and dactyl, avoiding the more regular and predictable iambic foot and pentameter length as he contemplates his uncertain future. Frequently a restless and sometimes agitated tetrameter seems to echo Kooser's physical state as he recovers from surgery and radiation and reflects his emotional state. Lines resist easy scansion as Kooser's future resists certainty.

This apparent irregularity moves the reader into the emotional content as surely as the narrative even as the clock ticks at its own regular pace. The poems, threaded along the regularity of the month and date, repeat like a mantra, "I am here, I am here," signaling the poet's survival and reminding the reader that he is here giving witness to life for as long as he is able to walk and write. Uncertainty, however, is established with the first dated poem, "November 9," where "the distance (or can that be the future?) / is sealed up in tin like an old barn."

Seemingly accurate descriptions, frequently employing similes, of animals, trees, and other aspects of the poet's natural world are juxtaposed with more allegorical aspects of the world, often by metaphor. These contribute to a fable-like quality that grows in intensity from the six shooting stars Kooser observes on November 17 that were "Celestial notes / . . . struck from the high end of the keyboard" to "December 22," when Kooser reports it is "Five below zero," and "the cold" is a palpable, living entity as it is a biting reminder of the physical world: "The cold finds its way through the wall / by riding the nails, common ten-penny nails," and "you can imagine the face / of the cold, all wreathed in flying hair, / its long fingers spread, its thin blue lips / pressed into the indifferent ear / of the siding." The house itself comes alive, on December 26, when it "cracks its knuckles," initiating conversation. Its furnace yawns, and in one of its rooms "the lampshade is drowsy, / its belly full of a warm yellow light."

Outside, Kooser creates the same effect, pairing and often

melding accurate physical description with fabulist. On November 18, "Cloudy, dark and windy," as the poet walks by flashlight,

> my circle of light on the gravel road
> swinging side to side,
> coyote, raccoon, field mouse, sparrow,
> each watching from darkness
> this man with the moon on a leash.

The world is frequently strange, as open to radical change as it is familiar, once again reflecting the poet's emotional state. On February 7, "Cloudy. Light rain in the night," a "noisy flock of starlings" are "moving / an entire 19th century garment factory / into the future." These continuing dual levels attained by keen physical description and allegorical aspects enable the reader to join the poet on his walks along the literal road while acknowledging that each day has its own "story," and although each person makes his or her own journey, it is on a metaphorical road that we all travel.

Winter Morning Walks is, however, first of all Kooser's story. His health is never far from his consciousness or ours, and the possibility of death sounds with every footfall. Conscious of his father's mortality, the first dated poem directly restates the theme of fate, and life creaks under his feet as he goes. Images related to health are often quietly imbedded, as in the "hunter's cap burns like a coal," recalling the haiku that Kooser wrote during the early days of his illness. Gray is the predominate color of the early poems.

The reader is pulled in and along by the continuing story of illness, hope, grief, and the possibility of recovery. "Look at me now," the narrator calls, enjoining us to see him, alive but humbled by the knowledge of mortality (November 28). By December 2, we are fully engaged by imagery of sickness and health, the contrail of vapor, the footstep's residue in gravel, the necessity of going on, to be buoyed by the knowledge that the foot sounding on the gravel gives notice that he is (and we are) alive. "The poems are often playful," David Mason observes, "but never remote from death; they display a quality that Frost called 'play for moral stakes.'"

As the year draws to a close, having filled his "lungs with hope," Kooser sets out "fast and hard / against this silence," both in his daily walks and his daily writing. He speaks directly about the text of time, the year of loss closing like a book behind him. "The opening pages forgotten, / then the sadness of my mother's death / in the cold, wet chapters of spring" gave way to the "featureless text of summer / burning with illness," and then, when he begins to write, the "first hard frosts" of autumn (December 31).

By Kooser's six-month medical report, in December 1998, when "a good chance at the 5-year recovery period" seemed feasible, he batched selections of the new poems and sent them off to *Shenandoah* and *Midwest Quarterly*, and settled on *Winter Morning Walks: Postcards to Jim Harrison* as a volume title. His plan was to continue writing these poems following his morning walks "until I have maybe 150, then cut out the 50 weakest and see if I have a little book." The future looked hopeful.

On Valentine's Day Kooser makes explicit his many-faceted connection between birds and life, writing and spirit that has remained *soto voce* until now. The junco scribbles (February 12), the hawk "with gleaming yellow eye" waits for (March 7) "each delectable metaphor . . . right under the beak of the poet," recalling, for example, the Great Blue Heron of *Weather Central*'s "Etude" and "A Poetry Reading."

Surgery and radiation are episodes in the poet's journey set in motion years earlier by his parents. Though the preface poem explicitly includes the poet's father, it is important to note that his parents both worked at Tilden's when they met in Ames in the mid-1930s. Their presence can be felt throughout the poems as they can throughout the poet's life.

On "March 18" Kooser sees "the season's first bluebird / . . . one month ahead." Feeling lucky, the poet sets off for his "cancer appointment," grateful for the life and world he has been given. On March 19, a day for which no poem is included, Kooser had his quarterly exam; he writes to Harrison that "I have learned that the biggest problem with cancer is not the disease but the depression and anxiety that go with it."

On March 20 Kooser "was up and out on the road with my camera this morning, so I could photograph the sun rising right at the end of the road," for the moment, at least, dispelling shadows of illness. The final poem ends on the vernal equinox.

"My cancer experience was filled with anger, depression, and chaos," he said; "writing gave me order." Kooser elaborated in a speech to the Alaskan Chapter of the American College of Physicians: "I was dealing with something huge, ominous, and cha-otic—there was no structure to it, no order. I remember how I seized one day on something Bill Lydiatt said to me. . . . 'The progress of a tumor has a kind of order to it, that if it spreads it'll go down your neck into your thorax and so on.'. . . this is certainly not good news, but to me, the fact that a cancer could have any kind of order to it was sort of—I could get hold of that. It meant something. All this poetry writing was also trying to establish order. If I could come home from a walk in the middle of this feeling lousy and make a little square of words with every one in its perfect place, then I had seized a little bit of order. I began doing that, and immediately, day after day, I began feeling better."

As Kooser's year of survival drew to a close, he held the long-planned memorial service for his mother and on Easter Sunday mailed the edited manuscript containing one hundred selected poems to Harrison. In April the poet celebrated his sixtieth birth-day. In May Carnegie Mellon accepted *Winter Morning Walks* for publication. Kooser is at work in his converted corncrib studio on a large painting of a snowdrift melting at the edge of a field, which will be used for the book's cover illustration. "I was looking at it," he writes to friends, "and these words come to mind: Trust snow to keep its secrets." A year later Kooser lost his mentor, Karl Shapiro, who had suffered from poor health for some time.

Awards for *Winter Morning Walks* were quick in coming: in 2000 the James Boatwright Award, *Shenandoah*; the Nebraska Arts

Council Merit Award in Poetry; and the Mari Sandoz Award of the Nebraska Library Association. The following year it received the Nebraska Book Award. In December 2001 Rutledge was named editor of the *Lincoln Journal Star.* Kooser returned to work on two manuscripts in progress prior to his illness, *Local Wonders*, a prose memoir, and *Braided Creek*, an exchange of short poems with Jim Harrison. Life was good.

CHAPTER TWENTY-ONE

Local Wonders

When God wishes to rejoice
the heart of a poor man,
He makes him lose his donkey
and find it again.

—Epigraph, *Local Wonders*

Informed by a close brush with mortality, Kooser returned to writing with gusto, adding to and arranging short autobiographical pieces written over the previous twenty years, as Leonard Nathan had urged him to do. He looked to several books as models, including Hal Borland's *Sundial of the Seasons* and Donald Culross Peattie's *Almanac for Moderns*, as he arranged his work. "For beautiful, clear prose, touched with good humor and generosity," he says he looked to the essays of E. B. White. "No other writer," Kooser continues, "approaches him when it comes to make me feel good about being alive."

The proverbs, from an anthology of adages the poet found at a yard sale, provide a delicate spine along which Kooser threads his short essays and add a timeless quality to *Local Wonders*. "Reading his collection of essays," reviewer Steven Harvey writes, "is a bit like running into Lao Tsu and Confucius in line at the hardware store."

Although Kooser does not mention *Walden* as an influence, he does seem to be following Thoreau's recommendation from his first essay, "Economy": "every writer, first or last, [should write] a simple and sincere account of his own life, and not merely what he has heard of other men's lives; some such account as he would send to his kindred from a distant land; for if he has lived sincerely, it must have been in a distant land to me."

Dedicated to his son, who lived in a "distant land" for much of his growing up, *Local Wonders* is not so much a formal autobiographical statement, complete with facts and dates and chronological development, as it is an attempt to convey the sum and essential substance of Kooser's life. The poet describes early on Jeff's return to Nebraska to live with him and Kathleen for three years while he finished college and his grief when his son graduated and moved on. "It had been," Kooser writes, "the best time of our lives, having him near." The memoir is his legacy.

Although the focus of this discussion is poetry, it is important to note that even in his prose, Kooser's approach is pastoral, directing his reader's attention to the individual life lived with awareness of the surrounding natural world and to the joy it offers. Nature as an outward manifestation of an overarching spiritual idea is not overt in Kooser as it was for Thoreau and Emerson, but it is clearly part of the whole of life though which human beings can learn about themselves. Like Thoreau, another walker, who collected notes for two years while living next to Emerson's pond outside Concord, the poet threads observations, anecdotes, and recollections written over the years he has lived beside his own pond outside of Garland.

Both writers see the seasons as analogous to human development. "The seasons and all their changes," Thoreau wrote in his *Journal*, "are in me." Kooser divides his memoir into seasonal sections nearly equal in length, beginning with spring and concluding with winter, as though to underscore his age. Time's passage energizes the memoir; not only does the reader see the year pass before her or his eyes, but there is a depth of time. The present is enriched and informed by memories of past events and loved ones, many of whom are familiar from Kooser's poetry, and reminds us of human patterns through time in much the same way as his postcards did in *Local Habitation & a Name*.

While Thoreau sees in wilderness a way to maintain balance, for Kooser, civilization is often an infringement. "People in the country can come to believe," he writes, "that any change occurring at a rate more accelerated than the unfolding of the seasons must be viewed with skepticism. . . . you can put just about anything over on a small community if you go about it slowly." Some of his own neighbors, corn and soybean growers, may see the poet as a "city slicker," part of a rural gentrification project, but Kooser is clearly on the side of his Seward Country compatriots, concerned about dumping of hazardous chemicals in the landfill, shutting down a local school in favor of consolidation, and the gradual development of housing tracts to provide a bedroom community for Lincoln workers. "Little by little, the countryside shows more and more signs of change. . . . The orange stakes go up on the hillsides, followed by white PVC pipes marking new wells. Then a new gravel lane appears . . . As the Bohemians say, "money is a master everywhere."

Metaphor, which abounds throughout *Local Wonders* as it does in *Walden*, is contained within the frame of the journey conceit. Kooser prefaces his memoir with the lay of the land, the downward pitch of the state from the Rockies to the Missouri River, before leading us down the road of geography and geology to the Bohemian Alps settled by the Czechs and Germans in the late nineteenth century, then home. "Go a mile and a half straight north from the bend, turn east, and follow that road along the ridge for a quarter mile," he writes, and "turn right at the first corner," offering directions so clear that students have found their way to the poet's front door.

Early in the first section Kooser, who describes himself as "in his sixties," is painting along a country road in his 1992 Mercury Topaz, converted into "a rolling art studio." While he paints, a farmer from a house up the road comes by to ask him if he needs help. "No," Kooser answers, "I'm just painting a picture." He interprets the farmer's look: "he'd never run into anything quite like that before."

The poet/painter does not invite the farmer into an exchange, and we are not surprised when he rolls up his window to return home.

On the other hand, Kooser proves to be not so different from his farmer neighbors. Thoreau remarked many years ago, "I have frequently seen a poet withdraw, having enjoyed the most valuable part of a farm, while the crusty farmer supposed that he had got a few wild apples only. Why, the owner does not know it for many years when a poet has put his farm in rhyme, the most admirable kind of invisible fence, has fairly impounded it, milked it, skimmed it, and got all the cream, and left the farmer only the skimmed milk."

Within the first few pages of *Local Wonders*, Kooser travels to the "sidewalks in Lincoln ... slippery since last weekend's snowstorm," through memory, to the ballroom dancing lessons in the church basement in Ames, and back outside on an overcast day to dig a posthole. Kooser's own motion is reinforced by a host of events: snow falls, water runs, people mow yards and clean out garages, his younger dog Alice runs, digs holes of her own, and pesters Buddy, his older dog, all by page ten. The pace continues throughout the book, urging the reader on as it underscores the passage of time and the brevity of life. When Kooser sees his father's hands in his own, palms "turned up as if to catch this fleeting moment as it falls away," he envisions them folded across his own chest in the coffin.

"The conveyances in which Death comes riding arrive in all manner of guises," including the weed-sprayers, in a "red-and-white '78 Ford pickup, creeping along at maybe five miles an hour." Unlike Kooser's Mercury fitted for the making of art, this rig has been outfitted with an air compressor and white plastic tank "sloshing with a milky fluid," deadly herbicide. The two temporary county workers wear no protective clothing or masks and are, he writes, "likely shortening their own lives." "The Czechs say," he reminds the reader, "'Do not spit into a well; you do not know when you will drink out of it yourself." An insurance underwriter for more than thirty years, Kooser is aware that death is always close at hand.

The "nurturing and sustaining power of family," according to Harvey, sets Kooser apart from Thoreau and other nature writers.

The poet includes fond memories of his parents and many relatives. He also includes stories of his friendships. Abstract painter Stewart Hitch, his friend since their days at the University of Nebraska, is commemorated with a variety of stories in *Local Wonders*, in which the reader views the friendship of the two men as well as the Bohemian Alps through which they travel. Hitch, who had lived in New York City since the early 1970s, returned to Nebraska one summer to buy a vacant tavern in Valparaiso, not far from Garland. With Kooser's help, he was renovating the space into a studio and living quarters where he hoped to spend a few months each year. Hitch's time in Valparaiso was short; he died in 2002 in Manhattan, the year *Local Wonders* was published.

Memory is the mother of the muses. Travel by means of remembrance is a way to hold the past to the present as is the glue Kooser applies to his mother's cutting board, enabling both memories and the board to exist into the future. "We are always trying to find footing on the damp edge of the future," he writes, "but to most of us, the dry sand of the past feels firmer under our sneakers."

Kooser renders his trip to the dentist June 1, 1998, so vividly, it is as though we accompany him. The temperature is in the "low seventies" as he drives into Lincoln, "lush and green" on a "perfect early summer" day. For the next six months, while undergoing and recovering from the radiation treatments, he travels again, this time in his imagination, to the gentle curve of the Mississippi from the overlook south of Guttenberg.

In autumn the morning walks began, and in January he discovers "a string of Burlington Northern boxcars . . . rust red against a clear sky." He has previously used images of the train in his poems, "Late Lights in Minnesota," "Another Old Woman," and "Snakeskin," for example. There could hardly be a better symbol of both connection and isolation for Plains dwellers than train cars, which 150 years or so ago brought settlers and supplies west into the heart of the North American continent. "The odd car for there is always an odd car in a string like this," he continues in *Local Wonders*, "like the one dark kernel in every ear of corn, is on this bright subzero day red, white and blue. Its paint is so fresh it looks sticky. *Columbia*, it reads, a lost word from America's past, a word like *liberty*, like *republic*, a word with the smell of black powder."

The close observation of seasons and of life, human and otherwise, is at the heart of *Local Wonders* as it is of his poetry. What Virginia Woolf wrote about Thoreau's work is applicable to Kooser's. Writing in the *Times Literary Supplement*, she remarked that "When we read 'Walden,' we have a sense of beholding life through a very powerful magnifying glass. To walk, to eat, to cut up logs, to read a little, to watch the bird on the bough, to cook one's dinner—all these occupations when scraped clean and felt afresh prove wonderfully large and bright."

"The aim of the poet and his poetry is finally to be of service," Kooser quotes Seamus Heaney, "to ply the effort of the individual work into the larger work of the community as a whole." This is the message of Robert McCloskey's Lentil, with whom Kooser identified; the fictional boy learns the harmonica and through his music serves his town. "Writing poems is, after all, a public service," Kooser advises in "More Letters to a Young Poet," part of *Midwest Quarterly*'s tribute to German poet Rainer Marie Rilke. "A poet serves a community," he continues, "and each poem ought to be thought of as a gift to the reader," an idea he credits to Lewis Hyde.

Gary D. Schmidt, who has written extensively about Robert McCloskey and his place in children's literature, notes that "in the midst of this dreadful world [World War II and after] . . . [there] appeared a series of books that celebrated childhood, family, friendship, the natural world—in short, life itself." McCloskey's vision "is one of absolute affirmation of the permanence and beauty and significance of the world." This might be said of all Kooser's work, but especially of *Local Wonders*. While "Clickety-clickety," the seasons, years, decades go by, the world is to be appreciated, relationships celebrated.

"Life is a long walk forward through the crowded cars of a passenger train," Kooser writes as *Local Wonders* draws to a close, "the bright world racing past beyond the windows." He has also become

Lentil's Colonel Carter riding the train of life. "And so it goes, car after car, passage to passage, as you make your way forward.... So much of the world, colorful as flying leaves, clatters past beyond the windows while you try to be attentive to those you move among." This passage is reminiscent of Kooser's description of his father in "Lights on a Ground of Darkness" as he moved through the nursing home where his wife's father and brother lived: "Now as he [his father] rushes through people calling and calling to him, his heart tapping in his ears, he feels how frail and light he may soon become. He wants more gravity; he wants to hold himself down, to keep himself together for a little longer, to cherish the softening muscles wrapped like weights around his bones."

Kooser, whose father died on New Year's Eve in 1979, wrote the final "train" section of *Local Wonders* on another New Year's Eve over twenty years later. "Often around the holidays, I find myself writing a deeply reflective piece like that, and this one fit nicely at the end of the book," he said in an interview. "I wanted the book to end in an upbeat way, and even though I'm talking about life inevitably coming to an end, at the end of that section, everyone raises their glasses in a toast, an affirmation." It is also about artist and art. "Think about your place in the world, your place in a community, all those fellow passengers, strangers and friends," he urges. "You'll be a better person for it and, by extension, a better writer."

"This is the life I have chosen," he writes in *Local Wonders*. "Driving east, the globe spins beneath me, the marigold yellow centerline on the old Lincoln Highway like a stripe on the whistling top. State Center rushes into the past, bright yellow leaves [of his art, I would say] flying behind." Kooser's final rendering of the journey metaphor, the long walk through the train cars, suggests he is well aware that he is walking toward the great engineer in the sky, who wears "his striped cap" and "red bandanna around his neck," as the train follows the ever narrowing tracks ahead.

Although a sense of human kinship has always been important in his work, community emerges as an essential ingredient in both his life and work in his later writings: *Winter Morning Walks: One Hundred Postcards to Jim Harrison*, *Local Wonders: Seasons in the Bohemian Alps*, and, with Jim Harrison, *Braided Creek: A Conversation in Poetry*, published in 2003.

Harrison, two years older than Kooser, is a prolific writer. Originally a poet, he published five volumes of verse before his first (of fifteen) novels, *Wolf: A False Memoir* in 1971. A Zen practitioner for more than thirty years, Harrison has written about nature and the impact of place on its inhabitants. The poetry of both men reflects walks along gravel roads, through the woods, and, figuratively, through time.

With *Braided Creek: A Conversation in Poetry*, Harrison and Kooser acknowledge that their walks, if not on the same terrain, have been parallel, their lives like a stream of the river Time. To reinforce the spiritual grounding of place and the importance of friendship, the book is dedicated to Michigan-born writer Dan Gerber, Harrison's long-time friend and Zen teacher, with whom he founded the magazine *Sumac* (1968–1972).

Kooser notes in his preface to *Winter Morning Walks* that he and Harrison had several years earlier "carried on a correspondence in haiku." After treatment for cancer, Kooser returned to editing the poems into the book-length collection. He pasted Harrison's and his own poems on two sets of note cards and then looked at how each played against or echoed the other and from that fashioned a braid of words. "How one old tire leans up against / another," the book opens, "the breath gone out of both," setting the stage for a wide variety of short meditations on life in general, aging, friendship, joy, nature, writing, to name only a few. Good humor and physicality, hallmarks of both poets' individual works, are pervasive. "The wit of the corpse / is lost on the lid of a coffin" and "Republicans think that all over the world / darker-skinned people are having more fun / than they are. It's largely true."

Harrison says the decision not to disclose the writer of each poem seemed to come naturally. "Ted had cancer a couple years ago and his poetry became really overwhelmingly vivid," he said. "And then we decided why not correspond in terms of these short walks or haikus," he continued, "because that was the essence of what we wanted to say, so we've been doing it for several years and we hope to publish the book with nobody knowing who wrote each poem. It transcends the ego. Just publish it collectively." Kooser notes, "At times . . . I no longer remember who wrote which."

Although death may seem just around the corner, the two men celebrate joyful and fulfilling lives with a view to the future that is intoxicating: As if homage to the Rubaiyat of Omar Khayyam, they write: "Which way will the creek / run when time ends? / Don't ask me until / this wine bottle is empty."

Kooser was feted in June 2003 by the University of Nebraska Press. Long-time friends, along with representatives from the university, Nebraska Arts Council, and many others, were on hand to pay tribute. That same year *Local Wonders* was selected as a finalist for Barnes & Noble's Discover Great New Writers Award for nonfiction. The memoir also received *ForeWord* magazine's 2003 Gold Award for Autobiography, the Friends of American Writers Prize, Honorable Mention in Society of Midland Authors nonfiction award, and the Nebraska Book Award for nonfiction.

Kooser's poem "In the Hall of Bones" was included in the 2003 *Best American Poetry*, edited by Yusef Komunyakaa. In 2004 Kooser, along with Harrison, received the Society of Midland Authors Poetry Prize.

Kooser found his donkey again, and happy trails stretched before him.

CHAPTER TWENTY-TWO

Delights & Shadows

Just now, if I look back down
the cool street of the past, I can see
streetlamps, one for each year.

—From "Just Now"

Although integral to his work as a writer, Kooser's interest and experience in the visual arts are not well known. As a young boy, he drew before he wrote, apprenticed with and worked as a professional sign painter for many years, and in college considered a career in painting. Even after choosing poetry as his primary art form, Kooser has continued to paint, draw, and photograph the world around him. When he introduces himself in his memoir, *Local Wonders*, he is parked alongside a country road in a car he has converted into a traveling art studio. He initially identifies himself as "an amateur painter" and then as a "Sunday painter," but before long he seems to conflate pen and brush. Painting, he writes, is his way "of trying to be a tulip, pushing my way out of the tight white bulb of winter and opening a little color against the darkness." This nexus of dark and light, along with human affinity with nature, is his aesthetic dwelling place, one that readers are familiar with from his poetry. Chiaroscuro, well known as a technique that renders form through the contrast of light and dark in painting, has long been favored by Kooser. In a 2006 interview he described the technique of chiaroscuro, standing in his office on the third floor of Andrews Hall at the University of Nebraska–Lincoln and nodding to the three self-portraits by Louisiana artist Amanda Hext that hang on his office wall. "This is what makes this work, the chiaroscuro," he clarified, pointing to the light and dark areas of the paintings, and explained the layering of paints, the application of a coat of green earth in order to depict shadow.

As a literary technique, chiaroscuro is, broadly speaking, an effect achieved by the juxtaposition of opposites (or extreme differences) to render meaning. Contrasting subject matter or aspects of theme, for example, can be juxtaposed: life and death, joy and gloom, pleasure and pain, or light and dark. Though chiaroscuro is most often associated with the visual, the technique may also be extended to the other senses as well. Symbols, meter, sound, and so on, may rely on chiaroscuro for their full affect. A popular and very rich example of its various literary uses is to be found in *The Scarlet Letter* by Nathaniel Hawthorne.

When the ravages of time and the richness of life, always among Kooser's major preoccupations as a writer, took center stage in his work following his diagnosis of throat cancer in 1998, chiaroscuro emerged as one of his primary poetic devices, and the relationship between his practice and knowledge of the visual arts became explicit. *Winter Morning Walks: One Hundred Postcards to Jim Harrison*, tracing his treatment and recovery, relies on visual chiaroscuro for its cover—Kooser's painting, *Old Snow*—and internal graphics as well as literary chiaroscuro. (The original poems affixed to the face of postcards and mailed to the poet's long-time friend, writer Jim Harrison, are works of visual art in their own right.)

Kooser elaborates on the essential relationship between his own literary use of light and dark and the artistic chiaroscuro in *Winter Morning Walks* during a discussion of George C. Ault's painting *August Night at Russell's Corners* in the permanent collection of the Joslyn Art Museum in Omaha. The 1948 painting, Kooser writes, "seems to have the simple premise: old buildings that in daylight would be so familiar that a person living in Russell's Corners wouldn't even notice them become exotic and mysterious in the light from a commonplace bulb. Ault," the poet continues,

> made four paintings of this same midnight crossroads, each from a slightly different angle. . . . But their effect upon me is identical. I can feel my will joining with that of the feeble light in its struggle to push back the darkness, darkness that has already begun to affect and alter the familiar, making it strange and exciting. I wrote:

> *If you can awaken*
> *inside the familiar*
> *you need never*
> *leave home.*
> Local wonders.

For his ninth full-length collection of poetry, *Delights & Shadows*, Kooser chose *August Night at Russell's Corners* as the cover image. The painting amplifies the title while making overt the correspondence he sees between literary and visual chiaroscuro.

As the collection's epigraph he borrows a line from Emily Dickinson's 1862 letter to Thomas Higginson: "The sailor cannot see the North but knows the Needle can." Kooser reminds readers at the outset that human mortality, death—the unseen North—both haunts and informs our lives. The poems that follow suggest, often by contrast, that human awareness of death and death itself are complimented by human memory and imagination by which we revisit the past and transform everyday life into art—for our own pleasure and appreciation as well as for others.

Each of *Delights & Shadows*'s four sections employs chiaroscuro in ways that are both painterly and literary, capturing the light of existence as it shines from the inevitable darkness beyond. In "Walking on Tiptoe," section 1, old men, middle-aged women, children, a college student, a biker, restaurant patrons, shoppers, mourners, a woman navigating a wheelchair, and an ice skater travel at various velocities and in a variety of ways; their stories flicker before us as they head toward a destination always certain if not always seen. Life is light, filled with a cacophony of movement and sound; death is dark, silent, and still.

Although neither memory nor imagination can stop time, both allow, as section 2, "The China Painters," demonstrates, a means by which we may preserve the past; their works of art are (de)lights that shine from the darkness. Kooser's use of chiaroscuro continues in section 3, "Bank Fishing for Bluegills," where his interest in and practice of drawing and painting become explicit. These poems include a still life, a series inspired by Winslow Homer, artifacts from natural history and county museums, and everyday tools. Each serves as a historical document by which we can glimpse and appreciate the past. As *Delights & Shadows* draws to a close, the final thirteen poems, section 4, personalize themes raised in the initial thirteen; here Kooser addresses the inevitability of his own death and his place within the natural world. Examples from each of the sections will suggest the various, subtle, and fresh ways Kooser uses literary chiaroscuro.

In the title poem of section 1, "Walking on Tiptoe," the poet juxtaposes human beings with other animals and suggests what we may have lost with our evolutionary gain and how that loss might, at least momentarily, be transcended through the imagination. The poem sets the tone of the entire collection:

> Long ago we quit lifting our heels
> like the others—horse, dog, and tiger—
> though we thrill to their speed
> as they flee. Even the mouse
> bearing the great weight of a nugget
> of dog food is enviably graceful.
> There is little spring to our walk,
> we are so burdened with responsibility,
> all of the disciplinary actions

that have fallen to us, the punishments,
the killings, and all with our feet
bound stiff in the skins of the conquered.
But sometimes, in the early hours,
we can feel what it must have been like
to be one of them, up on our toes,
stealing past doors where others are sleeping,
and suddenly able to see in the dark.

While other animals naturally walk and run on tiptoe, giving them speed and grace, "we," as a species, have become flatfooted and slow. Animals are light-footed, while "we" are weighted down: the contrast of the chiaroscuro rubric. Whether an evolutionary loss or one fashioned by a supreme being, the poem does not yet address; regardless of cause, there is "so little spring to our walk."

With lines 8–12, the poet's allusion to the first book of the Bible, Genesis, becomes apparent; humans are "burdened with responsibility," and as "disciplinary actions" have "fallen to us, the punishments, / the killings" have left us—the poet keeps our attention on our feet—"bound stiff in the skins of the conquered." Kooser subtly recalls God's command to the newly minted male and female to "Rule over the fish of the sea and the birds of the air and every creature on the ground."

By association and juxtaposition, Kooser brings the reader to the collection's major organizing principle (as it was in a more oblique way in *Weather Central*), the Judeo-Christian "beginning": the "earth was without shape and empty, and darkness was over the surface of the watery deep. . . . God said, 'Let there be light.' And there was light!" When God saw "light was good," he separated the light from dark.

The seventeen lines that make up the poem vary in length and rely on sound to support meaning. Long open *o*'s and liquid *l*'s pull us into the poem like a story at bedtime. "I sound out every syllable as it relates to the others," Kooser says. The third and fourth lines, of six and seven syllables respectively, quicken, suggesting human thrill.

The poem as a whole is a study in the use of sound. Line 8, the longest of the poem, is composed of twelve syllables. Working with plosives—*b, d, d, p, b, t*—Kooser accentuates the burden of responsibility that human beings have shouldered. This continues into the next line, heavy with the *d, p, t,* accompanied by the hiss of the *s.* Lines 8 through 10 slow considerably with three words with the longest syllabic count in the poem: "responsibility," "disciplinary," and "punishments." Already, Kooser has introduced the double-*l* sound that reverberates three additional times during the darkest movement of the poem, lines 11–13, visually reminding the reader of our delight, our "thrill," at their speed. *S* sounds that scurry throughout the poem accentuate the reader's imagined speed, as "up on our toes, / stealing past doors where others are sleeping," "we" are "suddenly able to see in the dark."

"Walking on Tiptoe" is a good example of the "Kooser sonnet," typically a poem of ten to twenty lines that generally follows the sonnet structure, itself dependant on literary chiaroscuro for its organization and form. As Karl Shapiro and Robert Behm note in *A Prosody Handbook*, although the traditional sonnet is composed of fourteen lines, there is flexibility of form. "The sonnet," they write, "is large enough to allow the poet to set forth a problem and then go on to solve it (or find it insoluble); to present a situation and then interpret it; to move in one direction and then to reverse that direction completely." Longer sonnets date back to Shakespeare's time. As an example, Shapiro and Behm note the eighteen-line Act 1 sonnet in *Romeo and Juliet.*

Kooser uses sentences (rather than lines) to signal the traditional cognitive movement within the poem. The six opening lines are composed of two related sentences: the first sentence, three and a half lines long, offers the observation that a long time ago human beings began walking flat-footed while other animals still ran on tiptoes, and "we thrill to their speed." The second sentence, of two and a half lines, extends recognition of the animals' abilities with the example of the mouse, graceful while bearing a great weight, a nugget of dog food. The following six sentences outline the human predicament that has resulted. Responsibility has its price: "our feet / [are] bound stiff in the skins of the conquered."

With line 13 comes the sonnet's turn or volta, signaled by the word "But," which begins a sentence as well as the line. The poet shifts from the difference between other animals and human beings to the lightness (note the pun), even joy, that the imagination can provide. Despite loss of speed and grace and the predicament of being in charge, "sometimes, in the early hours," before there was light, we can imagine the stealth and quickness.

In the ordinary the poet catches sight of the extraordinary. An *ars poetica*, "Walking on Tiptoe" is another kind of creation story, where "in the early hours" a poet catches sight of the extraordinary, sparking the poem into being. Light dawns; the poem begins to form. "We catch a glimpse of something, from time to time," William Carlos Williams, wrote in his autobiography, "which shows us that a presence has just brushed past us, some rare thing—just when the smiling little Italian woman has left us. For a moment we are dazed. What was that? We can't name it." This is what Kooser glimpses in the night and throughout *Delights & Shadows*: "a new, a more profound language," Williams continues, "underlying all the dialectics offers itself. It is what they call poetry. . . . It is actually there, in the life before us, every minute that we are listening, a rarest element, not in our imaginations but there, there in fact. It is that essence which is hidden in the very words which are going in our ears and from which we must recover underlying meaning as realistically as we recover metal out of ore." This "radiant gist," is a narrative thread running, like a vein of precious metal, throughout section 1.

Kooser's people are nearly always in motion tiptoeing, walking between tables of a garage sale, heading toward an examining room, or, as in the "Student," transformed into a turtle emerging from the sea, lumbering across campus toward the university library, known colloquially simply as "Love" after its benefactor. Each moment is a heroic act in the all-too-short drama of human life.

Image, metaphor, and allusion move from poem to poem and

serve as leitmotifs offering a layering, or perhaps a spiral leading to an underlying, continuing narrative. In "Gyroscope," for example, the navigational tool often employed as a child's toy to illustrate balance and orientation "spins and leans" like Earth, introducing by means of "one of the smaller worlds" the physical laws of being and relationship. By extension, the poem alludes to those patterns that can only be learned by practice and experience. The girl is ten, safe and warm in the "sleepwalking pose" in a glassed-in porch (reminiscent of Grandma Kooser's porch in *Local Wonders*), while February, the month of cold winds and snow, remains outside the girl's immediate experience. She is the archetypal maiden, Kore, on the porch of adolescence, learning to master this small world, "the last / to balance so lightly in our hands" before the onset of puberty when innocence is lost and balance may become more difficult to maintain.

"Skater," the section's final poem, captures the ecstatic moment as the long, thirteen-syllable lines show the elegant movements of the skater as she moves toward transformation. The skater's actions parallel both the crane, to whom she is compared, and poetry, with its leap of metaphor; she is not so unlike the tiptoer who is up at night to catch a moment of joy.

Section 2, "The China Painters," celebrates the preservation of loved ones through their work, in this case a form of art itself. The title poem, composed of one sentence carefully divided into eighteen lines, preserves family artisans, who "have set aside their black tin boxes." They have left behind their well-used tools: their "scratched and dented, spattered" paint box and "dried-up rolled-up tubes." The specific box Kooser describes once belonged to his wife's grandmother. Colors dazzle again as the poem names them: "alizarin crimson, chrome green, / zinc white, and ultramarine." Vials of gold powder are half full; death frequently comes before we are finished with our work.

Attention to the details of the art making continues: "stubs of wax pencils; / frayed brushes with tooth-bitten shafts" used to reproduce "clouds of loose, lush roses, / narcissus, pansies, columbine," on china that is "spread like a garden / on the white lace Sunday cloth." In one of Kooser's seamless reversals, the painters seem to disappear into the very blooms they have painted. The final two lines extend the life-as-garden metaphor with a simile, and the souls of the painters are imagined as bees, their world as "nothing but flowers." Like the bees produce and store honey, the painters distill and preserve the beauty around them.

The power of the imagination and the force of the creative act, as Kooser suggests in "Memory," the list poem that follows, can be likened the natural force of the tornado. "Spinning up dust and cornshucks / as it crossed the chalky, exhausted fields," Kooser begins, the tornado "sucked up into its heart" a myriad of things, "hot work, cold work, lunch buckets, / good horses, bad horses, their names / and the names of mules that were / better or worse than the horses," and continues for nearly the total thirty-eight lines of the one-sentence whirlwind of recollection. The fast-paced lines are pushed by a variety of descriptive verbs swept on by sound—"rattled," "dented," "shook," "cranked," "broke," "turning," "taking," "crossed," "undid," "plucked," "peeled," "reached down and snatched up"—until line 26, where the meter slows into a series of heavy accents. Here the poet moves from possessions to the people themselves, "uncles and cousins, grandma, grandpa, / parents and children one by one," holds them "like dolls," looking "long and longingly into their faces," before setting them back "in their chairs," before the "blue and white platters of chicken / and ham and mashed potatoes /still steaming before them." His wind, whirling with memories, suggests an exhalation of breath triggered by these recollections: "suddenly, with the sound like a sigh, drew up / its crowded, roaring, dusty funnel" of items and emotions. The caesura at the middle of the poem's last line emphasizes the hinge or *tertium comparationis* of the comparison: "and there at its tip was the nib of a pen."

In "Ice Cave," the poet returns to Turkey River valley in Clayton County, Iowa. The poem's long lines carry us to Ira Friedlein's farm, where the swapping of family stories is preserved. Kooser warns against the pitfalls of the purely anecdotal poem. "In recent years, more and more poems have taken on an anecdotal manner," which when they are read "a hundred years from now" will likely be met with a "so what? . . . something seems to be missing." But the poems in *Delights & Shadows*, particularly those in part 2, are examples of how a poem might have started in the anecdote and then moved beyond it. "The story itself," Kooser reminds us, "is merely the material. You have to do something special with that material, if you want it to be a poem."

This section contains two of Kooser's best-known epistolary elegies: "Mother," which originally introduced his essay, "Lights on a Ground of Darkness," and "Father," written on the ninety-seventh anniversary of his father's birth. Both poems, like "A Letter" from *One World at a Time*, emerge from stories and then move beyond them. Kooser's poems preserve his family though the artifacts and accounts that they have left behind: Aunt Sticky (Ruth Stickfort) in "Flow Blue China," Uncle Jack Mayo in "Creamed Corn," and Pearl Richards, his mother's long-time friend, whom the reader meets in "Pearl." (Readers of Kooser have already met Pearl's parents, Amy and Rob Hansel, the inspiration for Nels and Lydia from "An Old Photograph" collected in *Sure Signs*.)

"A Jar of Buttons" could have been simply an anecdotal poem about one of his mother's button jars; instead it becomes a core sample of the past. Poems are containers, even urns; no wonder this section is filled with so many: cups and pots, tin boxes, even natural "containers," the wind that picks up and funnels the past. As "Creamed Corn" suggests, not all memories are pleasant.

Kooser's vivid images are a reminder of his interest in and practice of drawing and painting. Among his favorite painters is Robert Henri (1865-1929), whose roots in Nebraska are well known; a retrospective of his work to mark the centennial of his birth was held at the Sheldon Museum of Art in fall 1965, two years after Kooser's arrival in Lincoln. *The Art Spirit*, a compilation of Henri's writings, is very close to the poet's own attitude toward process of art. He also admires painters of the Ashcan School, a group of early twentieth-century realists, including Henri, George Luks, John Sloan, William Glackens, and others. While "Modernism was going in another direction," he says, "these people were still trying to do something with proletarian things."

Given Kooser's work, it is not surprising that he would lean toward artists who, according to Dennis Wepman, deliberately rejected "the refined subjects and styles that dominated the art of the time in favor of commonplace, even sordid, aspects of the life of American cities." Kooser's aesthetics repeatedly echo Henri's *The Art Spirit*. Greatly influenced by Ralph Waldo Emerson, as well as Walt Whitman, Henri has much to offer writers. "I've been marking passages that would be useful to student writers," Kooser says. "There's a lot to learn from that whole group of people [the Ashcan School]," including John Sloane's diaries of that period.

In section 3, "Bank Fishing for Bluegills," Kooser chooses paintings by Winslow Homer, a variety of art-related images, and artifacts that serve as historical documents, some personal and some cultural, to address his larger themes of mortality and human awareness of the sweetness and brevity of life.

The section's title poem has the feel of a still life and, Kooser says, has "much in common" with a Homer or Sargent watercolor. "Good watercolor paintings," he continues, "look like the artist dashed them off, although it takes a tremendous effort to do that." He also sees similarities between the processes of painting and poetry, both built from an image. The revision process is similar," he observes, the "standing back, looking at it, giving it a little time, then going back in, correcting things. . . . For the small poem of twelve or fourteen lines, there might be thirty or forty versions by the time I'm done. My revisions are toward a kind of clarity and freedom so that—and this would be a parallel with painting—it appears the poem came off the brush like a stroke of watercolor without any effort whatsoever."

"Bank Fishing for Blue Gills" seems a painting, just as the subject, a boat, seems a man, and then seems to become the man. The reversal and re-reversals, a distant relative of the sonnet's volta, rather than posing a problem for the reader, present a delight. Composed of three sentences, the poem opens with a description of what the poet sees from the bank as he fishes, setting up his metaphor, creating the stillness of the poem. "The empty aluminum boat" nudged by the breeze of time becomes human, the fat man who has fallen asleep and dreams of, staying with the metaphor, when he was young and small. The man is to the boat as the boy was to the plastic bucket. The end rhyme of the first two lines, "boat" and "rope," the word "wallowing" in line 3, as well as "boy" at the end of line 5 are open *o*'s that pull and then open the reader into the past as well as into the comparison. The rhythm of the opening lines matches the movement of the boat lulling the reader into a sort of reverie.

Kooser keeps the rope of comparison taut. The sentence that follows runs four lines, itemizing the points of comparison as the subject of the comparison (the *tenor*) is clarified. The progression of the poem mirrors that of the sonnet, but instead of presenting a situation, to use Shapiro's terminology, and then to begin to interpret it, Kooser seems to offer the *vehicle*, the subject from which the poet will borrow attributes for his comparison before introducing the *tenor*, the subject of the poem to which they are attributed. The poet seems to move in one direction and then reverse direction completely, much like the boat drifting back and forth, the hypnotic movement of lake and wind currents.

The final three lines more clearly articulate the subject of the poem, and the boat remains as vivid to the reader as the man. The tether of man to world is physical, palpable as we experience the tug on the rope in the imagination. Were it not for the poem's title, one might argue that the boat is the true subject of the poem. Were it not for Kooser's skill with metaphor, the reader might overlook the fact that the poem is also about the mystery and transformative quality of art. "If you think of a metaphor," Kooser writes, "as being a bridge between two things, it's not the things that are of most importance, but the grace and lift of the bridge between them, flying high over the surface."

"Four Civil War Paintings by Winslow Homer," a more traditional series of ekphrastic poems, follows. Kooser traveled to Kansas City, Missouri, to attend *Winslow Homer and the Critics: Forging a National Art in the 1870s*, a 2001 retrospective, held at the Nelson-Adkins Museum of Art. Homer (1836-1910) sometimes used his experience as a Civil War illustrator for *Harper's Weekly* as a basis for paintings, and many works illuminate the day-to-day lives of the soldiers.

The epigraph makes clear that the series is also about aesthetics; the passage from the May 31, 1865, edition of the *Evening Post* reads: "if the painter shows that he observes more than he reflects, we will forget the limitations and take his work as we take nature, which, if it does not think, is yet the cause of thought in us." The quote tells us at least as much about Kooser's view of the poet and of poetry as it does about the criteria for evaluating Civil War art. Like Homer, Kooser is interested in the common man.

"Some part of art is the art / of waiting—the chord / behind the tight fence of a musical staff / the sonnet shut in a book," the first poem of the series, "Sharpshooter" begins. "This is a painting of / waiting," Kooser tells us before going on to describe Homer's painting of the lone figure, a Union sniper, sitting quietly in a tree, rifle ready, waiting for the target to appear. The analogy is clear. The sharpshooter is also the poet sitting quietly, "his one open eye, / like a star you might see / in broad daylight, / if you thought to look up." One thinks of Henri here: "It is harder to see than it is to express. The whole value of art rests in the artist's ability to see well into what is before him."

"The Bright Side" (the Homer painting is also known as *Light and Shade*), second of the series, relies on chiaroscuro for its full effect as Kooser calls attention to race within the Union war effort. "Though they lie in the sun," up against an army tent in the Homer painting, the light "seems to soak / into their sweaty clothes / and their skin, making them / even more black than they were." African American soldiers, rarely allowed to serve in combat roles, frequently provided food and munitions to the front line, essential to the Union. Kooser underscores the point in an accounting in the poem's final lines, where "five black men" may "have taken on all of the load": "powder kegs," "bags / of potatoes," and "canisters of lead."

The three Confederate "Prisoners from the Front," distinctive in dress and attitude, stand in line. Descriptions, a study of contrasts, are succinct. The youngest, who wears "butternut regalia, is handsome"; the cap on his red hair is "cocked," while the old man wears a tattered coat and "slumps like the very meaning / of surrender, but his jaw is set." Art, Kooser suggests, allows us to revisit the war in a personal way. The eyes of the old soldier are "like flashes / from distant cannon (we have waited / a hundred and forty years / to hear those reports)." The third soldier, "hot and young and ornery," is posturing in his "floppy hat, brim up" with his "military coat unbuttoned / hands stuffed in his pockets, / his mouth poised to spit."

Against the Confederates, Homer has juxtaposed the Union general, dressed in his "neat blue uniform, the cavalry / Saber and fancy black hat." The observer, painter and poet alike, has in his power, as the young captive with "mouth poised to spit," to affect general's mood, which provides painting and poem with a tension that seems to issue from the event itself.

In counterpoint to, or perhaps to balance, "Sharpshooter," the final poem of the series, "The Veteran in a New Field," depicts a returning soldier, who has discarded his Union army jacket, dark and nearly invisible at field's (and painting's) edge and has taken up a scythe at harvest time. Juxtaposed against the literal and metaphorical dark, the golden sun-lit wheat field lies before him. Although the war is over, the veteran will carry a new awareness into his life as a civilian: "Where he has passed, the hot stalks spread / in streaks, like a shell exploding, but that is / behind him. With stiff, bony shoulders / he mows his way into the colors of summer."

Throughout this section, images act as artifacts, juxtaposing present and past: the outline of tools on the pegboard, "like the outlines of hands on the walls / of ancient caves," preserve the past while illustrating what has been lost. Nickel vases on the four corners of the horse-drawn hearse on display at the Seward County Museum at Goehner, described in "At the Country Museum," the Pflueger and South Bend fishing equipment on the yard sale tables in "Casting Reels," the horse that carried us into the nineteenth century when horses pulled plows and buggies, and displays of past life at Morrill Hall, described in "In the Hall of Bones," all remind us life passes by as it continues.

Kooser's interest in and awe of the visual artist is nowhere more apparent than in "A Box of Pastels," one of the few poems in which the poet uses the first-person singular. After a college reading in Philadelphia he dined with a faculty member in the English Department who had, among other mementos from the Modernist period, a wooden box containing the pastels of Mary Cassatt. Although the poem begins with a memory of the evening—placing the "wooden box / in which a rainbow lay dusty and broken" on his knees—it is a meditation on Cassatt herself.

The thirteen poems of section 4 in many ways mirror the collection's initial thirteen. Just as section 1 speaks of our species' past, so does the final section, with images of glaciers, the ancient oak that falls in the Cumberlands, offering an afterimage that is both personal and aesthetic. In "Tectonics," "even one lush green island . . . may slide under the waves / like Atlantis, / scarcely rippling the heart." The sonnet "After Years," which resonates with the work of Ralph Waldo Emerson, considers the image of the loved one as memory recedes.

"That Was I," as critic Wes Mantooth notes, "seems like a crucial statement from a poet who has so often put impersonal observations of strangers into poetry." Many of the poems that comprise *Delights & Shadows*, Mantooth concludes, "emerge naturally from a careful consideration of how the enterprise of writing poems about people intersects with the more important enterprise of living among people." The "I" is no longer the teenage boy in "a leather jacket" with "duck's-ass hair" from "Home Town" written many years earlier. He has grown up and is now an older man who travels to the small towns located in his Bohemian Alps.

The "I" of the poem is archetypal as well as personal. In this case Kooser achieves the two levels of meaning in part by the uncommon syntax of the refrain (called a "burden"), and in part by a distancing, more impersonal description of the presenting figure in each of the three stanzas: "that older man," "the round-shouldered man," and the man "down on one knee." In each case we are invited to observe, as with chiaroscuro, the central figure. In each case the imagined reader is asked to examine the older man closely. In each case time moves on: morning of the first stanza evolves into the afternoon of the second and approaches dark in the third. Though time cannot be stopped, there is still cause for delight.

The first stanza is set in the small town of Thayer, population of seventy, York County, about twenty-eight miles west of his residence. The reader finds "the older man . . . sitting / in a confetti of yellow light and falling leaves" in the horseshoe court overgrown with grass, "like old graves." Then the poem turns: "but I was not letting / my thoughts go there [to courts/graves]." Instead the poet is "looking / with hope to a grapevine draped over / a fence in a neighboring yard, and knowing / that I could hold on," suggesting attachment, even communion, with the earth and others.

In Rising City, a town of about four hundred residents located in Butler County, forty-one miles north and west of Garland, the setting of the second stanza, the reader comes upon "the round-shouldered man" walking the Main Street of the abandoned Mini Golf range. The world he finds before him is "abbreviated"—the "plywood store, / the poor red school, the faded barn"—it is not far-fetched to conjecture, like the abbreviated versions of the classics, Cliffs Notes, originally developed by Rising City native Clifford Hillegass. Not even in the "little events" of the miniature Mini Golf world "could a person control his life." The metaphor with which he compares human loss of control, "the snap / of a grasshopper's wing against a paper cup," is haunting.

Staplehurst Cemetery, just outside of the town it serves, is about seventeen miles west of Garland, closer than that as the crow flies, in the heart of Seward County. It is evening, and Kooser/Everyman is "down on one knee." The poet imagines that the reader sees him as "some lonely old man" trying to make out a name on a stone. Instead, he is the poet kneeling in awe of the "perfect web" of a "handsome black and yellow spider," another miniature world. The spider, small though it may be, is "pumping its legs" trying to shake the poet's footing "as if I were a gift, an enormous moth / that it could snare and eat." This attempt to reverse the food chain is both absurd and comforting as it places human beings within the context of nature. The spider, long associated with the creative act, reminds the reader of the three Fates, the alteration ladies of Greek mythology, whose task it is to spin, measure, and cut the thread of life.

Mortality and hope, death and light, run throughout the fourth section. Lyrics are predominately softer; birds, long-held symbol of the spirit, flit through the pages. The "Screech Owl," "a bird no bigger than a heart," "calls out" in an aural chiaroscuro, "again and again" from the "center of darkness." The poem "The Early Bird," composed of one sentence divided into thirteen lines, six couplets, and a final singlet, hauls up each dawn with "its sweet-sour / wooden-pully notes" so that, like water from a well, we, in the last line, may drink. This early bird is a song bird, much like the poet at his desk at five singing his own song. But the preoccupation of one's later years continues, making its way into the poet's vision of the world, natural and manufactured. With age comes the pairing down of concerns, as in "A Spiral Notebook." Even so, awe remains. Memories of loved ones visit by day and by night in dreams, as in "Starlight," Kooser's two-line poem in which falls, "All night, this soft rain from the distant past."

Delights & Shadows begins with the dawn of the human race and ends with the twilight of one man, riding the winged chariot of human life as though it were a day in time. As "A Happy Birthday" opens, the poet recalls sitting at an open window reading until it was dark. "I could easily have switched on a lamp," he says, but he wanted to be mindful of the moment, "to ride this day down into the night." Recalling the image of his father's hand smoothing the fabric at Tilden's and the unrolled bolt of the quarry road that introduces *Winter Morning Walks*, the poet smoothes "the unreadable page / with the pale gray ghost" of his own hand.

As he moves into darkness, he does not, as Dylan Thomas urges, "rage, rage, against the dying of the light." Kooser's poem is closer to Czeslaw Milosz's nine-line "Gift," in which he describes a moment of transformation and light. "Nature's first green" may be gold, as Robert Frost writes, but as the poem's title suggests, "Nothing gold can stay." Day ends; the "pale gray ghost" of the poet's hand—the same hand that held the pen through which memories funnel into art—is still visible, still chiaroscuro, still speaking to the future.

CHAPTER TWENTY-THREE

"The Ripening Odor of Praise"

I can feel the thick yellow fat of applause
building up in my arteries, friends,
yet I go on, a fool for adoration.

—From "Success"

As Kooser was wondering what to fix for supper Friday evening, August 6, 2004, the telephone rang. He thought it might be his wife calling from Washington DC, where she was on the Pulitzer Prize selection committee in beat journalism.

When he answered, he heard a man's voice. "Ted Kooser, the poet?" Prosser Gifford, director of scholarly programs for the Library of Congress, introduced himself and then asked if Kooser would consider becoming the next U.S. poet laureate.

"I was completely flummoxed," the poet reports. "After we'd hung up, I tried to reach my wife," he reflects. When that proved unsuccessful, he tried to collect himself, "taking deep breaths, pacing back and forth, looking for something to do with my hands. I dislike travel, am fearful of strange places, and had always been terrified of public speaking. How was I going to handle the job of being a public poet?"

Practical matters intervened; by now several DVDs on the chair by the door were past due at the Seward video store. He grabbed the disks and hurried out to the garage. Still preoccupied by the call, Kooser demolished his driver's side mirror on the door frame as he backed out. "Oh, Jesus!" he thought. "First the poet laureate and now this!"

Further distracted by the damage to his car, he drove straight to Bern's Body Shop for an estimate. Soon he was headed back home, "the mirror swinging, thinking about being the poet laureate of the United States, scared to death, beating up on myself for doing such a stupid thing to my Intrepid." Then he noticed the DVDs on the seat where he had tossed them. "It was to be like that for months," he says.

Later that evening he reached Rutledge and several friends, and after soul-searching over the weekend, Kooser said yes to the appointment when Librarian of Congress James Billington called to formally extend the invitation. Kooser would serve as thirteenth poet laureate consultant in poetry to the Library of Congress from October to May, receiving a stipend of $35,000, endowed by the late Archer M. Huntington. Among those who previously held the position were his mentor Karl Shapiro, Elizabeth Bishop, Robert Frost, Billy Collins, Gwendolyn Brooks, and Louise Glück. Although the press release announcing the appointment issued by the Library of Congress notes that Kooser is the "first Poet Laureate chosen from the Great Plains," the position is not new to Plains natives. Probably best known among Plains poet laureates, or poetry consultants as they were called until 1986, are William Stafford, born in Hutchinson, Kansas, in 1914, and Gwendolyn Brooks, born in Topeka in 1917. More recently Mona Van Duyn, born in Waterloo, Iowa, less than a hundred miles from Kooser's birthplace, served the 1992–1993 term. Richard Eberhart (Austin MN) and William Jay Smith (St. Louis MO) are also former laureates.

For the next two years (the poet's tenure was extended with a second term) his life changed dramatically. "It was overwhelming at first," Rutledge says. "We'd get home at 8 o'clock and the phone system was jammed and the e-mail system was jammed." Letters, notes, and cards accumulated in a large bin on the front door until they could be read and answered.

Before Kooser's first official duties the poet traveled north to Deadwood, South Dakota, where he read with Jim Harrison at the South Dakota Festival of Books in September. While back in Nebraska, he chanced upon the work of artist Amanda Hext in a student gallery at the university. Hext's paintings, which characteristically employ chiaroscuro, included "three absolutely stunning portrait heads" that stopped Kooser in his tracks. He purchased these paintings and eventually commissioned her to paint his official U.S. poet laureate portrait. The following month the poet was in Washington DC for a celebratory luncheon with friends, family, and fans, the opening of the annual literary series with his installation as poet laureate, and to speak at the National Book Festival.

As Kooser traveled, he considered on what he might focus during the coming year. Each laureate set his or her own goals: Joseph Brodsky, for example, initiated poetry in airports, supermarkets, and hotel rooms. Maxine Kumin started a popular series of poetry workshops for women at the Library of Congress, while Rita Dove brought together writers to explore the African Diaspora through the eyes of its artists. Robert Hass organized a "Watershed" conference, inviting noted novelists, poets, and storytellers to talk about writing, nature, and community. During his two terms, Billy Collins began Poetry 180, bringing a poem each morning to high school classrooms.

"The way to broaden the audience for poetry," Kooser wrote in his journal during the autumn, "is to offer poems that are of some use, poems that answer questions, pose solutions to everyday problems, but, more important, provide new ways of perceiving the world." The idea of making poetry available through local newspapers was slowly beginning to take shape. In an interview with Tobin Beck, Kooser acknowledged the importance of English teachers and his own interest in assisting them in the teaching of poetry. With the emphasis on national standards, he acknowledged, there seemed to be "less room for the arts altogether, and poetry included." Over and over in meetings with journalists he stressed the importance of poetry as a way to more closely engage the world in order to enrich one's life.

During the four months that followed, Kooser traveled extensively. While in Arlington, Kooser attended a national convention of press associations and tried out his idea of offering national newspapers a free weekly poetry column. "They were wary," he says, "but willing to have a look." "I lobbied him," Rutledge says; "I advised him about it's got to be free; it's got to be short." On a trip to Chicago to read for *Poetry* magazine, Kooser broached the idea of a poetry column with John Barr and Steve Young at the Poetry Foundation; they were enthusiastic from the beginning. By the following April "American Life in Poetry," under the sponsorship of the Poetry Foundation, the Library of Congress, and the UNL Department of English, would become a reality, offering the poem "Neighbors" written by David Allan Evans, poet laureate of South Dakota.

By Christmas Kooser was happy to return, even for a short time, to the routine of domestic life. In his journal he wrote, "It would be a great pleasure to go to the small engine repair shop and order a new chain for my McCullough chain saw, or maybe to just clean the gutters." He was busy while home in Nebraska. NETV featured the poet in mid-December in its weekly news journal "Statewide." The following day he received an honorary degree of letters from the University of Nebraska.

As the year drew to a close, Kooser tallied up the work he had accomplished during his first months as poet laureate: twenty-nine interviews and twenty public appearances. "The lifelong introvert had found himself," he says, "fueled by dutifulness, in an extended frenzy of extroversion."

Travel, readings, interviews, e-mail, phone calls—and awards— resumed after the holidays. On February 1 Kooser was in Washington to introduce his selections, Martin Walls and Claudia Emerson, for the $10,000 Witter Bynner Foundation fellowships, administered by the Library of Congress, for promising poets.

When you learn to play the harmonica, you never know what

might happen, as Robert McCloskey's Lentil learned so well. Kooser was both Lentil and Colonel Carter as he stood before his admirers on February 8 in Lincoln for an "Evening with Ted Kooser," at the Lied Center for Performing Arts. In addition to reading to a capacity audience, Kooser spoke about what it was like to be poet laureate and his philosophy of poetry. Lincoln mayor Coleen Seng presented Kooser with a key to the city.

Although he still woke early to write and still revised extensively, he no longer sent out his work because, he said, "even the worst of them would get published." Come mid-February nearly five hundred women received his annual valentine postcard-poems. For a poet whose sympathies lie with Emerson's idea of cosmic harmony and whose poems are frequently lighted with images from the heavens, Robert Linderholm's decision to name an asteroid after the poet was much appreciated. An amateur astronomer from Cambridge, Nebraska, Linderholm, who has discovered a number of asteroids, has made it a tradition to name them after Nebraskans, including Standing Bear, Mari Sandoz, and Willa Cather. Asteroid 24,918, Tedkooser, has a relatively stable orbit and is visible every several years.

February 2005 saw publication of *The Poetry Home Repair Manual: Practical Advice for Beginning Poets*, dedicated to Kooser's good friend and fellow poet Charles Levendosky, who died the preceding year. The men met in the mid-1980s. Also an editorial page editor and columnist for the *Casper (WY) Star-Tribune*, Levendosky, advocate for first amendment rights until his death, inspired Kooser, as both "poet and citizen."

The Manual reflects lessons learned from mentors and from the actual experience of writing, teaching, and thinking about poetry for over four decades. A poet's education, Kooser believes, consists mostly of reading the poems of others, a relationship with the poetic tradition as well as contemporary poetry, and in the practice, writing, and revising of poem after poem with the reader in mind. The purpose of poetry, which he defines as "language brought to a kind of state of perfection is," he writes, "to reach other people and to touch their hearts." The perfecting—and every poet sets his or her standards—happens through "*extensive* revision," which he calls "the key to transforming a mediocre poem into a work that can touch and even alter a reader's heart."

Kooser focuses on craft, which, he believes, can be taught. His pedagogical approach is based on years of teaching poetry classes and workshops since the late 1960s, as well as by tutorial, since spring 2001. He says he became intrigued with the idea when Dana Gioia described his own tutorial given by Elizabeth Bishop. The inaugural tutorial, like those that have followed, began with a full-class meeting in Andrews Hall and ended with a reading of student work at the pond gazebo of Kooser's home, followed by dinner at the local tavern. Each week between the first and last classes, students met individually with the poet for a critique of their work.

Kooser was also particularly pleased with the publication of a special, limited edition of his essay *Lights on a Ground of Darkness* by the University of Nebraska Press. In March he returned to the Library of Congress for "A Literary Evening with John Prine and Ted Kooser." Kooser had followed the music of the well-known Illinois singer-songwriter long before the musician won the 1991 Grammy for *The Missing Years*. When they met, they discovered that both had been diagnosed with the same kind of cancer and had also undergone successful surgery and radiation treatments. On stage at the Coolidge Auditorium, the men swapped stories and talked about how they came about creating their works.

Later that month Kooser's *Flying at Night*, with selections from *Sure Signs* and *One World at a Time*, was published. Notices were positive, although reviewers tended to pigeonhole Kooser as a regionalist with a simplistic approach to poetry. The poet took it in stride: "When they praise you for your work, it's often fulsome and gassy, and then you feel like, 'Oh, come on, it isn't that good,' then on the other hand, if they come after you, it just hurts like the devil. So it's better really to just go on your way and be blissfully ignorant of what people are saying about you."

Attention soon returned to *Delights & Shadows* when it was

awarded the 2005 Pulitzer Prize for Poetry in April. "If being asked to be Poet Laureate had come as a shock," he reflects, "this was an even bigger one. I had no idea my book, *Delights and Shadows*, was even in the running." He learned of the award by e-mail from the university's public relations office asking him for an "immediate quote." "I staggered out into the front yard and lay down in a pile of leaves, looking up at the sky and wondering what could possibly be next. As I lay there, an *Omaha World-Herald* photographer drove down the lane."

More accustomed to travel, public speaking, and the generally fast-paced life of the last year, Kooser accepted the invitation of the Library of Congress's director of scholarly programs, Prosser Gifford, to serve a second year as poet laureate. Other awards came his way. "Small Rooms in Time," published in *River Teeth* in spring 2004, was included in the 2005 *Best American Essays*, and *Delights & Shadows* received the Midland Authors Award. Kooser marked the end of his first term as laureate with a lecture, "Out of the Ordinary," at the Library of Congress, looking back on his career and reiterating two interrelated themes found in his work: the poem is a way to show something special about ordinary life and a means to stay time.

Kooser's second year as poet laureate went by at the same hectic pace as the first. Some months the poet was "on the road"—and now "in the skies" as he began flying to more distant destinations—three weeks out of four. By early 2006, he was looking forward to the end of his appointment in order to have more time to himself and to fix up his two-room brick storefront that he had purchased for a studio in Dwight, Nebraska, a Czech community twenty miles from Garland.

Writing Brave and Free: Encouraging Words for People Who Want to Start Writing, written by Kooser and long-time friend Steve Cox, was published in the spring. Cox, who had been an acquiring editor for the University of Nebraska Press in the late 1970s, had moved on to the University of Arizona Press, where he is now director emeritus.

A highlight of the spring was Kooser's trip to Ames, Iowa, for Ted Kooser Day, on April 8, 2006. A self-guided tour map was available to those who wished to see his boyhood home on West Ninth Street, his grandmother Kooser's home two blocks away, the schools he attended, Tilden's Department Store, and other sites referenced in *Local Wonders*. The event included a poetry contest for school children K–12 and a reading at the city auditorium, where Kooser graduated from Ames High School in 1957. April was not without troubling news, however; Rutledge was diagnosed with breast cancer and began immediate treatment.

Kooser returned to Washington about once a month to attend to his duties at the Library of Congress. In spring he awarded the 2006 Witter Bynner Fellowships to Joseph Stroud and Connie Wanek. He also met with Pulitzer Prize composer Paul Moravec, who had been commissioned by Opera Omaha to write a piece based on *The Blizzard Voices*. Most of his time, however, was spent crisscrossing the nation. In a recap of his twenty months as poet laureate, Kooser figures that he had appeared in forty-seven states in front of approximately two hundred groups, ranging in size from small book clubs to audiences of over a thousand. "I was interviewed by the media—TV, radio, and spring on about 100 occasions. I received and answered hundreds of letters and e-mails, and have three fifty-five gallon Rubbermaid tubs full of letters and cards I received from well-wishers. My newspaper column, which I plan to continue indefinitely, is in 150–200 newspapers with a potential circulation of nearly 12 million readers."

Over the summer the Nebraska Repertory Theatre premiered a musical, *Local Wonders*, in Lincoln. Cowritten by Virginia Smith, the Theatre's artistic director and actor Paul Amandes, a professor of theatre at Columbia College in Chicago, the musical drew on Kooser's memoir and several poems for its text. Local actors David and Melodee Landis, directed by Robin McKercher, played Kooser and Rutledge.

"The ripening odor of praise" continued as Kooser's tenure as poet laureate drew to a close.

CHAPTER TWENTY-FOUR

"Bright Yellow Leaves Flying"

"This is the life I have chosen."

—*Local Wonders*

By September 2006 Kooser was able to return to his pre-laureate routine, writing in the mornings, painting in his Dwight studio, and teaching his poetry tutorial at the university. His literary life still took time—travel, readings, and mail—but not as much. Kooser's *The Blizzard Voices* was reissued, with a new introduction by the author, in anticipation of Opera Omaha's premier of an oratorio based on the poems. On September 20 Kooser received the Sower Award in the Humanities at the Lied Center of Performing Arts in Lincoln. Given annually by the Nebraska Humanities Council, the Sower recognizes contribution to public understanding of the humanities in the state. At the awards ceremony Kooser acknowledged his first teachers and his wife, Kathleen Rutledge, as his "first and best editor, my counselor and my best friend." Kooser and Rutledge celebrated twenty-nine years of marriage four days later.

About the same time Kooser was contacted by Dr. Bill Lydiatt, the surgeon who had treated the poet for cancer. Professor and director of Head and Neck Surgical Oncology at the University Nebraska Medical Center in Omaha, Lydiatt invited Kooser along with Mark

Gilbert, a Scottish artist, to take part in a pilot three-hour seminar for medical students and residents. The goal of the workshop, held in conjunction with Gilbert's exhibition of forty-two patient portraits, "Saving Faces: Art and Medicine," was to teach observation skills through drawing and poetry.

In June Kooser received some disturbing news. Leonard Nathan, whose health had been failing for some time, had passed away. For more than thirty years Nathan, "a whiz at cutting out unnecessary words," read and critiqued nearly every poem Kooser sent out for publication. In a memorial published in the *Prairie Schooner*, Kooser called Nathan "among the best and most intelligent writers of our age, and, more importantly, among the finest souls that we have been blessed to live our lives among." His wife, Carol, died within the year.

Kooser also announced his final mailing of his Valentine post cards. He sent his first card, "Pocket Poem," in 1986 to 50 women friends; by the 2006 mailing Kooser's list had grown to over 2,700 recipients nationwide. Not to worry, *Valentines*, a collection of his favorites, was to be published in 2008. Kooser dedicated *Valentines* to the memory of Laura Casari, a friend since his earliest days in Lincoln who had died two years earlier.

Beginning with *A Local Habitation & a Name*, the poet has been enamored by the postcard format that accommodates short poems and underscores the desire for relationship and communication. Illustrated by longtime friend Robert Hanna, the twenty-three poems are connected by sentiment, the color red, or the shape of a heart; most were published before in journals, previous Kooser collections, or fine art editions.

Kooser admits in the introduction to stealing the idea of valentines from a friend and neighbor, Dace Burdic, a woman, he writes, "who enjoys having fun." Originally printed on white first-class postcards, they were later embellished with a small red heart. Over the years Kooser sometimes sent his postcards to the Valentine, Nebraska, post office, with its heart-shaped holiday postmark, for mailing.

As Allan Benn notes, the twenty-three poems of *Valentines* "run an emotional gamut from the soft romance we expect in a Valentine to the hard-edged parades." The collection opens with "Pocket Poem," which calls attention to love's small gestures. Some poems are bittersweet: love gone wrong, love's detours, and affection in a world that is not always hospitable. "Chinese Checkers," for example, juxtaposes "two men in rags" playing checkers for candy and "laughing like crazy" with depersonalized "Commerce," who, like Big Brother, stands "behind mirrored windows, / disapproving."

Valentines celebrates the facets of love and its ramifications, not always what we might expect. "Barn Owl" is, perhaps, the most frightening because of its tender beginning that becomes potentially deadly as the movement within the poem advances. A sonnet, the form of the traditional love poem, it begins with the description of the barn owl, hidden in its nest, "a white heart woven of snowy feathers / in which wide eyes of welcome open / to you as you climb the rickety ladder / into my love." Kooser employs one of his characteristic turns, surprising, unhinging, and catching the reader unaware as he reveals the owl's beak at the center of its heart-shaped face, "a golden hook / the size of a finger ring," to hold the beloved, "plumpest sweetheart mouse of mine." Originally published in *Weather Central*, "Barn Owl" is a wonderful poem to read aloud. Students become enchanted with the unfolding of the sounds and rhythm of the lines, the seductive language, the heightened sense of romantic love, and are led forward by a compelling enjambment; they become "hooked" and then captured by the poem as it captures an aspect of love.

Benn points out that "*Valentines* has plenty of sex," calling "A Perfect Heart"—often misread as saccharine—"an exercise in double *entendre*." Seasoned love is celebrated in "In a Light Late-winter Wind," as one metaphor transforms seamlessly into the next, and in "Splitting the Order," where the details of movement and environment pull the reader into a café and an elderly couple's loving relationship. *Valentines* concludes with "Hog-Nosed Snake," according to Benn "as mischievously phallic as a poem could be," full of joy and discovery, written to his wife who, following her own successful treatment for cancer, retired as editor of the *Lincoln Journal Star*.

"It's only fitting," Kooser says, that "my last valentine should turn its attention back to her. You'll see that this last poem is indeed the poem of a man who has careened beyond the romantic into an altogether different age."

Hanna, whose pen and ink drawings accompany the poems, is well known in his own right for *A Nebraska Portfolio*, a book of drawings and watercolors that celebrate the state. A recipient of the Nebraska Architects Honor Award and the Central States Regional Honor Award for excellence in architectural design, Hanna writes in his introduction that his goal is to "give a glimpse of the world where they [the poems] were written . . . [and] reflect the aesthetic temper of Ted's writing space." Hanna introduces readers to Alice the dog, the Kooser acreage, his home and writing studio, the gazebo and pond, and his storefront in Dwight.

Recognition continued for Kooser and for Rutledge, who received an Alumni Awards of Excellence, Service to the Profession Award, in April for her work at the *Lincoln Journal Star*. The following month Kooser was awarded an honorary doctorate from SUNY's Bingham University. On his sixty-ninth birthday, Lincoln Public Schools broke ground for Kooser Elementary School. The poet attended along with Rutledge, his son, and granddaughter. "Of all the honors I've received," he said at the groundbreaking ceremony, "this is one that will mean the most to me over a long period of time."

September 12, 2008, saw the world premier of the oratorio *The Blizzard Voices*, composed by Pulitzer Prize-winner Paul Moravec. Commissioned by Opera Omaha under the artistic direction of Stewart Robertson, the oratorio incorporated earlier dramatic effects—skip rope rhythms, for example—that were part of the Lincoln Community Playhouse Gallery Theatre production in 1981. For six singers and a chorus, the score offers a timeless quality in which men and women wrestle for survival. Additions to the original text, from Job and the Psalms, recalling the fire and brimstone of Jonathan Edwards, change the mood and character of the story. For Kooser, a Plains native, weather is seen as a naturally occurring phenomena rather than punishment or reward by a supreme being.

While Kooser's relationship to religion has never been overt, he has often referred to writing poetry as a devotional act. Raised a Methodist, he attended the Unitarian church in Lincoln off and on for many years. In 2008 Kooser and his wife became active members of St. Andrew's Episcopal Church in Seward. In an essay, "Metaphor and Faith," Kooser begins with Robert Frost's well-known adage, "With so many ladders going up everywhere, there must be something for them to lean against," linking this world with, he hopes, the next. Using Frost's "The Silken Tent" as a template, Kooser's metaphor brings together "That abiding universal order" and the "worldwide diversity of beliefs." "My faith is, as I see it," Kooser concludes, "a kind of beautiful silken tent, and God is the *tenor* [of the metaphor] from which that *vehicle* lifts away."

Kooser continues to work in his rural Garland studio as well as in Dwight. His process remains very much the same as when he worked in insurance. An early morning writer, the poet makes his coffee and turns to his notebook, part diary and part workbook. "I start," he says, "by making a couple diary style entries about the weather and what I did last night or what I'm reading. . . . Then I break away and begin to let things fall into my mind. Sometimes I might write down a little list of things." After writing a few lines that seem to be heading in a particular direction, he copies them on to the computer and continues his work. "I have to do it early in the morning . . . I think it's because when you are just waking up, your mind is groping for connections."

In Dwight, Kooser has filled his studio windows with artificial flowers salvaged from Lincoln thrift shops. He has painted door and window casings with a variety of flowers, hearts, leaves, and vines, reminiscent of Pennsylvania Dutch designs. "When people ask what I'm doing there," he says, "I tell them that I am The Artificial Florist."

The sign on the plate glass window to the right of the door reads: "Poetry Made and Repaired Here." Inside is the writing room with walls of books and a partners desk, moved from Rutledge's grandmother's home in Valentine. In the second room an easel stands ready. As Kooser suggests, quoting American sculptor Louise Nevelson, "The essence of living is in doing, not in the prizes."

Should a child drop by to visit Kooser in Dwight, out the back door a tall sturdy maple stands, lower limbs set just so for easy climbing. If it's Wednesday, friends are often treated to the lunch special up the street at Cy's Café, serving traditional Czech fare—roast pork, dumplings, and sauerkraut—for under five dollars. After lunch there might be time to walk over to the Assumption Catholic Church and go around back to visit the small brick chapel where a life-sized replica of St. Cecilia, patron saint of music, rests in peace. After the walk back to the studio, Kooser waves good-bye and returns to work.

On other days Kooser joins friends in Lincoln for lunch and conversation. Publishing continues. New poems have begun to appear in literary journals, and *The Poets Guide to the Birds*, an anthology of poems coedited with Judith Kitchen, was published in 2009 by Anhinga Press. For the last several years Kooser's son has lived nearby, and on April 15, 2009, the poet welcomed his second grandchild, Penelope Helen, into the family.

To celebrate his seventieth birthday, Kooser and Robert Hanna traveled to the Nebraska sandhills to offer workshops in memoir writing and watercolor. While visiting Valentine, the poet donated to the Cherry County Historical Society a replica of the house that he constructed after the home of his wife's grandparents on Cherry Street. Although miniature, the house, featured in Kooser's essay "Small Rooms in Time," is six feet long, nearly three feet wide, and weighs over two hundred pounds. As precise in his carpentry as he is in his poetry, Kooser laid a dining room floor with small slats of hardwood and fashioned a black-and-white checkered floor in the kitchen.

Kooser Elementary School was formally dedicated in fall 2009. The poet, who donated his portrait by artist Amanda Hext to the school, spoke before a crowd of three hundred and reminisced about his own elementary school experience at Beardshear in Ames. He recalled his teachers—"Miss Carlson, Mrs. Thompson, Miss Mabie, Miss Kirby—as well as Mr. Ben Shockley, who kept the furnace going and mopped up after us." Kooser noted that "What makes any school memorable is not its name or its location but the people who give their lives to the education. I am a poet today," he continued, "because Miss Edith Kirby, whom I remember so well, right down to the elevated shoe she wore on one foot, showed me the pleasures of poetry. . . . It's the teachers in this world who do the most important work of all." Candlewick Press, which published Kooser's first children's book, donated 160 books to the new Kooser Elementary School library to celebrate the school's opening. *Bag in the Wind*, "the story of a plastic bag," was published in February 2010. Later that year Kooser donated $25,000 to begin an endowment fund for the school.

In May at the Ojai Music Festival composer Maria Schneider premiered *Winter Morning Walks*, based on Kooser's collection of the same name. Several months later the musical version, *Local Wonders*, opened in Lincoln to favorable reviews. Cowritten by Paul Amandes and Virginia Smith and directed by Smith, the musical was performed by Amandes in the role of Kooser and Anne Hills as Rutledge in the Johnnie Carson Theatre at the Lied Center. The University of Nebraska–Lincoln acquired the poet's correspondence, journals, notebooks, and other materials for further study of his work.

Literary retirement doesn't appear to be in Kooser's plans. His second children's book, *House Held Up by Trees*, based on a deserted house near Garland, appeared in 2012, as did a fine arts chapbook, *Together*, published by Brooding Heron Press. A short film adaptation of the poem "Pearl," which appears in *Delights & Shadows*, was completed by Dan Butler in 2011. Butler, who plays Kooser, is joined by stage and screen actress Frances Sternhagen, who plays Pearl Richards. A special viewing was held at the Mary Riepma Ross Media Arts Center in Lincoln with a conversation between Butler and Kooser following.

Kooser is currently editing the new and selected poems of Jared Carter due out in spring of 2014. *Bell in the Bridge*, his third book for children, is also scheduled for 2014. Inspired by landscape painter Keith Jacobshagen's hardbound orange engineer's field books with drawings, watercolor sketches, and observations, Kooser has written *The Wheeling Year: A Poet's Field Book*, composed of "sketches and landscape studies made out of words," also to appear in the fall. Through his writing, Kooser continues to "honor and affirm life," his goal all along. His full-length poetry collection, *Splitting an Order*, will be published in 2014 by Copper Canyon Press.

At the eastern edge of Iowa, the Mississippi River still stretches along its sandy bank like a waking cat along the leg of a friend. In the valley that Marquette and Joliet traveled three hundred years ago, farm stands burst with honey, wine, and stacks of zucchini, watermelon, tomatoes, and corn; Jolly Ridge Road still runs out toward the Meyers' place. Although John Moser's Standard Oil service station no longer stands just south of Guttenberg, the small white house still serves as anchor for a Moser family business, Murray's Country Garden & Outdoor Store, owned by a Kooser cousin and her husband. In "House by the Road," Kooser writes,

> . . . where Liz Moser's white chickens
> stepped with such purpose over the lawn,
> a fleet of wet pallets with seedlings
> nodding in flats is lashed by green hoses
> to the dock of the present.

Many years ago Theodore Briggs Kooser pointed out artist Velma Rayness's house to his young son as they walked past. Today the poet that boy became has, by the side of Branched Oak Road in a corner of the Bohemian Alps, the "house just like hers" that he has always wanted for himself. "This is the life I have chosen," he described in *Local Wonders*, "one in which I can pass by on the outside, looking back in—into a world in static diorama, the world that Edward Hopper seemed to see. Driving east, the globe spins beneath me, the marigold yellow centerline on the old Lincoln Highway like a stripe on the whistling top. State Center rushes into the past, bright yellow leaves flying behind."

Ted Kooser is still on the move, and those "bright yellow leaves" are still flying.

Source Acknowledgments

Permission to quote from Ted Kooser's poems, letters, and prose (published and unpublished) is from Ted Kooser.

"In the Laundromat," by Ted Kooser, originally published in *Not Coming to Be Barked At* (Pentagram Press, 1976). Reprinted by permission from the author.

An earlier version of "Part Four: "American Scripture, 1980–1994: *Weather Central*" first appeared as "The 'In-Between': Landscapes of Transformation in Ted Kooser's *Weather Central*" in *Great Plains Quarterly* 19, no. 2, 1999.

Karl Shapiro's letters used by permission of the Shapiro Estate, Robert Phillips, literary executor.

"Etude" from *Weather Central*, by Ted Kooser, © 1994. Reprinted by permission from the University of Pittsburgh Press.

An earlier version of "Part Five: 'Feeling the Speed,' 1995–Today: *Winter Morning Walks*" first appeared as "When a Walk Is a Poem: *Winter Morning Walks, A Chronicle of Survival*, by Ted Kooser" in *Midwest Quarterly* 45, no. 4 (2004): 399–414.

["The quarry road tumbles towards me"] from *Winter Morning Walks: One Hundred Postcards to Jim Harrison*. Copyright © 2001 by Ted Kooser. Reprinted with permission from The Permissions Company, Inc., on behalf of Carnegie Mellon University Press, www.cmu.edu/universitypress.

"Walking on Tiptoe" from *Delights & Shadows*. Copyright © 2004 by Ted Kooser. Reprinted with permission from The Permissions Company, Inc., on behalf of Copper Canyon Press.

Notes

1. OFFICIAL ENTRY

3 **paid their hospital bill:** Kooser, *Local Wonders*, 52.

3 **Upstairs apartment on Carroll Avenue and subsequent information about growing up at 109 West Ninth Street:** Kooser, letter to author, July 15, 2002.

3 **Historic Old Town:** Anderson, "Old Town."

4 **Originally from Württemberg:** "Descendants of Johannes Michael Kosser," Kooser Collection, Don L. Love Memorial Library, University of Nebraska–Lincoln. Unless otherwise indicated, all Kooser correspondence, journals, workbooks, and unpublished materials quoted may be found in the Kooser Collection noted above.

4 **During the 1840s:** Hilton, "Education," 5.

4 **Hans Michael Kosser and Anna Maria Sybilla:** "Descendants of Johannes Michael Kosser."

4 **The town of Ames:** Black, "Ames Centennial History," 36.

4 **Grace E. Lang:** "Grace E. Lang," Iowa State Census Collection, 1836–1925 (1905), Ancestry.com, 13.

5 **The ingenious young boy:** Kooser, *Local Wonders*, 54–55.

5 **end of farm subsidies:** Hunter, "The Farmer Feeds," 13.

5 **forced to mortgage:** *Funk and Wagnalls New World Encyclopedia*, s.v. "Iowa."

5 **her first husband, Calvin Lake:** Lake, Florence's first husband, managed Ames Canning Company. Later Florence would marry Jack (Ralph) Mayo, who worked for Independent Lumber in Omaha. Kooser, e-mail to author, July 16, 2007.

6 **They married**: "Vera Deloras Moser and Theodore Briggs Kooser Wed in Dr. Allen's Home," *Clinton (IA) Herald*, October 20, 1937, 7.

6 **Ames Celebrated**: "Ames Diamond Jubilee Celebration," Ames Historical Society, June 25, 2007, http://www.ameshistoricalsociety.org/.

6 **the children's uncle Charlie**: "Derral C. Kooser," U.S. World War II Army Enlistment Records, 1938–1946, Ancestry.com; National Archives and Records Administration, U.S. World War II Army Enlistment Records, 1938–1946, http://aad.archives.gov/aad/series-description.jsp?s=3360.

6 **Mabel, with her daughter, Janice**: Langmack, e-mail to author, November 11, 2007.

6 **A total of**: "Men and Women Join the Military," *Iowa's World War II Stories*, Iowa Public Television, http://iptv.org/IowaPathways/mypath.cfm?ounid=ob_261.

6 **served in the Pacific**: "Margaret Lola Kooser," Ames Historical Society, http://ameshistoricalsociety.org/vets/ww2_vets_k/kooser_margaret_lola.htm. Margaret is the daughter of Belle Kooser, whose letter Ted Kooser will feature in his poem "A Letter from Aunt Belle."

6 **"It would eventually be proven"**: Kooser, *Local Wonders*, 107.

6 **"Spotter Cards"**: "World War II Aircraft Spotting Cards," Ames Historical Society, http://ameshistoricalsociety.org/exhibits/aircraft_spottingcards.

6 **"Though we were never"**: Kooser, *Local Wonders*, 107.

7 **descended from immigrants**: Kooser, *Local Wonders*, 107.

2. AN EMERGING IMAGINATION

8 **Even with the threat**: Kooser, *Local Wonders*, 108.

8 **If their parents argued**: Clark and Saiser, *Road Trip*, 224.

8 **"I could do no wrong"**: Clark and Saiser, *Road Trip*, 224.

8 **"soul-mates"**: Langmack, e-mail, November 2, 2007.

8 **"type of woman"**: Kooser, letter to Rev. Lloyd Brockmeyer, April 7, 1998. Thanks to Ted Kooser, who shared his letters with me when they were in his possession. Now his correspondence, journals, and other materials may be found in the Kooser Collection noted above.

9 **careful management**: Kooser, *Local Wonders*, 52–53.

9 **Teddy adored**: Kooser, *Local Wonders*, 55.

9 "The Necktie": Kooser, *Delights*, 31.

9 One long afternoon: Kooser, *Local Wonders*, 55.

9 worked hard: Langmack, e-mail, November 2, 2007.

9 "good at describing people": Meats, "Tribute," 335.

9 named manager: According to Kooser, when his father was sixty, he was transferred to the Cedar Rapids Younkers, where he worked until his retirement at sixty-five in 1967.

9 over 8,300 Iowa men and women: Loren Horton, "Life Was Never the Same Again," World War II, Iowa Pathways: Iowa History Resources for Students and Teachers, http:iptv.org/iowapathways/mypath.cfm?ounid=ob_261.

9 atomic strike: "Survival under Atomic Attack," Ames Historical Society, http://ameshistoricalsociety.org/exhibits/events/atomic_attack.

9 by many accounts: compiled from conversations with and e-mails from Judith Kooser Langmack, Norton Mezvinsky, Edward Mezvinsky, and Larry Christie.

10 Saturday afternoons: McNeill, "Some World War II Memories in Ames, Part Two." *Intelligencer*. Ames Historical Society. http://www.ameshistoricalsociety.org/pdf/AHSNewsletter_2_05.pdf.

10 cowboy shirt: Kooser, *Local Wonders*, 51. "It still fits," Kooser writes, "though the style is quaint. . . . It's the kind of shirt Roy Rogers wore for the Saturday matinees when I was a boy."

10 Koosers belonged: Langmack, e-mail, November 11, 2007.

10 "my first experience": Kooser, *Local Wonders*, 6.

10 twenty books: Meats, "Tribute," 336.

10 "snow-bank punch": Kooser, *Local Wonders*, 6.

10 dramas of stabbings: Langmack, e-mail, November 11, 2007.

10 favorite game: Kooser, *Local Wonders*, 64.

10 hundreds of them: Kooser, *Local Wonders*, 86.

11 "big and small": Kooser, *Local Wonders*, 87.

11 Kooser describes his uncle: Kooser, *Local Wonders*, 132.

11 delighting the children: Kooser, *Local Wonders*, 86.

11 Mrs. Kooser hadn't wanted: Kooser, *Local Wonders*, 89.

11 Judy and Teddy spent: Kooser, *Local Wonders*, 132–33.

11 Some Saturday nights: Kooser, *Local Wonders*, 88.

12 Complications set in: "Mrs. Charles F. Kooser Dies of Heart Attack," *Ames (IA) Daily Tribune*, August 17, 1948. Her grandson's recollection is that she died at the Kooser home.

12 "silent, dark-suited old men": Kooser, *Local Wonders*, 89.

12 Uncle Tubby auctioned off: Kooser, *Local Wonders*, 89-91.

12 "loveliest whistle": Kooser, *Local Wonders*, 92.

13 "I tried hard to fit in": Kooser, *Local Wonders*, 142.

13 Lentil's story: Kooser provides a summary in Kooser, *Local Wonders*, 141.

13 wants to be special: Kooser, *Local Wonders*, 142.

13 bought himself a harmonica: Kooser, *Local Wonders*, 42.

14 "This book belongs to": Kooser, *Local Wonders*, 141.

3. SUMMERS IN PARADISE

15 The Paleozoic Plateau: Geological information about the area is from Prior, *Landforms of Iowa*.

16 valley's beauty: Kooser, "Lights," 4.

16 "door to the prairie": WPA *Guide*, 350.

16 Western Settlement Society: Jacobson, *Guttenberg, Iowa*, as quoted in "History" section of Guttenberg: Historic Rivertown website, www.cityofguttenberg.com.

16 Kooser's maternal: Information provided by Ted Kooser unless otherwise noted.

17 In 1851: G. Williams, "Immigration," Clayton Documents.

17 Three years later: Price, "John R. Moser," *History*, 286-87.

17 came ashore: Kooser, "Lights," 12-13.

17 counterforce contained: The author is indebted to Leo Marx's *The Machine in the Garden: Technology and the Pastoral Ideal in America* for his thoughts on the pastoral tradition in the United States.

17 fellow passenger: G. Williams, "Immigration."

17 Anna, widow: Kooser, "Lights," 18.

17 studied the portraits: Kooser, "Lights," 18.

17 They died within: Price, "John R. Moser," *History*, 286.

18 he and Elizabeth married: Price, "John R. Moser," *History*, 286.

18 caught fire: Kooser, "Lights," 19.

18 In their sixties: Kooser, "Lights," 19-20.

18 became life-long friends: "We always called her Aunt Sticky, because Mother called her Sticky. They were best friends all their lives, and it was Aunt Sticky who gave me that flow blue china I've written about [Kooser, *Delights*, "Flow Blue China"]. I loved her like a real aunt": Kooser, e-mail, July 16, 2007. "Lights" includes the description of a visit that he, his wife, his son, and Ruth Stickford

Kregel made to the Pioneer Rock Church just south of Guttenberg that Kooser's great-grandfather Morarend built in the 1850s.
Aunt Sticky died July 11, 1998, at the Guttenberg Care Center, four
months after the poet's mother.

18 **patch of blue, pink salmon, and yellow irises:** Kooser, "Lights," 5.

18 **"taking a midday nap":** Kooser, "Lights," 3.

19 **Because Guttenberg:** "Antagonism toward Germans and their
language escalated nationwide but [Iowa Governor William C.]
Harding became the only governor in the United States to outlaw
the public use of *all* foreign languages. . . . He was convinced that
destroying the vital bond of language within ethnic communities
would force assimilation of minorities into the dominant culture
and heighten a sense of patriotism in a time of war." See Frese,
"Divided."

19 **Teddy relished:** Kooser, "Lights," 5.

19 **The town and surrounding hills:** Kooser, "Lights," 15.

20 **even as an old man:** Kooser, "Lights," 17.

20 **dark curls:** Kooser, "Lights," 10.

20 **Summer visits included:** Kooser, "Lights," 32.

20 **Pete, who once worked:** Kooser, "Lights," 29.

20 **first cousin Harvey:** Information about Harvey Noack taken from
his obituary, "Harvey Noack Taken by Death," *Guttenberg (IA) Press*,
April 18, 1963, 4, unless otherwise noted.

21 **treasure trove:** Kooser, "Lights," 8, 9, 33.

21 **"We are learning":** Kooser, "Lights," 9.

21 **Other nights:** Kooser, "Lights," 10.

4. LOOKING THE PART

22 **"I love my dog":** Clark and Saiser, *Road Trip*, 223.

22 **"The Listeners":** Kooser, *Poetry Home Repair*, 9–12.

23 **On Saturdays:** Kooser, *Local Wonders*, 135.

23 **making posters:** Kooser, "Straight Answers."

23 **"A library is like an airport":** Kooser, *Local Wonders*, 89.

23 **small-town library:** Kooser, "Straight Answers," 31.

23 **Also important:** Kooser, *Local Wonders*, 65.

23 **"I've spent my life":** Kooser, *Local Wonders*, 66.

23 **state with a long:** Information taken from Andrews, *Literary History of Iowa* unless otherwise noted.

24 **Midwest literary movement:** Frederick, "Ruth Suckow," 4.

24 **Garland's early novels:** *Main-Travelled Roads* (1891), *Boy Life on the Prairie* (1899), *A Son of the Middle Border* (1917), and *A Daughter of the Middle Border* (1921), which won the Pulitzer Prize in 1922.

24 **Frederick Manford:** *The Golden Bowl* (1944), *Boy Almighty* (1945), and *This Is the Year* (1947), about the day-to-day life of a Frisian farmer, were particularly popular.

24 **long-time admirer:** Kooser, in conversation with author.

25 **acquaintance of Meredith Willson:** Kooser, in conversation with author.

25 **he was rebellious:** Clark and Saiser, *Road Trip*, 224.

25 **his relationship with:** Toth, phone interview.

25 **Kooser and Jack Winkler:** Puffett, "Nightcrawlers Club."

25 **according to Winkler:** Krapfl, "Ames Native." Kooser remembers it as a Ford engine.

26 **high school teacher:** Kooser, e-mail to author, July 26, 2005.

26 **"beatnik [Beat] poets":** Krapfl, "Ames Native."

26 **In a 1979 interview:** Tawney, "Interview," 41.

26 **"always interested":** Stillman, "Famous Poet."

26 **He elaborates:** Kooser, "Two Poets," 3.

26 **to be a famous poet:** Kooser, "Two Poets," 4.

26 **"there were girls":** Kooser, "Two Poets," 3, 4.

28 **dancing lessons:** "Country Club Hosts 135 Teen-Agers," *Ames Tribune*, June 25, 1956 (courtesy of the Ames Historical Society).

28 **"Susan and I were acquaintances":** Kooser, e-mail to author, June 23, 2009.

28 **apprenticeship with Mullica:** Information about Kooser's art training, personal interview, April 12, 2011, unless otherwise noted. "Gold Leaf" appears in Kooser, *Riding with Colonel Carter*.

28 **no question:** Langmack, e-mail, November 2, 2007. Judith went to Simpson College, Indianola, Iowa, to major in education and taught English in junior high school in Cedar Rapids for many years.

28 **visited his uncle:** Kooser Drive on the present ISU campus is named for Kooser's uncle Tubby, Herold L. Kooser. David Craft and Steve Jones, "For Whom It Is Named: Names of Halls, Buildings, Streets, Residence Hall Houses and Other Facilities at Iowa State University." University Archives, 2003 ed., http://www.public.iastate.edu/~isu150/history/forwhom.html.

28 **nine-mural design:** "About the murals," *Grant Wood Murals*, e-Library@Iowa State University, lib.iastate.edu/info/6292.

29 **spent his free time:** Kooser, *Local Wonders*, 143.

5. *KING, A DOG OF THE NORTH*

30 **King, A Dog of the North:** Information in this chapter relating to the King story is from Kooser, *Local Wonders*, 144–45. When I initially read this account, I was convinced that I had read that same book and was surprised to learn that Kooser had imagined it. Further research led to Rufus King's *North Star: A Dog Story of the Canadian Northwest* and Jack London's *Call of the Wild*. Dog stories are, as Kooser points out, "a staple of juvenile reading." "Sergeant Preston of the Yukon" was a long-time radio and then television favorite that featured Yukon King, the brave Alaskan husky.

31 **New Directions paperback:** Tawney, "Interview," 41.

31 **Most of a poet's education:** Kooser, *Poetry Home Repair*, xi.

31 **Soon he discovered:** Kooser, personal interview, January 16, 2006.

31 **"But the craft of careful writing":** Kooser, *Poetry Home Repair*, 4.

31 **"The first assignment":** Clark and Saiser, *Road Trip*, 227.

31 **"little sugary,":** Kooser, e-mail to author, June 6, 2006.

32 **He [Jumper] believed:** Tawney, "Interview," 42.

32 **put a premium on:** According to Dr. Richard Herrnstadt, a faculty member at the time, Jumper was well liked and dedicated to his students. He published short critical pieces on poets Emily Dickinson and E. E. Cummings, acted in Ames Community Theatre productions, and served as a theater critic for the *Ames (IA) Tribune* for many years. Herrnstadt, telephone interview.

32 **Kooser credits:** Tawney, "Interview," 42.

32 **Other members of the group:** Krapfl, "Ames Native."

32 **rallying point:** Christie, telephone interview.

33 **Kooser first encountered:** Tressler, e-mail, September 14, 2007. Subsequent information regarding their meeting is also from Tressler, unless otherwise noted.

33 **cache of Kooser's letters:** Dates of letters are included in text.

33 **circus mural:** The painting now hangs in Kooser's barn.

35 **tossed his $12 slide rule:** Krapfl, "Ted Kooser." Kooser took a class in literary criticism with Buell Lipa, professor of English at ISU and Susan Allen Toth's stepfather. Fortunately, Kooser writes, his

550-line rhyming poem in response to Pope's "Essay on Criticism"
has been lost. Kooser, e-mail to author, June 23, 2009.

35 **"I was certain"**: Kooser, *Local Wonders*, 84.

36 **took up residence**: Kooser, *Local Wonders*, 84.

37 **parents moved from Ames**: Kooser, letter to Brockmeyer, April 9, 1998.

37 **he roomed with**: Kooser, *Local Wonders*, 103.

6. MOVING GIBRALTAR

38 **"prophylactic measure"**: Kooser, to author, June 15, 2007.
Although approved by the FDA in 1960, pills were initially not
available in all U.S. states to married women until 1965 and not to
unmarried women until 1972.

38 **Kooser returned with his family**: Kooser, "Lights," 33.

39 **"He was by then"**: Kooser, "Lights," 31.

42 **kids fighting teachers**: Tawney, "Interview," 42.

42 **The high point**: "Tressler-Kooser Vows Said at Methodist
Church." *Marshalltown (IA) Times Republican*, November 19, 1963, 12.

43 **"I had no other skills"**: Tawney, "Interview," 42.

43 **"the glass windows"**: Kooser, *Local Wonders*, 143.

43 **Kooser mulled**: Kooser, "Karl Shapiro," 30.

7. THE MOVE TO NEBRASKA

47 **Ted and Diana Kooser**: Kooser, "Karl Shapiro," 30.

47 **Kooser remembers**: Kooser, "Review of *Reports*."

47 **trucking and railroad hub**: Sawyer, *Centennial History*, 235.

47 **"American alphabetical towns"**: Shapiro, *Reports*, 176.

48 **quickly settled**: Kooser, letter to author, February 15, 2008.

48 **undergoing substantial change**: Sawyer, *Centennial History*, 216.

48 **Clifford Harding**: Sawyer, *Centennial History*, 171. Husker football
fans may remember 1963 as Bob Devaney's second year as head
coach of the Nebraska Cornhuskers and Frank Solich's first year
as Husker fullback. Former football star Tom Osborne, who had
returned to the university after three seasons with the National
Football League and worked as a graduate assistant under Devaney, earned his master's degree in educational psychology the
same year. (Osborne, who received his doctorate in 1965, was
named head coach in 1973.)

48 **At twenty-two:** Labrie, "Karl Shapiro," 399–405.

49 **prestigious *Poetry* magazine:** Oostdijk, "'Someplace called Poetry,'" 346–57.

49 **geographic exclusivity:** Stewart, *Prairie Schooner Story*, 58, 69.

49 **Many would not:** Raz, personal interview. Hilda Raz served as the *Prairie Schooner*'s fifth editor (1987 to 2010).

49 **Shapiro seemed to enjoy:** Aronow, "Pulitzer Prize Winning Poet," 17.

49 **By the time Kooser arrived:** Kooser, "Karl Shapiro," 31.

49 **Nebraska was not:** Shapiro, *Edsel*.

49 **resigned his post:** "Karl Shapiro: 1913–2000," *Prairie Schooner*, http://webdelsol.com/Prairie_Schooner/html/shapiro.html.

50 **Kooser remembers his mentor:** Kooser, "Karl Shapiro," 31.

50 **"There were at least two Karl Shapiros":** Lemon, personal interview.

50 **"Brooks and Warren":** Olson, personal interview.

50 **railed against:** Shapiro, *Edsel*, 148–50.

51 **Whitman was:** Shapiro, "Maleboge," 51. Shapiro, with department chair James E. Miller Jr. and colleague Bernice Slote, published *Start with the Sun: Studies in Cosmic Poetry* in 1960. The collection of essays examined the "enduring vitality" of Walt Whitman and, according to Miller, a "daring enterprise, flying in the face of the dominant literary voices of the time" (Miller, "Karl Shapiro," 45). What the collection of essay points to is the impact of the work of Alexander von Humboldt, whose notion of the Cosmos, a "harmoniously ordered whole," on Emerson, Thoreau, Whitman, and many of the poets who followed. Laura Dassow Walls's *The Passage to Cosmos: Alexander von Humboldt and the Shaping of America* is indispensable reading, Whitman was said to have written *Leaves of Grass* with a copy of Humboldt's *Cosmos* on his desk. Like Thoreau, who copied passages of Humboldt's works into his own notebooks, Whitman made Humboldt's thought his own and incorporated much of Humboldt's thinking into his poetry. Humboldt's thought has made its way, some would say nearly undetected, into the work of Frost, Kooser, and many others writing today. A study of Humboldt's impact on American poetry is long overdue.

51 **In the classroom:** Kooser, interview with author, January 16, 2006.

52 **poetry workshops:** Kooser, interview with author, January 16, 2006.

52 **Kooser found inspiration:** Kooser, "Karl Shapiro," 30.

52 **end of the first semester:** Kooser, "Karl Shapiro," 31.

52 **method of instruction:** Shapiro, *Edsel*, 114.

53 **"we often took long drives":** Kooser, "Karl Shapiro," 32.

53 **stop to walk the fields:** Tressler, personal interview.

54 **"Where I was from":** Kooser, interview with author, June 6, 2006.

8. *JOURNEY TO A PLACE OF WORK*

55 **If you really want:** Kooser, "Karl Shapiro," 31.

55 **"I thought, what the hell":** Tawney, "Interview," 42.

56 **answering queries:** Kooser, letter to author February 15, 2008.

56 **the poet wrote:** Kooser, to Wilber Gaffney, July 25, 1964.

56 **Poet Don Jones:** letter to author, June 8, 2006.

56 **the pay was good:** Tawney, "Interview," 42.

56 **"visited English classes":** Kooser, "Karl Shapiro," 32.

57 **visual artists:** Kooser, interview with author, April 12, 2011.

57 **The group talked:** Kooser, interview with author, April 12, 2011.

57 **touchstone:** Kooser, interview with author, April 12, 2011. Henri, whose father hailed from Nebraska, spent many of his childhood summers in the state.

57 **"so very many poets around":** Kooser, interview with author, June 28, 2008.

57 **Lebsack's Tavern:** Kooser, letter to author, February 15, 2008.

58 **Poet Don Welch:** Welch, e-mail to author, May 5, 2008.

58 **Bill Kloefkorn:** Kloefkorn, personal interview.

58 **Roy Scheele:** Scheele, personal interview.

58 **he was increasingly discontent:** Shapiro, *Edsel*, 177; Evalyn Katz and Karl Shapiro were divorced January 1967.

58 **He continued to teach:** A thinly disguised account of Shapiro's last years at the university is chronicled in *Edsel*.

58 **Stryk observed:** Stryk, *Heartland*, xxii.

59 **"It is my hope":** Stryk, *Heartland*, x.

59 **pastoral impulse:** Barillas, *Midwestern Pastoral*, 12.

61 **the pastoral focuses:** Barillas, *Midwestern Pastoral*, 12.

60 **reflection of place:** Kooser, letter to Jones, August 20, 1967.

61 **provides a window:** Kooser, "Small Rooms in Time," 2.

61 **read proofs:** Kooser, letter to Virginia Faulkner, January 27, 1969.

61 **my intention:** Kooser, letter to Virginia Faulkner, January 27, 1969.

61 **despite his memories:** Kooser, journal entry, March 5, 1969.

61 **followed up on a lead**: Kooser, journal entry, March 6, 1969.

62 **cover proofs**: Kooser, journal entries, March 8 and 14, 1969.

62 **fan letter**: Kooser, letter to Glück, May 28, 1969.

62 **draft preface**: Kooser, journal entry, August 22, 1969.

62 **story about Elmo**: Kooser, journal entry, August 24, 1969.

9. OFFICIAL ENTRY BLANK

63 **Its epigraph**: Kooser, *Official*, 2.

64 **worldview emerges**: Kooser's concern with the poetry world might seem exaggerated unless seen in context. Not only did his mentor, Karl Shapiro, as poet and as editor, play an influential role in the world of publishing, but many poets of the time, perhaps any time, were publicly anxious about the merit of their poems—see Sylvia Plath's 1960 poem "Stillborn," for example—and their place within the tradition. Dana Gioia, in "My Confessional Sestina," published in *Poetry* 1983, uses Kooser's phrase "official entry blank" to describe the workshop sestina.

66 **As Gaffney notes**: Gaffney, "Prairie Poems," 421-22.

66 **dramatic monologue**: Don Jones, with whom Kooser exchanged drafts, sees the poem as an example of Kooser's adeptness with dramatic monologue. He writes: "Aunt Belle is a bit demented, tactless, reportorial, digressive, resourceful, dirt-dishing, pitying, self-pitying, neighborly, and even oddly cheerful with her deadly gruesome news. The tonal shifts, the ladylike rhythms, the polish are so convincing that Aunt Belle becomes as complexly real as Browning's duke (of 'My Last Duchess')." Jones, letter to author, June 8, 2006.

67 **continuing influence**: Kooser, *Poetry Home Repair*, 9-12.

68 **Kooser acknowledges**: Tawney, "Interview," 41.

68 **"strange surrealism"**: Kuzma, "Ted," 375.

68 **"Coming upon Official Entry Blank in 1969"**: Gioia, "Anonymity," 91.

69 **Murray's review**: Clipping provided to author by Diana Tressler.

70 **"difficult days"**: Kooser, journal entries, October 2 and November 10, 1969.

70 **colored by the turmoil**: Kooser, journal entry, October 8, 1969.

70 **trapped at work**: Kooser, journal entry, November 6, 1969.

70 **in hopes of obtaining**: Kooser, letter to Dudley Bailey, October 10, 1969.

70 **Just before Christmas:** Kooser moved in with friends, Charlie and Christie Tisdale, at 2345 R Street for about six months before renting his own apartment at 1720½ C Street.

70 **Writing to a friend:** Kooser, letter to Steven Osterlund, undated (last week of December 1969 or early January 1970).

10. RUNNING ON EMPTY

71 **Herold Kooser, died suddenly:** "Herold L. Kooser Died Monday," *Ames (IA) Daily Tribune*, August 2, 1971.

71 **He stood at the bedside:** "My Grandfather Dying," *Local Habitation* 3.

71 **John Moser died:** "Services for John R. Moser," *Guttenberg (IA) Press*, December 6, 1972, 9.

71 **"I found myself buried":** Kooser, *Journey* 11.

72 **"An insurance policy":** Kooser, *Journey*, 12.

72 **Long-time friends:** Mij (Hitch) Laging, personal interview; Kooser, letter to Will Jumper, July 5, 1970. Hitch's business card for "Nebraska Haulers" can be found in Kooser's personal brown scrapbook in his possession.

72 **"How much your poem":** Kooser, letter to Nathan, January 7, 1970.

72 **he announced:** Kooser, letter to Osterlund, July 20, 1970.

72 **In his journal:** Kooser, July 4, 1972.

73 **a predental major:** Kuzma, personal interview.

73 **he still had no response:** Kooser, letter to Jones, December 14, 1970. Swallow had recently accepted Jones's second book, *Miss Liberty, Meet Crazy Horse*.

73 **future editor:** Hilda Gregory [Raz], review of *Grass Country*, 88.

74 **beginning to loosen up:** Tawney, "Interview," 42.

74 **as Dana Gioia notes:** "Anonymity, 106."

74 **"consistently elegiac":** Gustafson, "Review of *Grass County*," 37.

74 **"increasingly and consistently visual:** Tawney, "Interview," 43.

75 **"You don't have to explain yourself":** Clark and Saiser, *Road Trip*, 225.

75 **Country life:** Kooser, journal, March 28, 1972.

75 **McLoughlin (later Lombardi) had returned:** Lombardi, personal interview.

76 **second collection:** Kooser, letter to Jumper, March 22, 1972.

76 **tentatively titled:** Kooser, letter to Shapiro, March 13, 1972. Kooser's original title may have been an allusion to a line from

the chorus of the song "Red Wing": "Oh the moon shines tonight on pretty Red Wing." Although it was written early in the century (1907) with music by Kerry Mills and lyrics by Thurland Chattaway, I remember my grandfather singing the song to himself while he worked. The song was likely made popular again by John Wayne, who sang it in the movie *Old Oklahoma* in the 1940s.

76 **The Heart-Shaped Box:** Kooser, letter to Atheneum, March 30, 1972.

76 **recently back from Colombia:** Luschei, e-mail to author.

76 **anthology of Nebraska poets:** Kooser, letter to Luschei, April 1, 1972.

76 **Kuzma's request:** Kooser agrees in a letter to Kuzma, April 21, 1972.

76 **things were looking up:** Kooser, journal entry, June 21, 1972.

77 **Viking also asked:** Kooser, journal entry, July 17, 1972.

77 **Inspired by Wilson:** Joan Barnes, "Fell Donates Cartoons to Archives," *Scarlet*, May 1, 2008, http://www.unl.edu/scarlet/ archive/2008/05/01/story5.html. Kooser's cartoon may be viewed at http://www.flickr.com/photos/unlcomics/3490604753/.

77 **In October:** Ann A. Hancock, letter to Kooser, October 3, 1972.

77 **as did Scribner's:** Kooser, journal entry, December 7, 1992.

77 **teaching credentials:** Kooser, journal entry, November 29, 1972.

77 **Twenty Poems:** "Bridges in the Woods," "Selecting a Reader" (from *Official Entry Blank*), "Composing at Midnight," "How to Foretell a Change in the Weather," "The Failed Suicide," "Late Lights in Minnesota," "Bridesong," "Anniversary," "They Had Torn Off My Face at the Office," "Words on a Man who Never Missed a Day of Work," "Grating a Brain," "Airmail from Other," "September was Empty," "Building a Bird," "A Dead Man Driving a Car," "Anne," "Domestics," "My Grandfather Dying," "Eyes," and "Advice." Some of these poems are discussed in chapter 11.

77 **"the darkest [collection]":** Lombardi, personal interview.

78 **"Cold hard poems":** Kooser, "Two Years."

78 **"I was empty":** Kooser, "They Had Torn Off my Face in the Office," *Twenty Poems.*

11. A LOCAL HABITATION AND A NAME

81 **welcome news:** A copy of Luschei's offer, dated March 19, 1973, is included in the Kooser collection along with his response.

81 **"really solid":** Kooser, letter to Luschei, March 28, 1974? (question mark by Kooser).

81 **Kooser himself notes:** Kooser, "Glenna Luschei," 48.

82 **"strongly regional"**: Kooser, letter to Luschei, March 18, 1973. Poems from *Official Entry Blank* to be considered for inclusion are "A Letter from Aunt Belle," "Gifted Hands," "Old Man at Supper," "Gas Station," "Windmill," Hampshire Sow," "Prize Bull in a Fair Pavilion," "Abandoned Farmhouse," "The Corpse of an Old Woman," and "Rooming House." Poems he suggested deleting from the current manuscript include "The Mother of a Boy Killed in Vietnam," "The Waster," "A Suicide," and "Moth (?)." Kooser would eventually withdraw his name for consideration for the laureateship. At this time, however, his eye is on marketing the new collection. He writes to Luschei, "I don't care about the title, but we could sell *lots* of books during the period of interest that this thing will generate."

82 **graduate seminar**: Kooser, interview with author, April 12, 2011.

82 **addressed his debt**: Kooser, "What Is American about American Poetry," *Poetry Society of America*, http://www.poetrysociety.org/psa/poetry/crossroads/qa_american_poetry/ted_kooser/.

82 **Williams had asserted**: W. C. Williams, *Selected Essays*, 130.

82 **to be confused**: Dijkstra, introduction, 8–9.

83 **Through "appearance: surfaces, sounds"**: quoted by Dijkstra, introduction, 7.

83 **"We are Americans"**: quoted in Wagner, "William Carlos Williams: Unity," 138.

83 **As the poet wrote**: W. C. Williams, *Collected Poems*, 1:183.

83 **Midsummer's Night Dream**: 5.1.12–17.

84 **"wondering how he wound up"**: Kooser, *Journey*, 3.

85 **"I put everything"**: Kooser, personal interview, June 17, 2008.

85 **acts as metaphor and metonym**: While a metaphor is a comparison of one thing to another (based on similarities) without the use of "like" or "as," a metonym is a figure of speech that works by the association of one thing with another.

85 **Red-winged blackbird**: Thirty years later, in "Dishwater," *Delights*, Kooser writes of the "glorious rainbow" formed from the water droplets from his grandmother's dishpan that become a bridge "over the redwing blackbirds in the tops of the willows" out back of her house just outside Guttenberg.

85 **The common and colorful**: Johnsgard, *Birds*, 430. When American children "Sing a Song of Sixpence," however, they are singing about the European blackbird, a relative of the robin.

85 **"Prairie Spring"**: According to James Woodress, Cather's biographer, the novelist had seen Jules Breton's painting of a peasant girl stopping on her way to work to listen to the song of a lark at the Chicago Art Institute. Her use of the allusion in the novel's title was to "suggest a young girl's awakening to something beautiful" (Woodress, *Willa Cather*, 259).

Shapiro used the lark in a similar fashion. "There Are Birds," an early poem, "defends," according to Robert Phillips, "the 'ever-singing larks' against the hawks. The poem," he continues," is not only about war, hawks verses doves, but also the value of pure song and artistry in a predatory, warring world" (Phillips, "Poetry, Prosody," 149). Kooser may also be alluding to "The Red-wing Blackbird," a poem by William Carlos Williams; Kooser's imagined reader has undergone modification since *Official Entry Blank*. Now the poet is writing for a wider group of readers: friends, compatriots, and neighbors, other members of the "human flock."

85 **red-winged blackbird as poet**: Kooser, *Poetry Home Repair*, 3.

85 **describe the landscape**: Vendler, *Poems*, 253.

86 **poem's composition**: Kooser, *Poetry Home Repair*, 31.

86 **"The poem is"**: Kooser, *Poetry Home Repair*, 31.

86 **During the 1970s**: Davidson, *Broken Heartland*, 15–18.

86 **real structure**: Kooser, personal interview, June 17, 2008.

87 **"When you encounter a poem"**: Vendler, *Poems*, 255.

89 **church/garage unites heaven and earth**: Denise Levertov, whose work Kooser appreciated, had defined "the poet—when he is writing" as "a priest, the poem is a temple; epiphanies and communion take place within it" in 1968 at the Hopwood Lecture at the University of Michigan ("Origins," 47).

"God is a straw in a straw,'" Levertov continues, "The strawness of straw, the humanness of the human, is their divinity; in that intensity is the 'divine spark' Hasidic lore tells us dwells in all living things." Kooser may also be referencing John Donne's Sermon VII, "God . . . is a straw in a straw" within the poem itself. Levertov references Donne in "Origins." "Art and religion . . . are the same thing in the end," Cather was fond of saying, as Susan Rosowski reminds us (*Voyage Perilous*, 69).

89 **"poetry is metaphor"**: Liebman, "Robert Frost."

91 **"first glance the callous"**: Gioia, "Anonymity," 105.

91 **like the paintings**: Hopper's paintings that hang at the Sheldon

Museum of Art include *Room in New York*, *The Evening Wind*, *Night Shadows*, and *Town Square*.

91 **in Williams's words:** quoted in Wagner, "William Carlos Williams: Unity," 138.

91 **Kooser calls them:** Kooser, personal interview, June 18, 2006.

92 **section designed:** Kooser, letter to Luschei, March 18, 1974[?].

92 **well-known lament:** W. C. Williams, *Collected Poems*, 2: 226.

12. SINGING THE SHEPARD'S SONG

93 **"Yes, I do":** Cole, "Trade Winds," 44.

93 **an admirer:** Kooser, letter to Luschei, June 1, 1974. On January 30, 1973, Cole contacted the poet asking him for permission to include "Get Your Tongue," originally published in *Evergreen Review*, in an anthology of short poems he was editing. Correspondence between the two men is included in the Kooser Collection.

93 **"a very unusual occurrence":** Kooser, "Glenna Luschei," 48.

94 **windmill on the cover:** The design and printing of *Local Habitation* were handled by Kooser in Lincoln. See, for example, Kooser, letter to Luschei, March 28, 1974(?).

94 **"regional poetry in the finest sense":** Contoski, "Words," 144.

94 **"enforce the rural":** Gustafson, *Poet*, 45.

94 **"Kooser offers a rich":** Glahn, "Ted Kooser," 133.

94 **does not characterize it:** Vinz, review, 120.

94 **"none of the 'nature fakery'":** Vinz, review, 119.

94 **tension between:** Stryk, introduction to *Heartland II*, xvii.

95 **as William Barillas argues:** Barillas, *Midwestern Pastoral*, 12.

95 **redefinition of the form:** Barillas, *Midwestern Pastoral*, 3.

96 **beginning with:** Barillas, *Midwestern Pastoral*, 12.

96 **came upon a poem:** Kooser, "In Memoriam," 193.

96 **In a tribute:** Kooser, "In Memoriam," 193.

96 **the poet recounts:** "Out of the Ordinary," 2–5. Born in Vergas, Minnesota, in 1922, Marxhausen, after a stint as a translator in World War II, obtained a degree in biology from Valparaiso University in Indiana on the GI bill and went on to study art at the Chicago Art Institute. A versatile artist and energetic proponent of the arts as means of discovery, Marxhausen received his master's degree in fine arts from Mills College in Oakland, California. An early advocate of sound sculpture, the artist traveled several times to New York to appear on *Late Night* with David Letterman.

97 **shown in the company cafeteria**: Kooser, "Out of the Ordinary," 5.

98 **"what was happening"**: Kooser, e-mail to author, June 14, 2008.

98 **"publish my own work"**: M. Sanders, "Interview," 103.

99 **keep his hands busy**: Kooser, e-mail to author, July 8, 2008.

13. *NOT COMING TO BE BARKED AT*

101 **As he acknowledges**: Kooser, personal interview, June 12, 2008.

101 **"a versified idea"**: Bly, *Sea*, ix.

102 **he defines the leap**: Bly, *Leaping Poetry*, 4.

102 **"the grudge American critics"**: Bly, *Leaping Poetry*, 18.

102 **is at the heart of this collection**: Kooser explains the power of *duende* in a letter to a friend, Lee McCarthy, dated November 2, 1999:

> Lorca, writing about flamenco, said that the art of flamenco resides in the dancer going right out to the edge of death and then drawing back. Great flamenco dancers apparently do dance almost to the edge of total collapse. So people with *duende* have had experience that has at some time taken them out to the edge and the experience has shaped their lives. There is also the sense in *duende* that life is lived more fully if death is kept with us. Thus at the great feast we keep the shadow of death in the room with us and this makes the food taste better. This is clearly what Joyce was playing with in "The Dead" in which everybody at the big dinner party is talking about the people who have gone before.

102 **"Greatest of all attempts"**: Frost, "Education."

103 **"metaphor-centered poems"**: Kooser, *Poetry Home Repair*, 130.

103 **"marvelous connections"**: Kooser, *Poetry Home Repair*, 140.

104 **1977 review**: Marcus, review of *Not Coming*.

104 **"impersonal observation"**: Kooser, *Poetry Home Repair*, 97.

104 **Kooser explains his attention**: Kooser, letter to Margot Fortunato Galt, September 15, 1999.

107 **"The proper response to a work of art"**: Kooser, *Poetry Home Repair*, 13.

14. *"WALKING HOME TO YOU"*

109 **closed on a house**: Kooser, journal, July 31, 1976.

109 **looked forward**: Kooser, journal, August 23, 1976.

110 **"It was a very cold day"**: information about the meeting, family,

and courtship, Rutledge, personal interview, unless otherwise noted.

110 **That night:** Kooser, journal, November 7, 1976.

110 **"I have at last":** Kooser, journal, November 12, 1976.

110 **Rutledge, a native Nebraskan:** Among Rutledge's relatives is her great-aunt Leta Stetter Hollingworth (1886–1939), a pioneer in education for gifted children. She received her bachelor's degree in writing and literature before obtaining her graduate degrees from Teacher's College at Columbia University in New York. Her *Psychology of the Adolescent* (1928) was the standard text for many years.

111 **Lombardi remembers:** Lombardi, personal interview.

111 **By March:** Kooser, journal, March 23, 1977.

111 **Patty Lombardi acting:** When Lombardi remarried, Kooser returned the favor and served as her "matron of honor."

111 **Prior to their vows:** Kooser and Rutledge, "Wedding Ceremony." Thanks to Diana Tressler for providing this document.

113 **anonymous and enthusiastic review:** "Lincoln Author's Novella."

113 **nineteenth-century Italian clerics:** This may allude to Cather's *Death Comes to the Archbishop. Hatcher*'s opening pages showing a bishop seated across from church fathers in much the same way as an American missionary bishop goes before cardinals urging them to appoint Latour bishop of New Mexico.

113 **field girl reflects:** Kooser, *Hatcher*, 5.

114 **Kooser's retrieval:** Luke, "Celebrating Kooser," 12.

114 **Über Land und Meer:** Stuttgart: Harald Fischer Verlag. <http://www.haraldfischerverlag.de/hfv/IZ/land_meer_engl.php>.

114 **driving to Cedar Rapids:** Kooser to Lee McCarthy, April 7, 1998.

115 **moving tribute:** Kooser, letter to friends, January 4, 1980.

115 **"There is little":** Shapiro, letter to Ed Ochester, April 15, 1979. Shapiro collection, Correspondence, Ransom Humanities Research Center, University of Texas at Austen.

15. *SURE SIGNS*

119 **universal order:** Kooser, *Poetry Home Repair*, 141.

120 **another of Cather's artists:** Cather, *Song*, 313.

120 **in his review:** Glahn, "Ted Kooser," 135.

121 **William Carlos Williams noted:** quoted in Wagner, "William Carlos Williams: Unity," 138.

122 **he quotes:** Kooser, *Poetry Home Repair*, 21.

127 **In a letter to Kooser:** Shapiro, April 15, 1979. Shapiro collection, Ransom Humanities Research Center, University of Texas at Austen.

127 **box of chocolates:** Gioia, "Poetry Chronicle," 617.

127 **while one may argue:** Stitt, "World," 662.

127 **"A first-rate collection":** Gioia, "Poetry Chronicle," 617–18.

127 **Charles Molesworth:** Molesworth, "Fondled Memories," 4.

127 **she notes Kooser's strengths:** Kinzie, "Haunting," 41.

128 **Stitt points out:** Stitt, "World," 662.

128 **Gilbert Allen:** Allen, "Measuring," 174–75.

128 **an interview published:** Tawnwy, "Interview," 46.

128 **"I do extensive revision":** Clark and Saiser, *Road Trip*, 225.

129 **Matthew C. Brennan summarizes:** Brennan, "Ted Kooser," 144.

16. COMMON GROUND

130 **according to Laurence Buell:** Buell, *Environmental Imagination*, 399.

132 **new literary journal:** Crane's work was familiar to the poet for a number of reasons: in 1969 the summer issue (vol. 43, no. 2) of the *Prairie Schooner* featured a special twenty-nine-page "Portfolio" on Crane, focusing on his visit to Nebraska during the winter of 1894–1896; in addition Will Jumper had completed his dissertation on Crane, for whom he never lost admiration.

132 **Crane's model:** Crane, "Blue Hotel," 1.

133 **Kearney or Lincoln:** M. Sanders, e-mail to author.

133 **"We ate hot dogs":** M. Sanders, "Portraits," 418.

133 **"fifth straight day":** Kaye, "Tin Camp," 41.

133 **nature took charge:** Information about the blizzard taken from David Laskin's *The Children's Blizzard* and W. H. O'Gara's *In All Its Fury* unless otherwise noted.

133 **Terry L. Flatt:** "One Succeeds."

134 **"coincidence of habitat":** M. Sanders, foreword, *On Common Ground*, edited by Sanders and Brummels, 15.

134 **Kooser was quick to take issue:** M. Sanders, "Interview," 102.

134 **In another interview:** Aronow, "Ted Kooser," 7.

134 **"it would be nice":** Aronow, "Ted Kooser," 7.

134 **Kooser was content:** Tawney, "Interview," 49.

135 **As Gioia notes:** "Explaining," 88–89. Nine years later, this essay, renamed "The Anonymity of the Regional Poet," will be included in Gioia's *Can Poetry Matter? Essays on Poetry and American Culture.*

135 **inspiring him:** Kooser, *Poetry Home Repair*, xii.

135 **"When I used to drink":** Clark and Saiser, *Road Trip*, 226.

136 **Recalling his history:** Kooser, "Sower Award," 11.

136 **seemed sudden:** Kooser, "Sower Award," 11.

136 **The poet made peace:** Aronow, "Ted Kooser," 6.

17. ONE WORLD AT A TIME

137 **first time:** Emerson was one of Frost's "four greatest Americans." See "Notes from the Academy," Frost's edited version of his acceptance speech for the first Emerson-Thoreau Medal, made by the American Academy of Arts and Sciences, October 8, 1958. Shapiro, too, had worshiped at Thoreau's altar, writing that he "is the best American scripture, and I never tire of the text," and gave a nod to Humboldt's basic notion of the Cosmos in his collection of essays (with Slote and Miller), *Start with the Sun: Studies in Cosmic Poetry*). Nature was, for Humboldt as it was for Emerson and Thoreau after him, an outward sign of the innermost human spirit. See Laura Dassow Walls, *Passage to Cosmos*.

137 **Like his friend Emerson:** Emerson, "Nature."

138 **When asked:** Harding, Days, 464; Thoreau, when asked by his aunt Louise if he'd "made his peace with God," answered "I did not know we had ever quarreled" (Harding 465).

138 **Kooser makes overt:** Philip Dacey, writing on Bly, marks a major philosophical difference between the Minnesota poet and his Nebraska neighbor: "Robert Bly can perhaps best be understood when regarded as a heterodox Lutheran minister successfully disguised as a poet. What motivates all his writings and talk is less a commitment to poetry as an art form than a deep desire to save souls, his own included. . . . he would save souls by an antipietistic development and maintenance of a healthy spiritual life with reference exclusively to this earth. 'The Kingdom of Heaven does not mean the next life,' he has written. 'The two worlds are both in this world.'" Dacey, "Reverend Robert E. Bly," 1.

138 **Like Frost:** Gerber, *Robert Frost*, 154.

138 **light/star motif:** Stars, one of Frost's reoccurring symbols, are in many cultures seen as representative of the human soul or spirit.

140 **words of Wendell Berry:** Berry, "Regional," 69.

141 **"I often see":** Hahn, e-mail to author.

142 **the streets of the Haymarket:** Although the area has undergone renovation (begun in 1985) and the streets are lined with restaurants, galleries, and coffee shops, industry still persists. Loading docks, rolling warehouse doors, and workers remain.

142 **investigated light and shadow:** "The artist," John Gardner wrote in *On Moral Fiction*, "lights up the darkness with a lightning flash, protects his friends the gods—that is, values—and all humanity without exception, and then moves on" (100–101).

143 **pop of the motorcycle:** "The motorcycle hummed under him," Gardner wrote in *The Sunlight Dialogues*, "and roared when he accelerated and popped and crackled when he cut back the spark for the sharp curve or the crest of a hill" (quoted in Silesky, *John Gardner*, 318).

143 **Hahn characterizes:** Hahn, "Common."

144 **Pictures of the probe:** By the time *One World at a Time* was published, Voyager 2 had traveled by Jupiter (1979) and Saturn (1981) and was heading out to Uranus and Neptune.

144 **The section's lead poem:** Hahn, "Common."

144 **Frost's farmer:** Gerber, *Robert Frost*, 143.

145 **Christopher Beach reminds:** Beach, *Cambridge Introduction*, 173.

145 **"artists are":** Pound, *ABCs*, 73.

18. *WEATHER CENTRAL*

148 **"All of my life":** Kooser, *Blizzard*, 1.

148 **"poems that follow":** Kooser, *Blizzard*.

148 **not taken:** Kooser, *Blizzard*.

148 **The winter of 1887–1888 started off:** Information about the blizzard taken from O'Gara, *In All Its Fury* unless noted.

149 **C. D. Burnley reported:** Laskin, *Children's Blizzard*, 158.

150 **provided a constant:** Rutledge, personal interview.

151 **according to Aristotle:** *Poetics*, 9.4.22.

152 **great blue heron:** No stranger to poetry, the heron was made familiar by Carolyn Kizer's poem "The Great Blue Heron." For both poets, nature is neither good nor evil; it is a lens through which we may see ourselves and our world more clearly. Both are transcendental rather than romantic in impulse.

152 **can be read two ways:** "Is" is understood as the present progressive tense, as in *the heron . . . [is] easing*, and may also be read as a continuation of the present perfect progressive, *I have been . . . easing ahead*."

153 **Kooser clarifies:** J. Smith, review, 31.
153 **Kooser has compared:** Stillman, "Famous Poet."
153 **Kooser confesses:** Kooser, *Journey*, 11.
154 **exhilarating work:** Kooser, *Poetry Home Repair*, 13.
155 **"Life poetry":** Slote, "Start with the Sun," 229-30.
155 **Shapiro's essay:** Shapiro, "Cosmic Consciousness," 30.
155 **"sense of identification":** Shapiro, "Cosmic Consciousness," 31.
155 **Shapiro notes:** Shapiro, "Cosmic Consciousness," 31.
156 **While it may be true:** Brennan, "Ted Kooser," 144.
156 **describes the in-between:** Heidegger, *Poetry*, 53.
156 **It is the place Bly describes:** Bly, *Leaping Poetry*, 3.
157 **He explains the symbol:** Kooser, *Poetry Home Repair*, 3.
157 **As Shelley writes:** Poet Edward Hirsch offers an interesting discussion about the "mysterious (visionary) relation" between Shelley's poet and auditor or audience in *How to Read a Poem*, pointing to philosopher Ted Cohen's explication of the metaphor and the intimacy that the figure of speech achieves (8).
158 **"No one is going to read":** Kooser, *Weather Central*, 22.
158 **A devoted chronicler:** Baker, "On Restraint," 34.
161 **"as universal as":** Gioia, Mason, and Schoerke, *Twentieth-Century*, 891.

19. "LIGHTS ON A GROUND OF DARKNESS"

165 **Kooser traveled:** His son, Jeffrey, lived in Rantoul, Illinois, at the time of Margaret's birth.
165 **"I am quite taken":** Kooser to the Nathans, January 12, 1998.
166 **He corresponded with Shapiro:** Kooser to Shapiro, November 21, 1986.
166 **In a letter to a friend:** Kooser to Tom Disch, January 6, 1998.
166 **To another friend:** Kooser to Chuck Woodard, January 13, 1998.
166 **have an opportunity:** Kooser, e-mail to author, March 27, 2001.
166 **According to Muir:** Muir, *Autobiography*, 224.
166 **As Muir wrote:** Muir, *Autobiography*, 48-49.
167 **"I was worried":** Kooser to Joe Survant, July 20, 1998.
167 **Kooser's letters trace:** Kooser to Joe Survant January 20, 1998, for example.
167 **he summed up:** Kooser to Reverend Lloyd Brockmeyer, April 7, 1998.

NOTES

168 **"iris in my garden"**: Kooser, "Mother," "Lights," 1; *Delights*, 43.
168 **His grandfather**: Kooser, "Lights," 12.
168 **significance of his family**: Kooser, interview with author, July 6, 2008.
169 **361 days**: Kooser, e-mail to Jeff Kooser, May 4, 1998.
169 **letter to friends**: Kooser to Pete Heckman and Lou Lower, May 5, 1998.
169 **e-mailed his son**: Kooser, to Jeff Kooser, May 13, 1998.
169 **either side of Highway 34**: Kooser, *Local Wonders*, 148.
169 **"awake half the night"**: Kooser to Leonard and Carol Nathan, June 2, 1998.
169 **"Coal in my tongue"**: Kooser quotes his notebook entry in a letter to Jay and Martha Meeks, September 15, 1998.
170 **preempting retirement plans**: Vera Kooser's memorial was held in Cedar Rapids in April 1999.
170 **imagined river and bluffs**: Kooser, *Local Wonders*, 149–50.
171 **"when his clutch"**: Kooser, *Local Wonders*, 150.
171 **felt as though**: Kooser, *Local Wonders*, 36.
171 **another blow**: "Ruth Kregel," *Guttenberg (IA) Press*, Garnavillo section, July 15, 1998.
171 **effects of radiation**: Kooser to colleagues (Kim, Dianna, Tracy, Chris, Mary Ann, Michelle, Sharie, and Holly), July 11, 1998. According to Kooser during a speech, "Poetry and Healing," given to the American College of Physicians in Alaska, he was also accepted into a trial program that included three doses of chemotherapy (Cisplatin) along with the radiation. Severe oral candida after the first forced his participation to an end.
172 **by September 15**: Kooser, letter to Jay and Martha Meeks.
172 **decided to take**: Kooser, letter to Deborah Cummins, September 15, 1998.
172 **"Then as autumn began to fade**: Kooser, *Winter*, 5.
172 **"sat at my desk"**: Kooser, letter to Jim Harrison, October 2, 1998.
172 **"An October Evening"**: Kooser, letter to Carol and Leonard Nathan, October 15, 1998.
173 **"biggest breakthrough"**: Kooser, letter to Carol Bly, October 13, 1998.
173 **On November 3, 1998**: Kooser, postcard to Jim Harrison, November 3, 1998.

20. WINTER MORNING WALKS

175 **Like much peripatetic literature:** Poet A. R. Ammons postulates in "A Poem Is a Walk" that the lyric poem and the walk are metaphorically related. In *Walks in the World* literary scholar Roger Gilbert, basing his theses on Ammons's 1967 essay, "A Poem Is a Walk," identifies the "walk poem" as a discrete poetic genre that has evolved from the Romantic lyric (ix, 6).

176 **Just as a reader:** Rosowski, *Voyage Perilous*, 62.

176 **object of a chase:** This is a race that leukemia won over his father in 1979.

176 **road becomes a path:** At the end of Shakespeare's *Midsummer Night's Dream*, from which Kooser's earlier title, *Local Habitation and a Name*, is taken, Theseus and Hippolyta are discussing both the poet's imagination and its influence on the reader or, in the case of drama, the spectator. Unlike the madman and the lover who also shape fantasies,

> The poet's eye, in fine frenzy rolling,
> Doth glance from heaven to earth, from earth to heaven;
> And as imagination bodies forth
> The forms of things unknown, the poet's pen
> Turns them to shapes and gives to airy nothing
> A local habitation and a name. 5.1. 13-18

177 **fates who determine:** Bulfinch, *Mythology*, 904.

177 **"Black Postcards":** Tranströmer, *Great Enigma*, 171.

177 **allude to Book Five:** W. C. Williams, *Patterson*, 234.

177 **The Tempest sounds:** 4.1.146-58.

177 **He invites us:** In "Christmas Eve," an earlier poem published in *Sure Signs* the year after his father's death, Kooser calls on images of fabric and hands to convey his flesh and blood relationship with his father: "Our common bones are wrapped in new robes. / A common pulse tugs at the ropes / in the backs of our hands." (Kooser, *Sure Signs*, 7-9).

177 **his father's hands:** Kooser, "Lights," 38-39.

178 **wrote to his friend:** Kooser, letter to Jeff Gundy, February 2, 1999.

178 **Slote, argues in her essay:** Slote, "Kingdom," 35.

179 **parallel those of Bunyan's pilgrim:** Bunyan, *Pilgrim's Progress*, 1.

179 **as careful a poet:** Kooser, "Poetry and Healing."

179 **"The poem needs insulators":** Shapiro, *Reports*, 167.

180 **"Anapest"**: Kooser, in conversation with author, February 12, 2001.

181 **recalling the haiku**: Kooser, letter to Jay Meeks, September 15, 1998.

181 **"often playful"**: Mason, review, 188.

182 **six-month medical**: Kooser, letter to Debra Winger and Arliss Howard, December 18, 1998.

182 **His plan was**: Kooser, letter to Lee McCarthy, December 31, 1998.

182 **writes to Harrison**: Kooser, letter to Jim Harrison, March 16, 1999.

183 **"up and out on the road"**: Kooser, letter to Richard Bausch, March 20, 1999.

183 **"My cancer experience"**: Tom O'Connor, "Portraits Provide Meaning, Security to Patients." UNMC News, University of Nebraska Medical Center, December 22, 2008, http://app1.unmc. edu/publicaffairs/todaysite/sitefiles/today_full.cfm?match=5233.

183 **Kooser elaborated**: Kooser, "Poetry and Healing."

183 **writes to friends**: Kooser, letter to Debra Winger and Arliss Howard, June 6, 1999.

21. *LOCAL WONDERS*

185 **"No other writer"**: "Meet the Writers: Ted Kooser." Barnes and Noble website, September 6, 2004. http://barnesandnoble.com/ writers.

185 **reviewer Steven Harvey writes**: Harvey, "Local Wonders," 135.

186 **first essay, "Economy"**: Thoreau, "Economy," 3-4.

186 **The poet describes**: Kooser, *Local Wonders*, 24-25.

186 **"The seasons"**: Thoreau, *Journal*, October 26, 1857, 127.

187 **"People in the country"**: Kooser, *Local Wonders*, 22-23.

187 **"Little by little"**: Kooser, *Local Wonders*, 22.

187 **"Go a mile and a half"**: Kooser, *Local Wonders*, xv.

187 **painting along a country road**: Kooser, *Local Wonders*, 3.

188 **Thoreau remarked**: *Walden*, 78.

188 **his father's hands**: Kooser, *Local Wonders*, 148.

188 **"Death comes riding"**: Kooser, *Local Wonders*, 39.

188 **"power of family"**: Harvey, "Local Wonders," 136.

189 **Hitch's time in Valparaiso**: According to Roberta Smith, Hitch exhibited his work in New York for more than thirty years. "His natural touch and distinctive sense of color earned him a strong underground reputation," Smith continues. His work may be seen in the permanent collections of the Brooklyn Museum of Art and the National Gallery of Art in Washington DC. R. Smith, "Stewart Hitch."

189 **"trying to find footing"**: Kooser, *Local Wonders*, 119.

189 **trip to the dentist**: Kooser, *Local Wonders*, 148.

189 **Burlington Northern boxcars**: Kooser, *Local Wonders*, 151.

190 **she remarked**: quoted in Buell, *Environmental Imagination*, 401.

190 **Kooser quotes Seamus Heaney**: Kooser, *Poetry Home Repair*, 6.

190 **Kooser advises**: Kooser, "More Letters," 390.

190 **Gary D. Schmidt**: *Robert McCloskey*, 149.

190 **"Life is a long walk"**: Kooser, *Local Wonders*, 152.

191 **"Now as he [his father] rushes"**: Kooser, "Lights," 37.

191 **"Often around the holidays"**: Kooser, personal interview, September 21, 2003.

191 **"Think about your place"**: Kooser, "More Letters," 390.

191 **"This is the life"**: Kooser, *Local Wonders*, 96.

192 **not to disclose the writer**: Bednarik, "Interview." One of the most interesting approaches to *Braided Creek* is a comparison by Nancy Bunge in *Midwest Quarterly* of the Harrison and Kooser conversation with the give and take between Marvin Bell, who moved to the Midwest to teach at the Iowa Workshop, and William Stafford, who was born and grew up in Kansas, published in 1983 as *Segues: A Correspondence in Poetry*. Bell and Stafford each wrote poems in response to the poems of the other. "The people of the Midwest," she writes, "have a finely honed ability to enjoy ordinary events," and both books, Bunge continues later, "commemorate the richness of ordinary life." She goes on, "But more persistently, *Braided Creek* suggests both explicitly and implicitly that aging gives one permission to relish life" (49).

22. *DELIGHTS & SHADOWS*

194 **identifies himself**: Kooser, *Local Wonders*, 3.

195 **August Night at Russell's Corners**: Kooser, *Local Wonders*, 94. There are at least four *Russell's Corners* paintings by Ault, all examples, Kooser points out, of chiaroscuro, which in drawing, painting, and the graphic arts refers to the rendering of forms through contrast between the light and dark areas.

195 **Kooser clarified**: Kooser, personal interview, June 28, 2006.

195 **Kooser elaborates**: *Local Wonders*, 94.

198 **"I sound out"**: Kooser, interview by Dan Wickett, January 25, 2005.

199 **A Prosody Handbook**: Shapiro and Beum, 135.

199 **Shapiro and Beum note**: *Prosody Handbook*, 136.

200 **"catch a glimpse"**: Williams, *Autobiography*, 360.

201 **box Kooser describes**: After the older woman died, Kooser epoxied its contents into place and then framed it as a gift for his wife.

203 **the pitfalls of the purely anecdotal poem**: Kooser, *Poetry Home Repair*, 84–85.

203 **"Creamed Corn"**: Kooser's uncle Jack (Ralph) Mayo died in 1975.

203 **favorite painters**: Kooser, interview with author, June 28, 2006.

204 **feel of a still life**: Kooser notes that the poem has "much in common" with a Homer or Sargent watercolor, noting that "Imagistic writing is like painting (Clark and Saiser, *Road Trip*, 224–25).

205 **"think of a metaphor"**: Kooser, *Poetry Home Repair*, 135.

206 **sometimes used his experience**: "Winslow Homer in the National Gallery of Art." National Gallery of Art. http://www.nga.gov/exhibitions/homerinfo.shtm.

206 **one thinks of**: Henri, *Art Spirit*, 169.

208 **"That Was I"**: Mantooth, "Spy," 32. The Mantooth essay is an excellent look at Kooser's use of the first-person singular pronoun.

208 **Many of the poems**: Mantooth, "Spy," 34.

208 **"Home Town"**: published in Kooser, *Official*.

209 **black and yellow**: The colors are reminiscent of those on the traditional Cliff Notes covers.

210 **The spider**: "That Was I" can also be read as an allusion, if not another tribute, to poet James Wright, whose work Kooser followed closely. Wright's posthumously published collection, *This Journey*, opens with the poet entering the Temple of Diana, asking for just one vine leaf, recalling Kooser's engagement with the grapevine in the first stanza. Wright, who was dying of cancer, was on a trip to his beloved Italy. In the poem "The Journey" Wright finds what he was looking for, perhaps what the "old man" in "That Was I" and the reader have all been seeking, a way to avoid thinking of death and all the while acknowledging it. Wright learns his lesson from a spider outside Anghiari, a medieval city in Tuscany.

23. "THE RIPENING ODOR OF PRAISE"

212 **Kooser was wondering**: The poet has told this story many times with a variety of small variations. This version is based primarily on Kooser's talk at Emory and Henry College, March 11, 2008, entitled "Two Years in the Catbird Seat: My Experience as U.S. Poet Laureate."

213 **poet laureate:** "About the Position of Poet Laureate," Library of Congress, June 9, 2009, http://www.loc.gov/poetry/about_laureate .html.

213 **"overwhelming at first":** Rutledge, personal interview.

214 **back in Nebraska:** Kooser, letter to Jim Harrison and Dan Gerber, September 19, 2004. Kooser describes Hext chiaroscuro technique, "almost like Vermeers in their luminosity," in the letter, "painted in built up glazes over green underpainting."

214 **Each laureate set:** "About the Position."

214 **broaden the audience:** Kooser, "Two Years," 14.

214 **In an interview:** Kooser, in Tobin Beck, "Transforming the Ordinary into the Extraordinary: A Profile of Ted Kooser," WorldandI .com. http://www.worldandi.com/subscribers/searchdetail.asp ?num=24312.Beck, "Transforming."

215 **"They were wary":** Kooser, "Two Years," 17.

215 **"I lobbied him":** Rutledge, personal interview.

215 **broached the idea:** Kooser, "Two Years," 17.

215 **"extended frenzy of extroversion":** Kooser, "Two Years," 18.

215 **"great pleasure":** Kooser, "Two Years," 19.

215 **tallied up:** Carlson, "Laureate Rounds," 1.

216 **"worst of them":** Kooser, interview with author, January 16, 2006.

216 **poet's education:** Kooser, *Poetry Repair Manual*, xi.

216 **purpose of poetry:** Kooser, *Poetry Repair Manual*, xi.

217 **by tutorial:** I was fortunate to be a member of Kooser's first tutorial. Weekly discussion was often augmented by short e-mail essays on metaphor, diction, titles, etc., which would eventually end up in the poet's *Poetry Home Repair Manual*.

217 **poet took it in stride:** Keenan, "Kooser's Everyday Poetics."

218 **"If being asked":** Kooser, "Two Years, 21.

219 **"Out of the Ordinary":** Kooser, unpublished manuscript.

219 **Ted Kooser Day:** "Ted Kooser Day," 8.

219 **crisscrossing the nation:** Carlson, "Laureate Rounds."

24. "BRIGHT YELLOW LEAVES FLYING"

220 **his first teachers and his wife:** Kooser, "Sower Award," 11.

220 **Kooser was contacted:** Karen Burbach, "Poet Shares Poems of Healing," UNMC News, University of Nebraska Medical Center, February 2, 2006, http://app1.unmc.edu/publicaffairs/todaysite/ sitefiles/today_full.cfm?match=2576.

221 **In a memorial:** Kooser, "In Memoriam," 192.

221 **list had grown:** Bartling, "Kooser's New Book," 1.

221 **Kooser admits:** Kooser, *Valentines*, vii.

222 **"emotional gamut":** Benn, "Mistaking Salt," 36.

222 **"plenty of sex":** Benn, "Mistaking Salt," 40.

222 **concludes with:** Benn, "Mistaking Salt," 45.

223 **"only fitting":** Kooser, *Valentines*, viii.

223 **Hanna writes:** Hanna, in Kooser, *Valentines*, ix.

223 **"Of all the Honors":** Reist, "Kooser Elementary School Dedicated," April 24, 2008; "Poetry in Motion," Lincoln Public Schools, April 29, 2008, http://www.lps.org/post/detail.cfm?id=918.

224 **"Metaphor and Faith":** Kooser, "Metaphor and Faith," 139–41.

224 **process remains:** Clark and Saiser, *Road Trip*, 225.

225 **Louise Nevelson:** Kooser, *Poetry Home Repair*, 6.

225 **hardwood dining room floor:** Vroman, "Big Donation," 1, 8.

225 **formally dedicated:** "Reist, Kooser Elementary School Dedicated," October 15, 2009.

225 **Recalling his teachers:** Kooser, unpublished manuscript.

226 **endowment fund:** Reist, "Endowment to Kooser," December 29, 2010.

226 **Kooser is currently:** Kooser, interview with author, November 1, 2012. Additional information on upcoming publications: Kooser, e-mails to author, December 6, 2012, January 19, 2013, and April 12, 2013.

227 **"House by the Road":** The full poem (unpublished) follows:

> The work that went into squaring the hedge
> with the shears (that deliberate snip)
> and the weekly labor of pushing the mower
> chattering over the grass, and my uncle
> clumsy on his knees beside the drive,
> splattering whitewash on his row of stones,
> what has it come to? My grandparents' house
> is a commercial garden center now,
> and where Liz Moser's lean white chickens
> stepped with such purpose over the lawn,
> a fleet of wet pallets with seedlings
> nodding in flats is lashed by green hoses
> to the dock of the present. And the flagstones

that led to their door, spaced as if to cross
a stream and sandy under bare feet,
were indeed crossing a stream, and now
they've sunken from sight, and I am
ankle deep in time and pink petunias.

227 **"bright yellow leaves"**: Kooser, *Local Wonders*, 96.

Bibliography

WORKS BY TED KOOSER

Bag in the Wind. Sommervlle MA: Candlewick Press, 2010.

The Blizzard Voices. St. Paul: Bieler, 1986. Reprint, Lincoln: University of Nebraska Press, 2006.

"The Chariot Cometh." *Sketch: Magazine of Student Creative Writing* 26, no. 3 (Spring 1960): 50–51.

Delights & Shadows. Port Townsend WA: Copper Canyon Press, 2004.

Flying at Night: Poems, 1965–1985. Pittsburgh: University of Pittsburgh Press, 2005.

"Glenna Luschei: In Appreciation." *Prairie Schooner* 78, no. 4 (Winter 2004): 45–92.

Grass County. Lincoln NE: Windflower Press, 1971.

Hatcher. Lincoln NE: Windflower Press, 1978.

"Here in Nebraska." *Script*, Fall 1967, 3.

House Held Up by Trees. Sommervlle MA: Candlewick Press, 2012.

"In Memoriam: Leonard Nathan, 1924–2007." *Prairie Schooner* 81, no. 4 (Winter 2008), 192–93.

Journey to a Place of Work: A Poet in the World of Business. Fargo ND: Institute for Regional Studies, 1990.

"Karl Shapiro Autobiography Includes Lincoln Years." Review of *The Younger Son and Reports of My Death* by Karl Shapiro. *Sunday Lincoln (NE) Journal Star*, April 15, 1990.

"Karl Shapiro in the Early Sixties." In *Seriously Meeting Karl Shapiro*, edited by Sue Walker. Mobile AL: Negative Capability Press, 1993.

"Lack-laughter." Letter to the *Lincoln (NE) Journal Star*, May 20, 1985.

"Lights on a Ground of Darkness." *Great River Review*, Fall/Winter 1998, 1–43. Reprinted as *Lights on a Ground of Darkness: An Evocation of a Place and Time*. Lincoln: University of Nebraska Press, 2005 (special limited ed.) and 2009.

A Local Habitation & a Name: Poems. Preface by Karl Shapiro. San Luis Obispo CA: Solo Press, 1974.

Local Wonders: Seasons in the Bohemian Alps. Lincoln: University of Nebraska Press, 2002.

"Metaphor and Faith." *Seminary Ridge Review* 13, no. 2 (Spring 2011): 139–41.

"More Letters to a Young Poet." *Midwest Quarterly* 44, no. 4 (Summer 2003): 389–390.

Not Coming to Be Barked At. Milwaukee: Pentagram Press, 1976.

Official Entry Blank. Lincoln: University of Nebraska Press, 1969.

Old Marriage and New. Austin TX: Cold Mountain Press, 1978.

One World at a Time. Pittsburgh: University of Pittsburgh Press, 1985.

"Out of the Ordinary." Unpublished manuscript. (Spoken version available at the Library of Congress. Webcast: www.loc.gov/)

"Poetry and Healing." American College of Physicians—Alaska Chapter meeting, June 26, 2008. http://www.litsite.org/index.cfm?section =Narrative-and-Healing&page=Narratives&viewpost=2&conten tid=2812.

The Poetry Home Repair Manual. Lincoln: University of Nebraska Press, 2005.

Review of *Reports of My Death*, by Karl Shapiro. *Lincoln (NE) Journal Star*, April 15, 1990.

Riding with Colonel Carter: An Essay and Two Poems. Grand Island NE: Sandhills Press, 1999.

"Small Rooms in Time." *River Teeth* 5, no. 2 (Spring 2004): 1–5.

"Some of the Things I Think about When Working on a Poem." *Midwest Quarterly* 40, no. 4 (1999): 439.

"Sower Award Winner Grateful for People and Places." *Nebraska Humanities* 11, 2007.

"Straight Answers from Ted Kooser." *American Libraries* 35, no. 11 (December 2004): 31.

"Success." *Kenyon Review* 30, no. 1 (January 1, 2008): 19–20.

Sure Signs: New and Selected Poems. Pittsburgh: University of Pittsburgh Press, 1980.

Ted Kooser Collection. Unpublished correspondence, workbooks, and journals. (Although Mr. Kooser has allowed the author access to these materials over the years, they are now housed at the Archives & Special

Collections, University of Nebraska–Lincoln Libraries. Correspondents are identified in text or in notes by first and last names along with date of composition.)

Together. Waldron Island WA: Brooding Heron Press, 2012.

Twenty Poems. Lincoln NE: Best Cellar Press, 1973.

"Two Poets." *Nebraska Humanist* (Nebraska Committee for the Humanities) 6, no. 1 (Spring 1983).

"Two Years in the Catbird Seat: My Experience as U.S. Poet Laureate." Emory VA: Emory and Henry College, 2008.

Valentines. Lincoln: University of Nebraska Press, 2008.

Weather Central. Pittsburgh: University of Pittsburgh Press, 1994.

"The Wedding Ceremony for Kathleen Rutledge and Ted Kooser," With Kathleen Rutledge. September 20, 1977. Unpublished manuscript.

"What Is American about American Poetry?" *Poetry Society of America,* March 12, 2006.

Winter Morning Walks: One Hundred Postcards to Jim Harrison. Pittsburgh: Carnegie Mellon University Press, 2000.

Writing Brave and Free: Encouraging Worlds for People Who Want to Start Writing. With Steve Cox. Lincoln: University of Nebraska Press, 2005.

PUBLISHED SOURCES

Allen, Gilbert. "Measuring the Mainstream—A Review Essay." *Southern Humanities Review* 17 (1983): 171–78.

"American Life in Poetry." Sponsored by the Poetry Foundation, Library of Congress, and University of Nebraska–Lincoln Department of English. http://www.americanlifeinpoetry.org.

Ammons, A. R. "A Poem Is a Walk." *Epoch* 18, no. 1 (Fall 1968): 114–19.

Anderson, Beth. "Old Town Named to National Register." *Ames (IA) Tribune,* January 26, 2004. http://iowa.amestrib.com/articles/2004/01/26/ames%20front%20page/10868565.txt.

Andrews, Clarence A. *A Literary History of Iowa.* Iowa City: University of Iowa Press, 1972.

Aronow, Ina. "Pulitzer Prize Winning Poet Karl Shapiro." *Omaha (NE) Sunday World-Herald Magazine of the Midlands,* February 26, 1984, 17.

———. "Ted Kooser of Lincoln: The Poet Who Works In the Executive Suite." *Omaha (NE) Sunday World-Herald Magazine of the Midlands,* June 26 1983, 6–7.

Baker, David. "On Restraint." *Poetry* 168, no. 1 (April 1996): 33–47.

Barillas, William. *The Midwestern Pastoral: Place and Landscape in Literature of the American Heartland*. Athens: Ohio University Press, 2006.

Barnes, Joan. "Fell Donates Cartoons to Archives." *Scarlet*, May 1, 2008. http://www.unl.edu/scarlet/archive/2008/05/01/story5.html. (The cartoon may be viewed at http://www.flickr.com/photos/unlcomics/3490604753/.)

Bartling, Kelly. "Kooser's New Book Chronicles 22 Years of Valentine's Prose." *Scarlet* 18, no. 3, January 31, 2008.

Beach, Christopher. *Cambridge Introduction to Twentieth-Century American Poetry*. Cambridge: Cambridge University Press, 2003.

Bednarik, Joseph. "An Interview with Joseph Bednarik: Jim Harrison." *Five Points: A Journal of Literature & Art* 6, no. 2 (June 2008). http://www.webdelsol.com/Five_Points/issues/v6n2/harrison.html.

Benn, Allan. "Mistaking Salt for Sugar: Ted Kooser's *Valentines*." *Midwest Miscellany* 40.2 (Fall 2012): 35-45.

Berry, Wendell. "The Regional Motive." *A Continuous Harmony: Essays Cultural and Agricultural*. New York: Harcourt, 1972.

Black, Helen. "Ames Centennial History for 100 Years." *Ames Community History*. Ames IA: Ames Centennial, 1964.

Bly, Robert. *Leaping Poetry: An Idea with Poems and Translations*. Boston: Beacon Press, 1975.

———, ed. *The Sea and the Honeycomb*. Boston: Beacon P, 1971.

Brennan, Matthew C. "Ted Kooser." *Dictionary of Literary Biography*. Edited by R. S. Gwynn. Vol. 105. Detroit: Gale, 1991. 143-50.

Brooks, Cleanth. *The Well Wrought Urn: Studies in the Structure of Poetry*. New York: Harcourt, Brace & World, 1963.

Brooks, Cleanth, and Robert Penn Warren. *Modern Rhetoric*. New York: Harcourt, Brace & World, 1961.

Buell, Laurence. *The Environmental Imagination: Thoreau, Nature Writing, and the Formation of American Culture*. Cambridge MA: Harvard University Press, 1996.

Bulfinch, Thomas. *Bulfinch's Mythology*. New York: Avenel Books, 1979.

Bunge, Nancy. "Influencing Each Other through the Mail: William Stafford's and Marvin Bell's *Segues* and Jim Harrison's and Ted Kooser's *Braided Creek*." *Midwest Quarterly*, September 2005, 33, 48-56.

Bunyan, John. *Pilgrim's Progress*. New York: Oxford University Press, 2009.

Butler, P. H. *Edwin Muir*. New York: Grove Press, 1962.

Carlson, Janet. "Laureate Rounds—Full Circle." UNL *English Department Newsletter and Calendar*, September 8, 2006, 1.

Cather, Willa. *My Ántonia*. Edited by Charles Mignon with Kari Ronning. Historical essay by James Woodress. Lincoln: University of Nebraska Press, 1994.

———. *One of Ours*. Edited by Frederick M. Link with Kari A. Ronning. Historical essay and notes by Richard C. Harris. Lincoln: University of Nebraska Press, 2006.

———. *O Pioneers!* Edited by Susan J. Rosowski and Charles W. Mignon with Kathleen Danker. Historical essay by David Stouck. Lincoln: University of Nebraska Press, 1992.

Clark, Shelly, and Marjorie Saiser. *Road Trip: Conversations with Writers*. Omaha: Backwaters Press, 2003.

Cohen, Ted. "Metaphor and the Cultivation of Intimacy." *Critical Inquiry* 5, no. 1 (Autumn 1978): 3–12.

Cole, William. "Trade Winds: Favorite Poet." *Saturday Review World*, November 1974, 44.

Conger, Cindy. "'Local Wonders' Traces Poet's Cancer Battle." *Lincoln NE Journal Star*, October 20, 2011. http:www.journalstar.com.

Contoski, Victor. "Words and Raincoats: Verbal and Nonverbal Communication." In Sanders and Brummels, *On Common Ground*.

"Country Club Hosts 135 Teen-Agers." *Ames (IA) Tribune*, June 25, 1956. (Courtesy of the Ames Historical Society)

Crane, Stephen. "The Blue Hotel." *Collier's Weekly* 22 (November 26, 1898).

Dacey, Philip. "The Reverend Robert E. Bly, Pastor, Church of the Blessed Unity: A Look at 'A Man Writes to a Part of Himself.'" In *A Book of Rereadings*, edited by Greg Kuzma. Crete NE: Best Cellar Press, 1979.

Davidson, Osha Gray. *Broken Heartland: The Rise of America's Rural Ghetto*. Iowa City: University of Iowa Press, 1996.

Dijkstra, Bram. Introduction to *A Recognizable Image: William Carlos Williams on Art and Artists*. New York: New Directions, 1978.

Eliot, Thomas Stearns. "Tradition and the Individual Talent." *The Sacred Wood*. London: Methune, 1920. http://www.bartleby.com/200/.

Emerson, Ralph Waldo. "Nature." Chapter 3 in *Nature: Addresses and Lectures*. Honolulu: University Press of the Pacific, 2001.

———. "The Over-Soul." Chapter 9 in *Essays: First Series*. 1841. Cambridge (MS): Belknap Press of Harvard University Press, 1980.

Federal Writers' Project. *The WPA Guide to 1930s Iowa*. Ames: Iowa State University Press, 1986.

Flatt, Terry L. "One Succeeds, One Doesn't, in Efforts by 2 Local Playwrights." *Lincoln (NE) Star*, January 5, 1981.

Frederick, John T. "Ruth Suckow and the Middle Western Literary Movement." *English Journal* 20 (January 1931): 1–8.

Frese, Stephen J. "Divided by a Common Language: The Babel Proclamation and Its Influences in Iowa History." *History Teacher* 39, no. 1 (November 2005): 59–88. http://www.jstor.org/stable/30036745.

Frost, Robert. "Education by Poetry: A Meditative Monologue." *Amherst Graduates' Quarterly* 20, no. 2 (February 1931): 75–85.

———. "Notes from the Academy." *Daedalus* 88, no. 4 (Fall 1959): 712–18.

———. "Nothing Gold Can Stay." *The Poetry of Robert Frost: The Collected Poems, Complete and Unabridged*. Edited by Edward Connery Lathem. New York: Holt, Rinehart and Winston, 1969.

Gaffney, Wilbur. "Prairie Poems." *Prairie Schooner* 43, no. 4 (Winter 1969/70): 420–21.

Gardner, John. *On Moral Fiction*. New York: Basic Books, 1979.

Gerber, Philip L. *Robert Frost*. New York: Twayne, 1966.

Gilbert, Roger. *Walks in the World: Representation and Experience in Modern American Poetry*. Princeton: Princeton University Press, 1991.

Gioia, Dana. "Explaining Ted Kooser." In Sanders and Brummels, *On Common Ground*. Reprinted as "The Anonymity of the Regional Poet," *Can Poetry Matter? Essays on Poetry and American Culture* (St. Paul: Graywolf Press, 1992. 93–112).

———. "My Confessional Sestina." *Poetry* 143, no. 1 (October 1983): 10–11.

———. "Poetry Chronicle." *Hudson Review* 33, no. 4 (Winter 1980–1981): 611–27.

Gioia, Dana, David Mason, and Meg Schoerke, eds. *Twentieth-Century American Poetry*. Boston: McGraw Hill, 2004.

Glahn, George von. "Ted Kooser: Searching for Signs." *Late Harvest: Plains and Prairie Poets*. Edited by Robert Killoren. Kansas City: BkMk Press, 1977.

Gregory [Raz], Hilda. Review of *Grass County*, by Ted Kooser. *Prairie Schooner* 46, no. 1 (Spring 1972): 88–89.

Gustafson, Richard. Review of *Grass County*, by Ted Kooser. *Poet & Critic* 6, no. 3 (1971).

———. Review of *A Local Habituation & a Name*, by Ted Kooser. *Poet & Critic* 8, no. 3 (1975): 45–46.

Hahn, Steve. "The Common Becomes Uncommon in Poet's Hands. *Sunday Lincoln (NE) Journal Star*, April 21, 1985.

Harding, Walter. *The Days of Henry Thoreau: A Biography*. New York: Knopf, 1965.

Harrison, Jim. "The Man Whose Soul Is Not for Sale: Jim Harrison." *Rendezvous: Idaho State University Journal of Arts and Letters* 21, no. 1 (1985): 26–41.

———. *Off to the Side: A Memoir*. New York: Atlantic Monthly Press, 2002.

Harvey, Steven. "Local Wonders: Seasons in the Bohemian Alps." *Fourth Genre: Explorations in Nonfiction* 6, no. 2 (2004): 135–36.

Heaney, Seamus. *The Place of Writing*. Atlanta: Scholars Press, 1989.

Heidegger, Martin. *Poetry, Language, Thought*. Translated by Albert Hofstadter. New York: Harper and Row, 1971.

Henri, Robert. *The Art Spirit*. Compiled by Margery A. Ryerson. Philadelphia: Lippincott, 1923.

Hilton, Robert T. "Education for Pioneers and Pioneers in Education." *Ames Community History*. Ames IA: Ames Centennial, 1964.

Hirsch, Edward. *How to Read a Poem and Fall in Love with Poetry*. New York: Houghton Mifflin, 2000.

Hunter, Linda Mason. "The Farmer Feeds Us All: Making Do during the Great Depression." *Des Moines Iowan*, March/April 2004.

Jacobson, James E. *Guttenberg, Iowa—The Limestone City of Clayton County: Its Architecture and History, 1854–1951*. Des Moines: History Pays! Historic Preservation Consulting Firm, 2001.

Johnsgard, Paul A. *The Birds of the Great Plains*. Lincoln: University of Nebraska Press, 1979.

Johnson, Jean H. Review of *Weather Central*, by Ted Kooser. *Southern Humanities Review* 30 (1996): 407.

———. "Two Visions." Review of *Weather Central*, by Ted Kooser, and *The October Palace*, by Jane Hirshfield. *Poet Lore* 90 (1995): 52–55.

Jones, Donald. *Medical Aid and Other Poems*. Lincoln: University of Nebraska Press, 1967.

Kaye, Fran. "Tin Camp Writers' Picnic." *NEBRASKAland Magazine* 62 (July 1, 1984): 40–44.

Keenan, John. "Kooser's Everyday Poetics." *Omaha (NE) World Herald*, February 6, 2005. http://www.omaha.com.

Kinzie, Mary. "Haunting." *American Poetry Review* 11, no. 5 (September/October 1982): 37–46.

Krapfl, Mike. "Ames Native Ted Kooser Honored for His Poetry." *Ames (IA) Tribune*, August 28, 2004. iowa.amestrib.com/articles/2004/08/28/import/12800777.txt.

———. "Kooser's Upbringing," *Ames (IA)Tribune*, August 28, 2004.

———. "Ted Kooser Threw His $12 Slide Rule into Lake LaVerne." *Iowa State University Visions*, ISU Alumni Association, Winter 2005. Available as "Finding the Profound in the Ordinary," http://visions.isualum.org/winter05/alumni.asp.

Kuzma, Greg. "Ted." *Midwest Quarterly* 46, no. 4 (2005): 372–78.

Labrie, Ross. "Karl Shapiro." *Dictionary of Literary Biography*. Vol. 48, edited by Peter Quartermain. Detroit: Gale, 1986. 399–405.

Laskin, David. *The Children's Blizzard*. New York: HarperCollins, 2004.

Levertov, Denise. "Origins of a Poem." Hopwood Lecture, University of Michigan, 1968. http://studiocleo.com/librarie/levertov/prsfrmset.html.

———. "Origins of a Poem." *The Poet in the World*. New York: Norton, 1974.

———. *O Taste and Sea*. New York: New Directions, 1964.

Liebman, Sheldon W. "Robert Frost, Romantic. (Poet)." *Twentieth Century Literature* 42, no. 4 (Winter 1996): 417–38.

"Lincoln Author's Novella Ludicrously Funny, Good." *Daily Nebraskan*, September 13, 1978.

Love, Glen A. *"Et in Arcadia Ego*: Pastoral Theory Meets Ecocriticism." *Western American Literature* 27, no. 3 (Fall 1992): 195–207.

Luke, Hugh. "Celebrating Kooser." *Sunday Lincoln (NE) Journal and Star, Focus Magazine* section, 12, November 12, 1978.

Lydiatt, William, and Perry Johnson. *Cancers of the Mouth and Throat: A Patient's Guide to Treatment*. Omaha: Addicus Press, 2000.

Makuck, Peter. "Heartlands." *Hudson Review* 58, no. 3 (Autumn 2005): 248–506.

Marcus, Mordecai. Review of *Not Coming to Be Barked At*, by Ted Kooser. *Lincoln (NE) Journal and Star*, January 23, 1977, 12F.

Mantooth, Wes. "The Spy in the Lobby: Impersonal Observation in the Work of Ted Kooser." *Midwest Miscellany* 40, no. 2 (Fall 2012): 23–34.

Marx, Leo. *The Machine in the Garden: The Technology and the Pastoral Ideal in America*. New York: Oxford University Press, 1964.

Mason, David. Review of *Winter Morning Walks*. *Prairie Schooner* 76, no. 3 (September 2002): 187–92.

McCloskey, Robert. *Lentil*. New York: Viking Juvenile, 1940.

Meats, Stephen. "A Tribute to Ted Kooser: An Interview." *Midwest Quarterly*, June 22, 2005, 335.

Miller, James E., Jr. "Karl Shapiro in Nebraska." In *Seriously Meeting Karl Shapiro*, edited by Sue Walker, 45–47. Mobile AL: Negative Capability Press, 1993.

Miller, James E., Jr., Karl Shapiro, and Bernice Slote, eds. *Start with the Sun: Studies in Cosmic Poetry.* Lincoln: University of Nebraska Press, 1960.

Milosz, Czeslaw. "Gift." *New and Collected Poems.* New York: Ecco, 2003.

Mitchell, Justin. "17 Nominees Forsake Poet Laureateship." *Lincoln (NE) Journal,* March 9, 1982.

Molesworth, Charles. "Fondled Memories." *New York Times Book Review,* October 12, 1980.

Muir, Edwin. *An Autobiography.* New York: William Sloan, 1954.

Murray, Roger. Review of *Official Entry Blank,* by Ted Kooser. *Denver Quarterly,* Winter 1970, 99–100.

Nathan, Leonard. "Sorry." *New Republic* 162, no. 2 (January 10, 1970): 25.

Nicodemus, Ron. *Findings: A Film about Reinhold Marxhausen.* Lincoln: Nebraska ETV Network, 1985.

O'Gara, W. H. *In All Its Fury, A History of the Blizzard of January 12, 1888, with Stories and Reminscences.* Collected and compiled by W. H. O'Gara on behalf of the Blizzard Club. Lincoln NE: Union College Press, 1947.

Oostdijk, Diederik. "'Someplace Called *Poetry*': Karl Shapiro, *Poetry* Magazine and Post-war American Poetry." *English Studies* 4 (2000): 346–57.

Phillips, Robert. *The Confessional Poet.* Carbondale: Southern Illinois University Press, 1973.

———. "Interview with Karl Shapiro." *The Art of Poetry* 36 (December 1984). http://www.departments.bucknell.edu/stadler_center/shapiro/interview.pdf.

———. "Poetry, Prosody, and Meta-Poetics: Karl Shapiro's Self-Reflexive Poetry." *Poetics in the Poem: Critical Essays on American Self-Reflexive Poetry.* Edited by Dorothy Z. Baker. New York: Peter Lang, 1997.

"Poet Shapiro Seeking 'Sign of Creative Life.'" *Lincoln (NE) Journal Star,* February 24, 1957.

Pound, Ezra. *The ABCs of Reading.* New York: New Directions, 1960.

Price, Realto E. *History of Clayton County: From the Earliest Historical Times Down to the Present.* Vol. 1. Chicago: Robert O. Law, 1916.

Prior, Jean C. *Landforms of Iowa.* Iowa City: University of Iowa Press for the Iowa Dept. of Natural Resources, 1991.

Puffett, John. "Nightcrawlers Club Stresses Safety on Drag Strip, Highway." *Ames (IA) Tribune,* July 30, 1956. (Courtesy of the Ames Historical Society)

Ransom, John Crowe. *The New Criticism.* Norfolk CT: New Directions, 1941.

Reist, Margaret. "Endowment to Kooser Will Help School as Will High School Endowments." *Lincoln (NE) Journal Star,* December 29, 2010.

———. "Kooser Elementary Kooser Elementary Dedicated, to Open in 2009." *Lincoln (NE) Journal Star*, April 24, 2008. http://journalstar.com/ news/local/kooser-elementary-dedicated-to-open-in/article_25e950ad -aa04-5018-aaad-905a4dc18a1e.html.

———. "Kooser Elementary School Dedicated to the Sweet Music of Poetry." LPS *News*, October 15, 2009.

Rosowski, Susan J. *The Voyage Perilous: Willa Cather's Romanticism*. Lincoln: University of Nebraska Press, 1986.

Sanders, Gerald Dewitt, John Herbert Nelson, and M. L. Rosenthall, eds. *Chief Modern Poets of England and America*. 4th ed. New York: Macmillan, 1962.

Sanders, Mark. "Interview with Ted Kooser." In Sanders and Brummels, *On Common Ground*.

Sanders, Mark. "Portraits of Kooser." *Midwest Quarterly* 46, no. 4 (Summer 2005): 415-20.

Sanders, Mark, and J. V. Brummels, eds. *On Common Ground: The Poetry of William Kloefkorn, Ted Kooser, Greg Kuzma, and Don Welch*. Ord NE: Sandhills P, 1983.

Schmidt, Gary D. *Robert McCloskey*. Boston: Twayne, 1990.

Sawyer, R. McLaran. *Centennial History of the University of Nebraska*. Vol. 2: *The Modern University, 1920-1969*. Lincoln NE: Centennial Press, 1973.

Shapiro, Karl. *Beyond Criticism*. Lincoln: University of Nebraska Press, 1953.

———. *The Bourgeois Poet*. New York: Random House, 1962.

———. "Cosmic Consciousness." In Miller, Shapiro, and Slote, *Start with the Sun*.

———. "Editorial." *Prairie Schooner* 30 (Winter 1956): 309-11.

———. *Edsel*. New York: Bernard Geiss Associates, 1971.

———. "Karl Shapiro Turns Barbed Pen on Scientific Mind, Youth, Midwest." *Daily Nebraskan*, July 18, 1961.

———. "Magician." *V-Letter and Other Poems*. New York: Raynat, 1944.

———. "A Malebolge of 1400 Books: Six Lectures by Karl Shapiro." *Carleton (College) Miscellany* 5, no. 3 (Summer 1964): 1-135.

———. *Person, Place and Thing*. New York: Reynat, 1942.

———. "Poetry and Family: An Interview with Karl Shapiro." By Andrea Gale Hammer. *Prairie Schooner* 55, no. 3 (Fall 1981): 3-31.

———. *Poems*. Baltimore: Waverly Place, 1935.

———. *Prose Keys to Modern Poetry*. Evanston IL: Row, Peterson, 1962.

———. *Reports of My Death: A Distinguished American Poet Looks at the Literary Life of Our Times*. Chapel Hill: Algonquin Books, 1990.

———. "Romanticism Comes Home." *Prairie Schooner* 31, no. 2 (Fall 1957): 182–83.

———. *V-Letter and Other Poems*. New York: Reynall and Hitchcock, 1944.

Shapiro, Karl, and Robert Beum. *A Prosody Handbook*. New York: Harper and Row, 1965.

Silesky, Barry. *John Gardner: Literary Outlaw*. Chapel Hill: Algonquin Books, 2004.

Slote, Bernice. "The Kingdom of Art." In *Kingdom of Art: Willa Cather's First Principles and Critical Statements, 1893–1896*, edited by Bernice Slote. Lincoln: University of Nebraska Press, 1966.

———. "Start with the Sun," In Miller, Shapiro, and Slote, *Start with the Sun*.

Smith, Jared. Review of *The Poetry Home Repair Manual* and Craft Interview with Ted Kooser." *New York Quarterly*, no. 62 (2006): 27–37.

Smith, Roberta. "Stewart Hitch, 61, Painter Who Merged Styles." *New York Times*, February 18, 2002. http://www.nytimes.com.

Steiner, George. *Errata: An Examined Life*. New Haven: Yale University Press, 1998.

———. *Real Presences*. Chicago: University of Chicago Press, 1989.

Stevens, Wallace. "Sunday Morning." *Harmonium*. New York: Knopf, 1923.

Stewart, Paul Robert. *The Prairie Schooner Story: A Little Magazine's First 25 Years*. Lincoln: University of Nebraska Press, 1955.

Stillman, Kevin. "Famous Poet Returns to Ames." *Iowa State Daily* online ed., April 20, 2005. http://www.iowastatedaily.com.

Stitt, Peter. "The World at Hand." *Georgia Review* 34 (Fall 1980): 661–70.

"Straight Answers from Ted Kooser." *American Libraries* 35, no. 11 (December 2004): 31. (Interview)

Stryk, Lucien, ed. *Heartland: Poets of the Midwest*. DeKalb: Northern Illinois University Press, 1967.

———, ed. *Heartland II: Poets of the Midwest*. DeKalb: Northern Illinois University Press, 1975.

Suckow, Ruth. "Middle Western Literature." *English Journal* 21, no. 3 (March 1932): 175–82.

Tawney, Robin. "An Interview with Ted Kooser." *Cottenwood Review* 21 (Fall) 1979.

"Ted Kooser Day: A Delight!" *Ames Historical Society Newsletter to Members* 2, no. 4 (Spring 2006): 8.

Thomas, Dylan. "Do not go gentle into that good night." *The Poems of Dylan Thomas*. New York: New Directions 2003.

Thoreau, Henry David. "Economy." *Walden*. New York: Modern Library, 2000.

———. *The Journal of Thoreau: 1875-1858*. Edited by Bradford Torrey and Francis H. Allen. Salt Lake City: Peregrine Smith Books, 1984.

Toth, Susan Allen. *Blooming: A Small Town Girlhood*. Boston: Little, Brown, 1981.

Tranströmer, Tomas. *The Great Enigma: New Collected Poems*. New York: New Directions, 2006.

Urschel, Donna. "Kooser & Prine: Illegal Smiles." *Library of Congress Information Bulletin*, April 2005. http://www.loc.gov.

Vendler, Helen. *Poems, Poets, Poetry*. Boston: Bedford/St. Martin's, 2002.

Vinz, Mark. Review of *A Local Habitation & a Name* by Ted Kooser. *Dacotah Quarterly* 42-43, no. 8/9 (Fall-Winter 1974-75), 119-21.

Vroman, Laura. "Big Donation Comes In for Cherry County Historical Society." *Valentine (NE) Midland News* 23, no. 39 (May 6, 2009): 1, 8.

Wagner, Linda Welshimer. "William Carlos Williams: Giant." *College English* 25, no. 6 (March 1964): 425-430.

———. "William Carlos Williams: The Unity of His Art." *Poetic Theory/Poetic Practice: Papers of the Midwest Modern Language Association*. Edited by Robert Scholes. Iowa City: Midwest Modern Language Association, 1969.

Walker, Sue. *Seriously Meeting Karl Shapiro*. Mobile AL: Negative Capability Press, 1993.

Walls, Laura Dassow. *The Passage to Cosmos: Alexander von Humboldt and the Shaping of America*. Chicago: University of Chicago Press, 2009.

Wepman, Dennis. "Robert Henri." *American National Biography Online*. February 2000.

West, Kathleene. "Land-Bound." *Land Bound*. Port Townsend WA: Copper Canyon Press, 1978.

Wickett, Dan. "Interview with Ted Kooser." *Emerging Writers Forum*, January 25, 2005. http://www.breaktech.net/emergingwritersforum/ (not a working URL at press time).

Williams, George. "Immigration: Gisiger, Mullet, Moser." IAGenWeb Project. http://iagenweb.org. (Clayton Documents maintained by Sharyl Ferrall)

Williams, William Carlos. *The Autobiography of William Carlos Williams*. New York: New Directions, 1967.

———. *The Collected Poems of William Carlos Williams*. Vol. 1, *1909-1939*. Vol. 2, *1939-1962*. New York: New Directions, 1991.

———. *Patterson*. New York: New Directions, 1963.

———. *Pictures from Brueghel, and Other Poems*. Norfolk CT: J. Laughlin, 1962.

———. "The Red-wing Blackbird." *The Collected Poems of William Carlos Williams.* Vol. 1, *1909–1939.* New York: New Directions, 1991.

———. *Selected Essays.* New York: Random House, 1954.

Woodress, James. *Willa Cather: A Literary Life.* Lincoln: University of Nebraska Press, 1987.

The WPA Guide to 1930s Iowa. Compiled and written by the Federal Writers' Project of the Works Progress Administration for the State of Iowa. Iowa City: University of Iowa Press, 2007.

Wright, James. *This Journey.* New York: Random House, 1982.

Young, Joanne. "Laureate Looks Back, Ahead." *Lincoln (NE) Journal Star,* February 12, 2006. http://www.journalstar.com.

UNPUBLISHED SOURCES

In addition to the author's formal interviews with Ted Kooser, information has been obtained from various conversations with and letters and e-mails from Ted Kooser over the years, beginning in 1997. Date and type of communication are provided in a note to the text quote whenever possible.

Christie, Larry. Telephone interview with author. January 25, 2010.

Cox, Steve. E-mail to author. June 11, 2009.

Hahn, Steve. E-mail to author. February 2, 2009.

Herrnstadt, Richard. Telephone interview with author. June 22, 2005.

Jones, Donald. Correspondence with author. June 6, 2007.

Kloefkorn, William. Personal interview with author. February 1, 2006.

Kuzma, Greg. Personal interview with author. April 17, 2003.

Laging, Mij (Hitch). Personal interview with author. March 12, 2008;

Langmack, Judith Kooser. E-mail to author. November 2 and 11, 2007.

Lemon, Lee. T. Personal interview with author. April 17, 2005.

Lombardi, Patty (McLaughlin). Personal interview with author. February 22, 2008.

Luschei, Glenna. E-mail with author. April 6, 2005.

Mezvinsky, Edward. Telephone interview with author. January 19, 2010.

Mezvinsky, Norton. Telephone interview with author. July 28, 2007.

Olson, Paul. Personal interview with author. February 1, 2006.

Raz, Hilda (Gregory). Personal interview with author. January 12, 2006.

Rutledge, Kathleen. Personal interview with author. July 17, 2008.

Sanders, Mark. E-mail to author. August 11, 2008.

Scheele, Roy. Personal interview with author. June 27, 2007.

Shapiro, Karl. Letter to Marjorie Loehlin. March 23, 1964. Included in Ted Kooser's brown scrapbook (unpublished and in Kooser's possession).

Toth, Susan Allen. Telephone interview with author. January 24, 2010.

Tressler, Diana. Personal interview with author. June 16 2007. E-mail dates are provided with corresponding text notes.

Welch, Don. E-mail to author. May 5, 2008.

Index

Kumin, Maxine, 214
Kuzma, Greg, 68, 72–73, 134

Laging, Maj (Hitch), 72
Lake, Calvin, 5
Lake, Florence Moser (aunt), 5
Lang, Grace E.(grandmother), 4–5,
   11–12
Langmack, Judith Kooser (sister),
   6, 8, 9, 11–12
lark, 245
Lebsack's Tavern, 57–58
Lemon, Lee, 50
Lentil (McCloskey), 12–14, 190–91
"Letter, A" (Kooser), 143
"Letter from Aunt Belle, A"
   (Kooser), 66–67
Levendosky, Charles, 216
Levertov, Denise, 245
Lewis, Sinclair, 24
libraries, Kooser on, 23
Liebman, Sheldon W., 89
"life-poetry," 155–56
"Lights on a Ground of Darkness"
   (Kooser), 16, 21, 166–67, 177–78,
   191, 203
Lincoln Benefit Life, 97–98, 130,
   136, 143, 166, 169–70
Linderholm, Robert, 216
"Listeners, The" (De La Mare),
   22–23, 67
"local," 82–83, 86–87
Local Habitation & a Name, A
   (Kooser), 76, 81–96
Local Wonders (Kooser), 185–93
Local Wonders (musical version),
   219, 226
Lombardi, Patty, 57, 72, 75–76,
   77–78, 111

Lorca, Federico Garcia, 102
Love, Glen A., 95
Luke, Hugh, 114
Luschei, Glenna, 76, 81, 244
Lydiatt, William, 171, 183, 220–21
"Lying in a Hammock on William
   Duffy's Farm in Pine Island,
   Minnesota" (Wright), 141–42
lyric poems, 87

Madrid IA, 40–42
Mallo, Gary, 10
Manfred, Frederick, 24
"Man Opening a Book of Poems"
   (Kooser), 68–69
Mantooth, Wes, 208
Marcus, Mordecai, 104
Marxhausen, Reinhold P., 96–97,
   246
Mason, David, 181
Masters, Edgar Lee, 149
Mayo, Jack (uncle), 203
McCarthy, Lee, 114
McCloskey, Robert, 8, 12–14,
   190
McKibben, Belle (aunt), 67
McLoughlin, Patty. *See* Patty
   Lombardi.
McLoughlin, Tom, 57, 72
McNally, Mary, 26
memorials, poems as, 141–43
memory: in *Delights & Shadows*,
   210; *Local Wonders* and, 189
"Memory" (Kooser), 202
metaphor: broken allegory and,
   178; Kooser on, 136, 205; *Local
   Wonders* and, 187; *Not Coming to
   Be Barked At* and, 101–8; versus
   metonym, 244; *Weather Central*

and, 151–60; *Winter Morning Walks* and, 180
"Metaphor and Faith" (Kooser), 224
metonym, 244
Meyer, Clarence, 20
Meyer, Parthenia, 20
midland poets, 58–60, 94–95
Midsummer Night's Dream (Shakespeare), 83–84, 89
Midwest literature, 23–24
Midwest Pastoral: Place and Landscape in Literature of the American Heartland, The (Barillas), 59–60, 95–96
Miller, James E. Jr., 239
Milosz, Czeslaw, 211
Molesworth, Charles, 127
monologue. *See* dramatic monologue
Monroe, Harriet, 24
Morarend, Dorothea Schroeder (great grandmother), 17
Morarend, Elizabeth D. (grandmother), 5, 15, 18, 20, 38
Morarend, John Dietrich (great grandfather), 17
mortality, 139–40, 165–69, 181, 191, 210
Moser, Alva (Elvy)(uncle), 5, 18, 115
Moser, Anna Marie Mulett (great grandmother), 17
Moser, Dorathea Magdalina Gisiger, 17
Moser, Elizabeth D. Morarend (grandmother), 5, 15, 18, 20, 38
Moser, Florence (aunt), 5
Moser, John R. (grandfather), 5, 15, 18, 20, 71
Moser, Mabel (aunt), 5, 6

Moser, Nicholas (great grandfather), 16–17
Moser, Vera Deloras. *See* Kooser, Vera Deloras Moser
"Mother" (Kooser), 203
Muir, Edwin, 166–67
Mulett, Anna Marie (great grandmother), 17
Mullica, J. Laverne, 28
Murray, Roger, 69–70

Nathan, Carol, 172–73, 221
Nathan, Leonard, 72, 96, 101, 138, 172–73, 221
Nevelson, Louise, 225
New Critics, 50–51
New Salt Creek Reader, 98. See also *Salt Creek Reader, The*
"New Year's Day" (Kooser), 92
nightingale, 85
Noack, Harold (mother's cousin), 20
Noack, Harvey (mother's cousin), 20–21, 39
Noack, Laura Morarend (great aunt), 20, 38
Noack, Pete (great uncle), 20
Northern Iowa University, 61–62
Not Coming to Be Barked At (Kooser), 100–108
"November 9" (Kooser), 180

Ochester, Ed, 115
"October Evening, An" (Kooser), 172–73
Official Entry Blank (Kooser), 61, 62, 63–70
"Official Entry Form" (Kooser), 64, 121